*The histories, the myths, the obsessions . . .
behind the greatest treasures in America*

CAPTAIN KIDD: The pirate with the most dire reputation for bloodletting—and buried treasure—in American history

KARL STEINHEIMER: A German pirate turned miner whose entire fortune was buried by an oak tree for his true love to find

CONFEDERATE GOLD: The billion-dollar treasure nestled on the grounds of a genteel Southern plantation

THE LOST DUTCHMAN MINE: A source of incomparably pure gold ore that has eluded hundreds of searchers

JOHN DILLINGER: The gun-toting gangster was shot to death—but what happened to the money he stole?

And many other mysterious treasures waiting to be discovered—maybe by you!

LOST TREASURE

A Guide to Buried Riches

BILL YENNE

BERKLEY BOOKS, NEW YORK

LOST TREASURE: A GUIDE TO BURIED RICHES

A Berkley Book / published by arrangement with
the author

PRINTING HISTORY
Berkley edition / February 1999

All rights reserved.
Copyright © 1999 by William Yenne.
Cover design by Erika Fusari.
Cover illustration by Dan Kirk.
This book may not be reproduced in whole or in part,
by mimeograph or any other means, without permission.
For information address: The Berkley Publishing Group,
a member of Penguin Putnam Inc.,
375 Hudson Street, New York, New York 10014.

The Penguin Putnam Inc. World Wide Web site address is
http://www.penguinputnam.com

ISBN: 0-425-16742-9

BERKLEY®
Berkley Books are published by The Berkley Publishing Group,
a member of Penguin Putnam Inc.,
375 Hudson Street, New York, New York 10014.
BERKLEY and the "B" design
are trademarks belonging to
Berkley Publishing Corporation.

PRINTED IN THE UNITED STATES OF AMERICA

10 9 8 7 6 5 4 3 2 1

Contents

Introduction

Lost treasure mythology has always been part of the collective consciousness of humankind. It has been woven into our folklore since the beginning of history, but unlike relics of the past that have become irrelevant, treasure mythology remains vital because, while it has a mythical dimension, it promises real and tangible riches. Certainly King Solomon's Mines is a very old story that still causes the hair on the back of a treasure hunter's neck to bristle a little bit. The gold in those mines would be just as valuable today as it was in Solomon's time.

The searches for the Ark of the Covenant and the Holy Grail have inspired centuries of unsuccessful quests, and the fact that they are still out there waiting to be found keeps the legend alive. Indeed, both of these treasures have been popularized for recent generations as the subjects of *Indiana Jones* movies. Clearly this is evidence of the power of lost treasure to fire the imagination and to become part of popular culture.

The popularity of these films and the box-office revenues they generated are indicative of a theme that will come up again and again in this book: The richest treasure in buried treasure mythology is not the treasure that is buried. In a sense, the treasure in buried treasure mythology is actually buried in the mythology itself. The mythology represents the *promise* of treasure as much as it represents the treasure. In the California gold rush that began in 1849, the biggest fortunes were not made by the people panning or digging for gold. They were made by the merchants who sold them the pans and shovels. A steak-and-eggs breakfast cost more in San Francisco in 1849 than it does today.

This book is a survey of a few of the more interesting lost-treasure stories that are interwoven in American history. It is also about those moments in American history that provide the backdrop for the treasure stories. Dreams of treasure and the lust for treasure have made history in the United States as often as the discovery of treasure has made history. Certainly the dreams of treasure and the lust for treasure have inspired more stories and more tales.

There are hundreds of exhausted and closed gold mines in the West whose locations are well known. They inspire the imagination not a bit. However, tales of mysterious lost mines, such as the Lost Dutchman Mine in Arizona, have inspired dozens—if not hundreds—of books and pamphlets, all-night discussions, and expeditions into inhospitable terrain. The mythology represents the *promise* of treasure as much as it represents the treasure. The mythology is stronger than the reality.

Tales of buried treasure and lost mines are part of local lore in every state and nearly every county. Such stories have been part of the history of what is now the United States since before there was a United States. Indeed, the original European obsession with America itself began not so much with a longing for adventure or a taste for spices, but with a lust for gold.

They told you in school that Columbus came here looking for spices. Yeah, sure. The Spanish galleons that sailed eastward from the Americas in the sixteenth century— groaning from the weight of their loads—were not sailing with holds filled with nutmeg!

In the case of the above-mentioned California gold rush, the hundreds of thousands of people who abandoned jobs, lifestyles, and families to scramble to California in

1849 and thereafter were not coming for the golden sun, the golden beaches, or the golden orange groves. When the clipper ships set out for the Isthmus of Panama or Cape Horn, their decks teeming with prospectors, the first passenger aboard was always the allegorical character in the stovepipe hat whose name was ''Mr. Greed.''

Meanwhile, these migrations—first of Europeans to the New World, and then of people from China, Chattanooga, and Charleston to California—were really migrations. Among those who came to merely dig and run were those who came to stay. For good or bad, they changed the demographics of vast lands forever. In 1848—a year before the ''rush''—James Marshall found a gold nugget in California's Sierra Nevada and set off a spark of excitement that created the biggest voluntary mass migration in modern history and one that literally created the state of California. The promise of gold was as important in the making of history as was the gold itself.

Of course, just as greed drove the 49ers in search of naturally occurring gold ore, so greed is a driving force among those who search for gold that has been buried, lost, or hidden by others. And just as migrations of merchants, settlers, and farmers followed the 49ers, so archaeologists and historians have struck a treasure of their own as they follow the treasure hunters and those who we would call— if we were being impolite—grave robbers. The treasure hunters came with a gleam in their eye and left secretly with pockets filled with gold coins. The archaeologists and historians came with a gleam in their eye, but they came away with a treasure they shared with the rest of us—they have given us a better understanding of our heritage or of a collective heritage we share with other human beings. The archaeologists and historians helped to give us the stories. The archaeologists have turned up long-forgotten artifacts, and the historians have turned up long-forgotten legends.

Of course, not all the stories are long forgotten. The Lost Dutchman Mine is as much a part of the mythology of Arizona as any story from that state's history. Along the eastern seaboard, pirate treasure is almost an essential element in the local lore in nearly every shoreline community.

And, of course, just as many of the stories are not long forgotten, many of the well-remembered stories are just not true. It doesn't make them bad stories, and in many cases they are pretty good stories. In the case of pirate treasure, the name "Captain Kidd" occurs frequently, and tourists shop for Captain Kidd souvenirs in places where the captain never set foot. And it wouldn't hurt business to tell them that. Tourists flock to England to walk in the footsteps of Robin Hood and Sherlock Holmes, even though those gentlemen left no footsteps in which to walk. It doesn't matter. I suppose that's why they call it mythology.

While he may have been exaggerated for commercial purposes, Captain Kidd *was* real. So was the Dutchman whose lost mine is so much a part of Arizona lore, and so were all the other characters mentioned in this book. They were as different as the centuries in which they lived, but they had a great deal in common. They were not merely greedy; they were obsessed with wealth. It was a peculiar obsession. It was not the same obsession as with the suited twentysomethings who sit at computer terminals high above Wall Street, nor even the suburban housewives and long-haul truck drivers who routinely buy their lottery tickets as they pay for their gas at the gas station. The treasure seekers in this book were a breed apart. If the treasure that was part of their obsession is worthy of consideration by the archaeologist, and the story that brought the treasure seeker into conjunction with the treasure is grist for the historian's mill, then the obsession is for the psychologist.

What, we might ask, is it about gold that tilts the mind? With addictions to drugs, there is a traceable pharmacological trail that leads us to the answer, but with gold, there is only mystery. The story of the human obsession with treasure, especially with gold, dates to the deepest prehistoric dawn of human civilization and continues to this day. If you want to see and touch gold, there are easy, safe ways to do so. Go to a jewelry store. Take a tour of Fort Knox. If you want to possess more wealth than 99 percent of the prospectors who ever saw "color" in their pans, simply work hard and invest wisely. But the search for lost, buried, or stolen treasure is not about the luster of gold, nor is it really about the value of gold. It is the obsession. In shaping lives as in shaping history, the power of the myth is at least as powerful as the power of the gold.

The obsession of the treasure hunter is probably best summarized by Frank Dobie, a man who wrote a lot about the treasures of Mexico and the Southwest in the 1920s. Wrote Dobie, "What men believe or fancy to be true, what they have faith in, whether phantom or fact, propels their actions. The hunter of precious metals is always a fatalist, no matter how civilized above superstition he may be. Deep in his heart he believes that somewhere out in the Sierras, the magic scales are awaiting him."

Gold is a cold, straw colored metal, but it ignites a fire in the soul. Christopher Columbus himself wrote, "Gold is the most excellent thing. Of gold, treasure is made, and he who possesses gold does what he wishes in the world."

Gold is attractive for its luster—because of its poor chemical reactivity, it occurs in a pure form rather than in a compound. And gold is attractive for its rarity—just 0.004 gram per ton of other material in the earth. It is hard to find, but not impossible. It is hard to find and even harder to not notice when you do.

Gold is useful for what it can be traded for, but it has always been more than a trading commodity. Since the beginning of recorded history, it was the basic form of wealth. It was a recognized medium of exchange from the Middle East to China, and in the Western Hemisphere—which had no traceable contact with the rest of the world—people had also concluded that gold had a value that transcended the intrinsic. Until the twentieth century, the international monetary system was based on the gold standard. The value of currency was defined in terms of a fixed quantity of gold; paper currency was freely convertible into gold, and both circulated as "money." From the late nineteenth century and the outbreak of World War I in 1914, the English pound dominated international trade, prices remained fairly stable, and all the world's currencies were backed by gold. With the upheaval in world markets that occurred during World War I, however, most countries dropped the gold standard, leaving the United States as the only Western country where paper money was still convertible into gold coins. In 1933 the incoming Franklin D. Roosevelt administration took the United States off the gold standard, a move that has been fodder for conservative animosity ever since.

Gold drives people and governments wild. Roosevelt jettisoned the gold standard to inflate the dollar, and he has been hated ever since. To this day, the United States is filled with groups who vociferously advocate, or even demand, a return to the gold standard. Roosevelt also made it illegal for Americans to own gold (except as jewelry and tooth fillings), and that ban survived for four decades.

Gold is so rare that rumors of its discovery inspire "rushes." When Columbus "discovered" Central America and the islands of the Caribbean, he touched off the mother of all gold rushes. A gold rush was the centerpiece of Spanish foreign policy for two centuries. And what a rush it was. In the eighteenth century, 80 percent of the gold found in the world was dug (or stolen) in America and taken to Spain. And the discoveries continue. In the United States, before the California gold rush of 1849, there was Georgia's Dahlonega gold rush of 1833 and then there was the Klondike gold rush of 1898. There have been smaller discoveries—including the Dutchman's in Arizona—that have inspired smaller rushes. Then, too, there are the discoveries about which little is spoken. This writer has been on the site of a certain eyebrow-raising discovery on the south fork of a river in California about which nothing *can* be spoken.

Gold is hard to get, but it is axiomatic that anything worth having is not easy to get. Nearly a century after the 49ers changed the course of history, Berwick "B. Traven" Torsvan wrote in *The Treasure of the Sierra Madre* (which John Huston turned into the legendary 1948 film of the same name with Humphrey Bogart), "You thought the gold would be lying around like pebblestones, and nothing to do but bend down and pick it up and go off with it by the sackful. But if it was as simple as all that, gold wouldn't be worth more than pebblestones.''

While Traven admits that gold is a wondrous thing to have, he tells us that it would not be worth having if it was easy to have. Traven also implies that the search for the treasure is as much a part of the experience as having it. Just as with Christopher Columbus, who discovered the richest bonanza of all time, Bogart's character in *The Treasure of the Sierra Madre* died neither rich nor happy. Bogart's character becomes a metaphor for the human obsession with gold. For him—as for the Spanish—gold was easy to find at first, but the psychological baggage that came with it proved to be an impossible burden.

As Traven clearly conveyed in *The Treasure of the Sierra Madre,* and as countless others have conveyed in other tales of treasure, the search inflames the mind and fires the spirit, but it is a wildfire that can flame beyond control. A word or two whispered about a lost mine or a buried strongbox will turn the most mild-mannered, most settled person into a Walter Mitty or a Jesse James. The treasure lore of the United States is an essential element of our history, of the most adventurous aspects of our history. It was treasure that inspired people to explore, to take chances, and to build the infrastructure made the lifestyles of both Mitty and James possible.

Billions of dollars were made in the gold fields of California, Arizona, and Colorado as well as in the silver mines of Nevada's Comstock Lode, but there are billions left undiscovered. There are lost mines and buried stashes of old Spanish gold throughout the American West.

In California, where the 49ers grossed a billion dollars a year for the better part of a decade and turned up one single ''nugget'' weighing 195 pounds, people still earn a good living panning for gold, and the hidden treasure stories— if you believe them all—contain enough value to pay off several national debts.

The Southwest, with its windswept mesas and labyrinthine canyons, has beckoned to treasure seekers for centuries. Ever since 1536, when Cabeza de Vaca stumbled, half dead, into Mexico City with tales of "seven golden cities," people have come into the Southwest to pursue treasures of mythical proportions. It is a place of real and well-documented gold and silver mines, as well as tall tales of stolen coins and fields of gold nuggets "the size of quail's eggs" bragged about by men in clapboard saloons, men who had not tasted whiskey for eighteen months, and by dying men who would never again see the sun rise.

The treasure lore of the United States is a cornucopia of lost Spanish mines, of gold and silver stolen from Mexican pack trains, hidden by Native Americans, stolen from churches, concealed by priests, and whispered about by paranoids with a past. It includes mines lost and found by Frenchmen, Dutchmen who were really Germans ("Deutsche" men), Dutchmen who were really Dutchmen, one-eyed strangers, English pirates, and Spanish conquistadors. The stories tell of silver, gold, precious stones, and Confederate coins stolen from Army convoys, cruel slavers, innocent travelers, guilty travelers, and people who disappeared without a trace.

A generation or two ago, stories of lost Indian or lost Spanish mines were still fresh in the minds of the loners and packers who lived in the hills of the West, or hard-to-reach villages on the Outer Banks, and these legends became a staple of pulp journalism. Tales were often related around flickering campfires to the eager ears of greenhorns by old Mexican men who were often part Indian or who had been raised by the Indians. Almost invariably, these old men were sure that for the right inducement they could find that mine again. Occasionally—not often, but often enough—they actually did.

Today, the old-timers who were adults in the early twentieth century are gone, taking their tales with them. Many of the more enduring legends were recorded for posterity, but a rich literature has grown obscure, more the stuff of dusty shelves of Tucson, Idaho Falls, or Helena used bookstores than of current tabloid journalism.

Many of America's treasures are associated with the

names of history's notorious rascals. On the eastern seaboard and the Gulf Coast you can practically tell where you
are by the name of the buccaneer that falls from the lips of
anyone describing pirate treasure. Out West there are stories
told from Texas to the Dakotas of blood-drenched loot hidden by Jesse and Frank James and their gang. In the Rockies, tales turn to Butch Cassidy and his Wild Bunch, and
in Montana they speak of Henry Plummer, who conducted
his reign of terror from behind a badge and died with his
boots on without divulging the whereabouts of a dozen supposed caches.

Treasure is elusive in a metaphysical as well as a physical sense. There is a story they used to tell in the mountains
of Grant County, New Mexico, that is a good allegory for
this. It is the tale of *Los Perros de la Niebla*—the Dogs of
the Mist.

It was nearing winter, the air was cold, the canyons were
filled with mist, and you could smell the snow coming. A
man and his dogs were deep in the mountains, hunting for
a bear, when he stumbled across a streambed filled with
large gold nuggets. Somehow, in his excitement, apparently
his gun went off, mortally wounding him. A day or so later
the dogs were seen in town, and people wondered what had
happened to the dogs' master. Around the neck of one dog
was a torn piece of the man's shirt. On it, written in blood,
were the words "Follow Dogs. I am Dying." Tied up in
the cloth was a huge nugget of almost pure gold.

Unlike the happy ending you'd expect if the story originated in Hollywood, searchers could not get the dogs to
lead them back to the man. They searched the misty mountains—probably until the snows finally came—but they
never found the man and they never found the gold. However, as the story goes, on misty days in those mountains,
you can still hear the distant barking of *Los Perros de la
Niebla.*

Treasure hunting is indeed like following dogs in the
mist. It is as much the mythology that keeps the treasure
hunters going as it is the gold. The *promise* of gold has
kept prospectors in the field for years. Their hearts remain

filled with fire even as their pockets remain empty. If there is a tangible story and just enough of a hint of location to keep them going, they never give up.

With the tangible, there is always something intangible that drives the treasure hunter—something more than the thirst for money. The odds are probably better with lottery tickets. Lottery tickets are certainly less work, but they are not magic.

Treasure *is* magic, a magic that transcends the monetary value of the gold or silver itself, a magic that comes from the legends that swirl about the treasure, and a magic that is part and parcel of the search itself, which often is transformed into a search of self-discovery, and the search itself becomes the ultimate treasure.

This book is about the search as much as it is about the treasure. The idea is to take the reader to the treasure through the story of how it got there, and then to take the reader to the treasure with actual directions to the vicinity of the place where it is hidden. These treasures were not lost or buried in mythical places, but rather in places that can be reached from real cities on real roads. The places are real, and there is good evidence that the stories are as real as any history. Perhaps they are slightly shaded in the telling, but they are true stories.

The places are as specific as we can get. This is to say that the directions given in this book will take you to a place that is tantalizingly close to the actual treasure. It will take you to a spot from which—if you were to be able to magically go back in time to that magic moment—you could see the Dutchman at the entrance to the mine, or Captain Kidd supervising the burial of a certain sea chest. We can take you to the place where you can sense the electricity of the legend. If we could take you to the place where your shovel would hit the strongbox, we would have gone there first, and yes, we would have the strongbox.

Please remember that legends and tales of treasure are just that. If the details about these treasure sites were specific, and if the gold was, as Traven wrote in *The Treasure of the Sierra Madre*, "lying around like pebblestones, and nothing to do but bend down and pick it up and go off with it by the sackful,'' someone already would have been off with it. It's not that simple. People have been searching for and dreaming of some of these treasures for years. It will take time and patience, and it will take care and research, but in that time and research you will find that the true treasure may very well be in the experience of the quest.

If the treasure is truly in the story and in the search itself, then we can give you the treasure. If the treasure is in standing in the same arroyo as the Dutchman, or in smelling the same cold, salty air as the captain, then we offer you this as your treasure map.

Chapter 1

CAPTAIN KIDD'S COUNTLESS CACHES

PLACE: *Maine to Delaware*

TIME PERIOD: *1699*

Few types of lost, hidden, or buried treasure troves are shaded with such color, or flavored with such romance, as pirate treasure, and few pirates—indeed, no pirates—are associated with more buried treasure up and down the East Coast of the United States than Captain William Kidd, who sailed the English main as the sixteenth century melted into the seventeenth, in days that are still recalled as the golden age of seagoing lawlessness.

Today, the local lore in parts of the eastern seaboard and the Gulf Coast are colored by the lore of the local pirate. You can practically tell where you are by the name of the pirate that is mentioned in the visitors' bureau brochure, or the name of the buccaneer that falls from the lips of anyone describing pirate treasure. While many of the treasures identified with these gentlemen may actually be tied (for local publicity purposes, of course) to loot stashed by pirates of lesser notoriety, each of these villains was extremely active in his respective area. If they whisper the name "Blackbeard," you are south of Cape May, New Jersey. On the Gulf Coast, if someone says "Billy Bowlegs," you may well be in the Florida panhandle, but if it's "Jean Lafitte," you might be anywhere from Mobile, Alabama, to South Padre Island, Texas. If they whisper "Captain Kidd," you're probably north of the mouth of the Delaware River, although you do hear about Kidd all the way down to Florida.

William Kidd was born in Greenock on Scotland's Firth of Clyde, downstream from the great shipbuilding port city of Glasgow. The best guess is that the year was 1645. As there was no promising future in Scotland in the seventeenth century, young men in Scotland who felt they had promise went to sea as soon as they could. Kidd shipped out when he was just a kid and ended up in the Caribbean, which was warmer and far more interesting than the chalky hills of Clydeside.

Records show that he took command of the privateer *Blessed William* in 1689 and participated a Royal Navy raid on the French-owned island of Marie-Galante. For those who may be under the impression that the term "privateer" is somehow synonymous with "pirate," it should be told that a privateer was—in the sixteenth century context of our story—simply an armed vessel that carried a license to attack ships belonging to a nation at war with the nation issuing the license, which was literally a "letter of reprisal." It was a way of getting soldiers—or, in this case, sailors—of fortune to do the work of the navy by harassing the merchant fleet of the opposing nation. In the seventeenth century, most European nations of consequence were in a state of war with many other nations of consequence. As for Britain, it was more or less in a state of perpetual war with Spain and France.

Privateering was a bit like bounty hunting, and a privateer was a private warship. In 1689 Captain Kidd was the captain of a private warship. This may have given the Scotsman pause to reflect about the pirating lifestyle, but it certainly left the taste in the mouths of Kidd's crew, who seized *Blessed William* and left poor William Kidd cooling his heels on the island of Nevis, while they ran off to become buccaneers. For those who may be under the impression that the term "buccaneer" is somehow associated with pirates, it should be told that such an assumption is exactly correct. Captain Kidd wasn't one yet, but soon he would be.

Rewarded for his privateering in the Marie-Galante attack, Kidd was given a captured French three-master by the governor of Nevis. With this ship renamed *Antigua,* the captain sailed forth, arriving in New York in the spring of 1691. It was here that the old sailor engaged in a bit of the sort of buccaneering to which men occasionally stoop—he courted and married a widow with money. Sarah Oort, presumably a member of one of the prominent Dutch families who still lived in Manhattan, had a substantial brick house on Pearl Street near the bustling tip of that island, and this became Captain Kidd's home ashore. But a captain ashore is no captain at all, and a captain can take it only so long, no matter how much money his wife has, so Kidd started entertaining dreams of going back to privateering.

In 1695 he traveled to London in search of financial backing for his scheme of hunting bounty on the bounding main. Here a friend of Kidd's, New York wheeler-dealer Robert Livingstone, introduced the captain to Richard Coote, Lord Bellomont, and the two became fast friends. In turn, his lordship spread the word around the House of Lords that Kidd needed backers. The plan was to form a sort of privateering corporation, buy a fast ship, and sail to the pirate-infested waters of the Indian Ocean. The privateer would then be used to capture pirate ships and recover stolen property, which would become the property of the shareholders of the corporation. Technically, a privateering license was good only against warships in time of war, but the keeper of the great seal at the Admiralty happened to be Lord Somers, one of Bellomont's cronies who was investing in the plan. Naturally, he was able to make all the necessary adjustments to the paperwork by hand. Lest anyone question the legality of the transaction, it should be added that King William III himself approved the deal. Their lordships had promised His Majesty a 10 percent cut off the top.

An alternative version of the story claims that it was King William himself who came up with the plan to exterminate the pirates and get rich at the same time. This telling of events suggests that His Majesty called a meeting of the prominent gentlemen in London and presented a plan for a private company that would wage war on the pirates and capture their stolen cargoes. These treasures would be divided among the members of the king's company in proportion to the amount of money each put up to start the venture. Not all seventeenth-century pirates were at sea. As Captain Kidd himself once said: "All men love to take what belongs to others; it is a universal desire; only the manner of doing it differs."

On April 10, 1696, Kidd set sail aboard a ship romantically dubbed *Adventure Galley*. She would carry 34 cannons and 152 men. The cannons were outfitted in England, and Kidd made for New York, where he had little trouble collecting a crew, despite the condition that none would be paid unless they seized some well-stocked "pirate" ships. Greed would sail with the *Adventure Galley* as the 153rd crewman, but disease would be a deadly stowaway.

In January 1697 the *Adventure Galley* and her crew were anchored off Madagascar, where Kidd hired additional crew to replace those who had died from a fever or, as it was then colorfully known, "the" fever. Among the new men were some who had crewed on pirate ships, and had a thing or two to tell the New York crew about the notion that nobody would be paid unless the *Adventure Galley* seized some well-stocked pirate ships. The thought of going home empty-handed started to chafe, and there was a growing sentiment for seizing *any* ship. Even William Kidd could see where things were leading. In August 1697, when the captain ordered "Mocha," he wasn't sending out for his morning coffee, he was setting sail for the Red Sea port of the same name, a port near which some especially lucrative plundering targets would soon be sailing.

The Islamic pilgrims making the annual hajj to Mecca would soon be heading home. Poor Bedouins set out across the desert sands aboard dromedaries, but rich Muslim merchant princes sailed past Mocha for Malabar aboard plush three-masters fitted with all the accoutrements of home and palace. This meant gold, jewels, dancing girls, and all the other things that warmed a pirate's heart. If Captain Kidd had never before had a stray thought about the buccaneering side of life, he was having them in droves now. The *Adventure Galley* had struck the English flag (the Union Jack didn't exist yet) and was flying the skull and bones when she made contact with a convoy of pilgrim vessels.

Ironically, Kidd's first firefight was with an English ship, the *Sceptre,* and Kidd panicked. This was his first taste of high seas piracy, at age fifty-two, and he lost his nerve. Fortunately, the *Adventure Galley* managed to get away from the English ship. Unfortunately, the *Adventure Galley* had failed to capture or board a merchant ship, and her itch crew had scored no gold, jewels, dancing girls, and all the other things that warmed a pirate's heart.

A few weeks later, Captain Kidd committed his first act of piracy, against an English trading ship off Malabar. The *Adventure Galley* had her plunder at last, but her crew turned ugly, and things got out of hand. They started torturing the merchant seamen. One thing led to another, and soon there were men dangling from a yardarm. One would like to imagine that William Kidd had imagined himself a gentleman pirate of the sort who would seize a ship's cargo, then toast her captain with shots of brandy before sailing away. If he had any such pretense, and we do not know whether he did, it died that afternoon off Malabar.

The privateer turned pirate was on the crime spree that would define the remaining years of his life and the memory of him that lives today in legend. To add to what had already transpired, on October 30 he killed a gunner's mate in a brawl on deck and secured a place for himself among a breed of men for whom blood on the hands is a baptism of initiation.

Through 1698 and into the early days of 1699, the *Adventure Galley* was the scourge of the Indian Ocean, plundering ships and murdering crews. Kidd seized an Armenian ship called *Quedah Merchant,* which carried immense treasure belonging to the mogul of India. Kidd sold the treasure, renamed the ship *Adventure Prize,* and took her as his own. Since the *Adventure Galley*—the property of the English lords—was getting a bit long in the tooth, he simply abandoned her, to sail away in the appropriately named *Adventure Prize*.

While few versions of the life of William Kidd dispute the fact that he captured the *Quedah Merchant,* and that she was a merchant ship, there has been growing interest in a long-suggested conspiracy theory that sees him being set up as a fall guy by the London gentlemen who put him in business. In England—even as Kidd was rampaging in the Indian Ocean—King William was in trouble. His political enemies had learned of the private venture and were protesting the use of the Great Seal of England in private enterprises that seemed to be little more than piracy. His Majesty slipped out of the controversy by declaring Kidd a pirate and issuing a warrant for his arrest.

The alternate version of this part of the story claims simply that Captain Kidd had done so much damage to the East India Company's merchant ships that His Majesty's government had no choice but to declare him a pirate. Still another variation may be that the lordships insisted he be designated a pirate because he took what they felt was *their* treasure.

With the spring of 1699, *Adventure Prize* reached the Caribbean. The old privateer had come back a buccaneer. As was the custom at the time, Kidd and crew put in at St. Thomas, where the Danes were accommodating brokers of plundered property. Kidd and company caught their breath and sold some goods, but the word that was on the narrow streets of St. Thomas was not so good as far as the captain was concerned. The Royal Navy had him at the top of their wanted list. In short, the warm and tropical Caribbean basin was as hot as a volcanic caldera for Captain William Kidd.

The theory of Captain Kidd as an innocent fall guy had Kidd surprised to learn that he was wanted for piracy. He had what amounted to be a license to plunder, and a royal license to plunder at that. It was now clear to him that he had become a scapegoat, a royal scapegoat.

In any event, Kidd was looking at the end of his short-lived buccaneering career. The long arm of the law was coming closer and closer, and he was starting to feel more and more like John Dillinger would when J. Edgar Hoover gave him the honorary title of "Public Enemy Number One."

As the story goes, Kidd set about off-loading the considerable plunder he had amassed since his crime spree off Malabar. Apparently he sold a great deal of it to the mercurial booty broker Henry Bolton, who did business on the isle of Hispaniola. He bought the sloop *San Antonio* for three thousand pieces of eight—Spanish gold coins about twice the size of an American quarter with a copper content of at least one-fourth—and sailed north. We know where he went—he was headed for the eastern seaboard of the English colonies that are now the United States—but we don't know exactly why.

Ultimately he wound up in Boston trying to stay out of jail, but in the meantime, who knows? As we know, few pirates—indeed, no pirates—are associated with more buried treasure up and down the East Coast of the United States than Captain Kidd. If so, how did it get there? We have to suppose that some of the treasure stories associated with him are untrue, but at the same time some are true. Estimates of the treasure he carried north from Hispaniola vary. He almost certainly did have an immense amount of gold in various forms, and it is suggested that this included an estimated eighty-two hundred pieces of eight, although he reportedly had offered the governor of St. Thomas forty-five thousand pieces of eight for a month's protection. Governor Laurents, not wanting to walk on the fighting side of the Royal Navy, had turned him down. So Kidd still had at least that much in April 1699. He landed in New York two months later with numerous bags of gold. Witnesses saw them. In the meantime, he may have hidden some of his treasure. According to legend, Kidd secreted the bulk of his ill-gotten wealth in caches from Maine to Florida, although he apparently did very little in the way of actual pirating on the eastern seaboard, and he would have had to have done all the hiding attributed to him in a five-month block of time.

Captain Kidd landed in New York in June 1699. Just a little more than three years had passed since he had begun the adventure that earned him revulsion in his own time and three centuries of legendary immortality. What then followed was a complex series of legal maneuvers in which Kidd called in all his favors in New York in an effort to stay out of jail. He started out with his friends in high places: His friend and patron, Lord Bellomont, was now Lord Royal Governor Bellomont of New York, Massachusetts, and New Hampshire. You couldn't get higher than that in 1699.

As the story goes, before taking care of business, Kidd casually passed some time in New York catching up on old times with acquaintances there. As might be expected, when the phrase "What have you been doing?" came up in conversation, it was Kidd who did most of the talking.

One can only guess what his wife had to say when he showed up on the Pearl Street doorstep. He was not arrested in New York, even though he was a wanted man. Either he kept a very low profile, or his standing in Manhattan kept the law on his side.

At last Kidd traveled to Boston, burying treasure in at least two places and possibly more as he went.

When Captain Kidd walked into Lord Bellomont's office, it had to have been one of the most awkward meetings that Boston would experience until the unpleasantries that were to begin in 1774. Here was the English governor of an area larger than England itself, greeting a man he had helped to get started on a voyage that made him the most wanted man in the world. Kidd sat down in His Lordship's office—with Bellomont and nervous members of the Massachusetts Council—and calmly related the tales of his three years at sea, or his three-year reign of terror, depending on your point of view. Legally he felt he was only doing what he was mandated to do. Lord Bellomont had helped see to it that Kidd was issued his privateering license to capture ships and recover stolen property, which would become the property of the shareholders of the corporation. Kidd had captured ships. Kidd had captured property.

Kidd was a royal licensee. Now he was briefing the man from the House of Lords who had facilitated his license. Even though a privateering license was good only against warships in time of war, Bellomont had twisted the arm of Lord Somers at the Admiralty to issue the amending paperwork. Even the king had nodded the royal noggin for 10 percent. As Bellomont knew, not all seventeenth-century pirates were at sea.

As the councillors squirmed in their chairs, Captain William Kidd, royal licensee, recounted the property he had seized while sailing under—and, admittedly, a bit outside of—a royal license. There were bales of calico, bales of muslin, bales of silk, tons of sugar, tons of hardware, and, of course, pounds—if not tons—of gold and silver. There wasn't much said about rape and murder or the innocent blood that stained the deck on which Kidd had stood the last time he saw Bellomont.

They say that Lord Bellomont whispered something about a royal pardon, but that Kidd should go now and come back in a day or so. They don't say whether Kidd knew that Bellomont was kidding.

On the way to his next meeting with the governor and the council, Captain Kidd found the police waiting. He ran. He was caught and dragged away, kicking and screaming for his patron and the whispered pardon. The only memo his patron posted to London that day was a notification that the criminal William Kidd was in custody.

Captain Kidd's next voyage—his last—was a February 1700 crossing of the stormy, snowy, frigid North Atlantic, which fittingly set the tone for the rest of his life. Thrown into London's hellish Newgate Prison, Kidd languished for a year before being called before Parliament to beg for mercy. He was, he told the wigged gentlemen, the most misunderstood seaman ever to explain himself before them. He was, in fact, the only seagoing pirate to testify before Parliament in its history. The old buccaneer calmly explained that he'd captured only two ships, and both of those were French, and hence enemy ships.

The trial was finally held at the Old Bailey in early May

1701. The prosecution did its job. They subpoenaed Lord Bellomont's records, they brought in a merchant who had been on the *Quedah Merchant,* and they even interrogated the slippery Henry Bolton, who had bought the ship and brokered Kidd's bales of calico, bales of muslin, bales of silk, tons of sugar, tons of hardware, and pounds—if not tons—of gold and silver.

Claiming to be the most innocent man ever sentenced at the Old Bailey, William Kidd went to the gallows at Execution Dock, overlooking the Thames a mile from the Tower of London, where executions are also part of the heritage. The necks of many pirates were snapped at Execution Dock through the years before Britain banned capital punishment for capital crimes, but today the pub that overlooks the site is named for just one: Captain Kidd.

The Only Place Where They Actually Found a Kidd Cache

Captain Kidd sailed north from the Caribbean a very rich pirate, and he arrived in Boston with relatively little in his pockets. It is well known that he buried it in various places along the way, and the search for those places has consumed the lives of hundreds of treasure hunters over the past three centuries. How do we know that he buried treasure along the way? Because treasure was found in two of the places the same year he put it there. These were found by following clues, and clues exist for many additional sites.

Gardiner's Island is located between Orient Point and Montauk Point on Long Island, like a jewel held delicately by a thumb and forefinger. It was here, late in 1699, that Lord Bellomont's constables recovered gold valued at about £14,000.

In John Gardiner's version of the story, Kidd had anchored his sloop off the island, and Gardiner rowed out to investigate. Kidd welcomed Gardiner aboard and explained that he was on his way to Boston to see Lord Bellomont.

He asked Gardiner's permission to land two bales of goods. The next day, Kidd exchanged some muslin and silks with Gardiner for a barrel of cider and six sheep, and the *San Antonio* sailed away. Three days later the ship returned to Gardiner's Island, and Kidd sent ashore a chest, a box of gold, a small bundle of gold, two thirty-pound bags of silver, and four bales of goods. With Gardiner's knowledge, the treasure was buried at Kidd's Hollow on the inshore side of the island.

Kidd is also known to have stopped at the mouth of the Connecticut River to put two chests of treasure ashore on Clarke's Island, where he entrusted them to the care of his old friend "Whisking" Clarke, who buried them on the island. These, too, are believed to have been recovered by Bellomont's constables, although some people have claimed that nothing was found on Clarke's Island.

What was confiscated on Gardiner's Island amounted to 1,123 ounces of gold and 2,353 ounces of silver. Did Lord Bellomont's men find it all? Those who still believe that most of it is still out there waiting to be found would like to think not. Those who believe that Kidd was a fall guy for Bellomont's own greed will tell you that His Lordship found a great deal more than he owned up to. On the wind-swept shores of Gardiner's Island, the word that is still whispered in the wind tells of "Captain Kidd's money pit" and a treasure that eluded the searchers of 1699 and all those who came after them over the past three centuries.

Where else did he bury portions of his amassed wealth?

Following the Penultimate Voyage of Captain Kidd

Between April 1699, when he left St. Thomas, and September 1699, when he was taken into custody in Boston, Captains Kidd sailed north on the last voyage he made in command of a ship. The sloop *San Antonio* made its way to New York and from New York to Boston and stopped along the way to bury treasure in two places. The conventional wisdom holds that these were not the only two, but nobody knows how many other stops or where. There are stories and there are clues. They can't *all* be true, nor can they all be false. The greatest liturgy of buried pirate treasure stories in the United States are associated with the *San Antonio*'s movements for those five months.

From Maine to Delaware and beyond, the stories of buried Captain Kidd treasure are almost as numerous as the inlets on the shores of the Atlantic Ocean and various sounds and bays. As noted above, many of these may actually be tied (for local publicity purposes, of course) to loot stashed by pirates of lesser notoriety, but Kidd did sail this way, he did have treasure to stash, and he did stash it somewhere.

For purposes of this overview we will begin at the northern terminus of his alleged travels and work south, although for one who is following this "treasure trail," the search may begin at any point. Specifically, we begin on the rugged coast of Maine. Today this area is a favorite of vacationers, but during the eighteenth and nineteenth centuries its hundreds of remote islands and inaccessible inlets made it a land of opportunity for pirates looking to stash their loot, and for people wishing to hide loot *from* the pirates. Specifically, the trail is mostly U.S. Highway 1—the mother of all the old U.S.-numbered highways—which begins on the St. Lawrence River at Fort Kent, Maine, and winds on down to Key West, Florida. In the 1950s much of the more direct and "important" sections of Highway 1 were superseded by the faster Interstate 95—and various toll and bypass interstate highways with the "95" suffix—but Highway 1 is the scenic alternative, and is generally closer to the shoreline, where the captain would have put the loot.

In Captain Kidd's day there was no road on the coast of Maine, and that which ultimately became U.S. Highway 1 existed only between New York and Boston as the Boston Post Road. Indeed, even today, much of U.S. Highway 1, especially through Connecticut, is referred to as "the Post Road."

Apparently Kidd did not get as far north as Washington County, where you can first see the sea from U.S. Highway 1, so the story starts in neighboring Hancock County, home to Acadia National Park, which was a pirate favorite because of its many inlets and islands.

Various eighteenth- and nineteenth-century pirates, including Kidd, are said to have stashed plunder at many places in Hancock County, although there are probably fewer sites than legend tells. The stories we hear today may include variations on tales of a single site that have been embellished to the point where they are now thought to be two or more treasures in the same area. Traveling to Penobscot Bay, and the lower Penobscot River area around Belfast, Sandy Point, and Castine, you'll hear many stories. Around these parts you will hear that Captain Kidd put in at various places on the lower Penobscot River area and down near Musselridge Channel in Penobscot Bay. There also are tales of buried pirate treasure—though not necessarily Captain Kidd treasure—on Monroe Island, which is on the west side of Penobscot Bay.

One of the more intriguing tales about the captain's fast sojourn in and around the Penobscot country involves the tantalizing and mysterious place known as "Captain Kidd's Money Cove" on Isle au Haut (Upper Island). Isle au Haut is actually in Knox County, but it is closer to mainland Hancock County, and it is reachable only by ferry from Stonington in Hancock County—unless you have your own boat.

To reach Isle au Haut, you turn south from U.S. Highway 1 onto Maine Route 15. This turnoff is between the villages of Orland and East Orland about a mile north (literally east, but in the northbound direction) of where U.S. Highway 1 crosses the Penobscot River. Drive south on Route 15 and plan to take your time, because it is a slow road. About thirteen miles south of the turnoff, you'll pass through Blue Hill, the last major town to be seen for a while, and the place where, if your gas tank is not nearly full, you should fill it. South of Blue Hill, Route 15 narrows for the ten-mile drive to the bridge to Little Deer Isle. A second bridge takes you to Deer Isle, while lies between Penobscot Bay and Jericho Bay. The scenery here is nothing but spectacular, and if you come for the view rather than for the gold, you will have hit pay dirt the moment you hit either of the isles named for the mammal species that owns the woods hereabouts.

Ten miles across Deer Isle from the bridge that connects it to the mainland is the town of Stonington, the ferry terminal for Isle au Haut. The ferry schedule for the ten-mile crossing changes occasionally, so it is best to call ahead. Since Acadia National Park owns about half of Isle au Haut and has a ranger station out there, you can get the Isle au Haut ferry information from them at (207) 288-3338.

As the ferry chugs across and the tiny island comes into focus through the fog, 543-foot Mount Champlain is the most prominent landmark, although there are three hills more than 400 feet high on the island, and these would have been the landmarks observed by Captain Kidd when he made his alleged flying visit back in 1699. The ferry approaches, threading its way among the numerous rocks and channels in the area, notably Merchant Island, which will be on your left as you are about two miles out, and Kimball Island, which crowds the northwestern shoulder of Isle au Haut, forming a mile-long channel called "the Thorofare" that is so narrow you could practically throw a piece of eight across. The ferry docks at the top of Thorofare at a place known locally as "Town Landing" but that shows up on maps as the town of Isle au Haut. The Acadia National Park Isle au Haut ranger station will be up on top of the hill on your right. If you haven't struck up a conversation on the ferry regarding Captain Kidd's Money Cove, now is the time and place. The folks in the town of Isle au Haut may look at you funny and chuckle. You aren't the first. Up at the ranger station, they'll humor you.

The island known as Isle au Haut has only about five miles of road, with less than half of it—mostly on the north side—paved. If you try to drive here in the winter, you have to depend on when things are plowed, but that is no time to be stumbling around the rocky shoreline looking for Kidd's Cove. In the summer there's a ferry that will take you to Duck Harbor, on the southwestern corner of Isle au Haut. From here, there is a pretty good network of trails maintained by the National Park Service that will take you out to places such as Deep Cove, Barred Harbor, and Head Harbor (named for Eastern Head, a rocky peninsula that has no trails—or at least none that are officially maintained).

Is Captain Kidd's Money Cove actually on Isle au Haut, or was it ever? If it was, is the money actually still in the cove, or was it carted away two or three centuries ago? The answers may well be—to quote the poet—blowing in the wind, because the wind is the only constant on Isle au Haut. It really does feel like the edge of the world out here, and it literally is the edge of the continent. When you gaze seaward from the tip of Eastern Head, the next landfall is Europe. If Captain Kidd came to Isle au Haut, he would certainly have been confident that it would be safe here until he got the royal pardon that Lord Bellomont had promised.

Driving south on U.S. Highway 1 from Hancock County, you'll pass through Knox County, then Lincoln County, where there is an alleged Captain Kidd's treasure, which is located on the Sheepscot River, which runs through the county seat of Wiscasset, flowing into the ocean down by Boothbay Harbor. With his sense of urgency, did the captain sail ten miles up the Sheepscot River? Those who believe the story will swear by it. On the eastern side of Squirrel Island in Boothbay Harbor there is a two-hundred-foot cave that is known as Kidd's Cave. Has it been fully explored? Some say yes and some just shake their heads slowly.

Over in Kennebec County there are also stories that Captain Kidd stashed some treasure about thirty miles up the Kennebec River in the vicinity of Hallowell, which is now a suburb of Augusta. From U.S. Highway 1 you can take Interstate 95, which merges into the Interstate 495 toll road about five miles south of Hallowell. There is another Captain Kidd site rumored to be across the Kennebec River near Pittston, but this may be a variation on the Hallowell story. With his sense of urgency, did Captain Kidd sail twenty-five miles up the Kennebec River? Those who believe the story will swear by it.

Sagadahoc County is particularly rich in both pirate and buried-treasure lore. Perhaps the county's most intriguing stories involve what is known as the Portuguese Seaman's Cache, which is said to include $50,000 in gold and silver coins. They are said to be near the ruins of an old tavern on the northern end of St. John's Island in Casco Bay. Also in this area south of U.S. Highway 1 there are Captain Kieff's treasure, located on Cliff Island; Dixie Bull's treasure, on Cushing Island; Edward Lowe's treasure, on Pond Island in Casco Bay; and Captain Kidd himself is associated with treasures on both Cliff Island and Jewell's Island in Casco Bay.

Back in 1900, a man from Nova Scotia is said to have showed up at Jewell's Island with a map purporting to show where Kidd's treasure was buried. He took an old sea captain into his confidence, and the two were seen to go up the beach together. The Nova Scotian was never seen again, but people later found that a large hole had been dug on the southeastern shore, and it looked as if a large object had been taken from it. Years later the skeleton of a man was found in the crevice of a rock covered with stones. The object, widely believed to have been an old sea chest, was never located, and is probably long gone. In a possibly related story, they say that the anchor of a ship at the mouth of the Sheepscot River once brought up an old sea chest by accident. The chest fell off and was never seen again.

South of Maine, U.S. Highway 1 and Interstate 95 squeeze through New Hampshire, a largely rural state with a short coastline. The state is dominated by the rugged White Mountains in the north, which blend into rolling hills in the south, toward the state's major population centers. It might be mentioned as an aside that one of the Granite State's most important legends recalls that while fleeing the American Revolution in 1775, English governor John Wentworth buried a strongbox filled with gold and silver coins along with six chests of silver and gold plate in a wooded area between Portsmouth and Smithtown in Rockingham County.

Other stories swirl around the rugged Isles of Shoals that New Hampshire shares with Maine. Numerous treasures have been buried here, both by the crews of wrecked ships and by pirates. Blackbeard buried caches on Londoner and Smuttynose Islands, while John Quelch buried gold and silver on the west side of Appledore Island, as well as on both Snake and Star Islands. Captain Sandy Gordon buried plunder on White Island. Curiously, the prominent treasure attributed to Captain Kidd is said to be at Rye Pond, near Antrim, New Hampshire, on U.S. Highway 202, fifty "crow flight" miles from the Atlantic, in Hillsborough County.

The only New England state without an Atlantic coastline, Vermont is not without legends of pirate treasure, including one attributed to Captain Kidd that is in the vicinity of Bellow's Falls, in Windham County, just across the Connecticut River from New Hampshire and about twenty "crow flight" miles farther from the Atlantic Ocean than Antrim. Most of the Captain Kidd stories around these parts date back to 1839, when men digging a canal found two Spanish silver dollars of a very early date. The fact that it was linked specifically to Captain Kidd is attributable more to the power of his legend than to the fact of his actually being in Vermont. Nevertheless, the Green Mountain State is filled with other tales, especially involving her granite crags and deep canyons, which verge on inaccessible because they are choked with vegetation in summer and with snow and ice in winter. Indeed, like several western states, rugged little Vermont boasts not one but *two* "Hell's Half Acres."

With his sense of urgency, would Captain Kidd have had the time or inclination to have traveled overland for three days to a week to bury plunder near Antrim or Bellow's Falls? This is not very likely, unless he had helpers or surrogates, and certainly they would have been back to reclaim it when the captain had his last dance on the London gallows just two years later.

Below New Hampshire, U.S. Highway 1 and Interstate 95 cross into Massachusetts, which was the largest and most populous of the New England colonies, and in whose capital Captain William Kidd breathed his last as a free man. Did he hide some of the famous plunder around Massachusetts Bay when he sailed toward Boston for his fateful rendezvous with Lord Bellomont? According to legend, Kidd did—especially on the Atlantic coastline of Essex and Norfolk Counties, although such sites attributed to him may be the plunder of other buccaneers, and credited to him because his name is more notorious in the literal sense of the word.

Other pirates are also credited, of course. Captain John Quelch buried a cache of gold and silver coins on Snake Island, off Cape Ann in the Isle of Shoals chain north of Boston, in Essex County. The area around Boston Bay abounds in pirate treasure lore. For example, Captain Avery's chest of diamonds and gold coins is said to have been buried on Gallops Island, just outside Boston Harbor. Captain Billie's "Lost Treasure" is thought to have been buried on Grape Island in Hingham Bay off Quincy. John Breed's treasure is said to have been buried on Swan Island, William Marsh's somewhere on Apple Island, and still more treasure in concealed caches on Calf Island, on Castle Island, on Grape Island, on Great Brewster Island, on Little Brewster Island, and on Hog Island. Captain Kidd's alleged Boston Bay stash was on Conant's Island.

Due south of Boston, U.S. Highway 1 passes through the state of Rhode Island, where stories of Captain Kidd treasures start to make sense historically. There is a strong indication that Kidd made several short trips out of port after his return to New York City in June 1699. Legend has it that he was caching loot on Long Island, but Rhode Island is near the end of Long Island, and Rhode Island's many coves and inlets were somewhat more secluded in 1699 than those of Long Island. Indeed, the islands and waterways in and around Narragansett Bay and Rhode Island

Sound were soon to become great favorites of eighteenth-century pirates, and today nearly every island and inlet has a story involving Captain Kidd.

Following the trail to the major Rhode Island sites associated with the captain begins with a drive down the eastern side of Narragansett Bay, although a day spent researching Captain Kidd lore at the state archives in Providence would be extremely useful in fine-tuning your search. Let the travelogue given below serve as your first set of clues. These are, in our experience, the six primary Captain Kidd sites in Rhode Island.

As you near the Rhode Island state line—and the Providence city limits—coming south from Boston on U.S. Highway 1, you will note that Highway 1 joins Interstate 95 about a mile north of the line but that there is a Highway 1 "Alternate" that does not. Take the Alternate in the direction of Pawtucket. If you are coming south on Interstate 95, Massachusetts exit 2 will be the Highway 1 Alternate. Drive south, through Pawtucket, to Rhode Island Route 114. If you are driving east out of Providence, take Interstate 195 across the Seehonk River and exit on Rhode Island exit 8, about two miles later. Drive south to Route 114.

Rhode Island Route 114 is known locally as the "Wampanoag Trail," after the tribe of Native Americans who lived here in the seventeenth century, when the English coming here for religious freedom started to settle on their land. It was the Wampanoags, and their leader, Massasoit, who welcomed and befriended the Pilgrims at Plymouth Colony and who sat down with them at the first Thanksgiving dinner eight decades before Captain William Kidd came calling on Narragansett Bay. Today's four-lane highway of the same name—and the numeric designation 114—was actually once a trail used by the Wampanoag people.

The ultimate destination on Route 114 is Newport, Rhode Island, the town that has been the home-way-from-home of the richest of the rich for more than a century. Individual houses in Newport are worth more than most towns in the United States. Newport is certainly a far cry from the lifestyle enjoyed by the Wampanoag people in the early seventeenth century. What an irony if this is the place where Captain Kidd buried his untold wealth. He would have liked it here. People in Newport like sailboats. On the other hand, with the skeletons in the closet of Newport society's past reputation, Captain Kidd's strongboxes are assuredly not the only intriguing secrets buried hereabouts.

Route 114 parallels the Massachusetts state line and the Barrington River to the town of Barrington, where it narrows to just two lanes. After just another eight miles, you'll see signs for the ferry to Hog Island. If you reach the bridge over to Portsmouth, you've come too far. Hog Island is the first point on this tour of the Narragansett Bay area that is an alleged Captain Kidd treasure site. Catch the ferry across to Hog Island, which is a surprisingly remote place, given its proximity to Providence and Portsmouth.

To reach the second and third sites, cross the bridge into Portsmouth and turn left on Rhode Island Route 177 East. You'll be rejoining Route 114 to get along to the third site, but for the moment a side trip is required. Immediately out of Portsmouth, you'll cross the Sakonnet River, a river so wide that it is more like a bay. It fact, where it flows into the ocean, it is actually wider than Narragansett Bay, where it leads into the ocean, But they call it a river, so it's a river. The eastern end of the bridge will set you in the town of Tiverton, where you should turn right and go south on Route 77. After about five miles you'll pass through Tiverton Four Corners, a town so small that it has only three corners. You'll see what we mean.

About eight miles farther on, Route 77 reaches a dead end in the village of Sakonnet. Straight ahead is the stormy North Atlantic, and on your right is the broad mouth of the Sakonnet River, with the city of Newport visible on the opposite shore, about eight miles away. They call it a river, so it's a river. Legend has it that Captain Kidd buried some of his elusive treasure near Sakonnet, probably on the shore here at the mouth of the Sakonnet River. Whatever havoc the effects of three centuries of storms and hurricanes may

have had on the shoreline, Sakonnet is still here, and that
says a great deal about staying power.

If you study a map large enough to include both New
York and Boston, it is clear that if someone was sailing
between the two and needed to put in long enough for a
quick digging expedition on a secluded shore, the mouth
of the Sakonnet River makes as much sense, probably
more, than any of the sites discussed thus far. You can
inquire in Sakonnet, and probably find someone who will
tell you as much as you want to hear about the Captain
Kidd treasure. If you don't hear what you want to hear, ask
for a second opinion.

To get to the third of the six suggested sites, backtrack
to Portsmouth, find Route 114 again, turn left, and follow
the signs to Newport. Yes, Newport, the playground of a
century of the richest if not the most famous contains a
Captain Kidd treasure site.

Entering Newport on Route 114, you'll pass through a
traffic circle and soon discover that Route 114 has become
Broadway. A couple of miles farther on, you'll be in the
heart of Newport's business district. Ask directions to
Touro Street and the Newport Historical Society, at 82
Touro Street. Find a place to park. As you will soon discover, the Newport Historical Society is a useful and interesting trove of information about Newport, and about the
fortunes and the fortunate who passed the hours here in the
Valhalla of Old Money. The museum offers changing ex-
hibitions of photographs, paintings, Townsend-Goddard
furniture, silver, and china, but more to the point, it has a
research library and an archival manuscript collection with
the earliest town records. Plan to arrive early, because they
close at noon except in the summer. Take our word for it
and call ahead to (401) 846-0813. Ask about Captain Kidd
and they'll probably mention Brenton Point, and there will
probably be a thing or two else that will perk up your ears.

To reach Brenton Point, head south on Bellevue Avenue,
past those gargantuan homes that make Newport Newport
and distinguish it from, say, Tiverton Four Corners. I would

guess that many of these homes have more fireplaces and more square footage than all the homes in Tiverton Four Corners combined, but that's only a guess. You'll pass The Elms, Château-sur-Mer—considered one of America's finest examples of lavish Victorian architecture and design—Rosecliff, the Astors' fabled Beechwood mansion—the summer home of William Backhouse Astor and *the* Mrs. Astor, once the undisputed queen of eastern society—and Belcourt Castle. They probably told you at the Newport Historical Society about the parties that once took place—and still take place—in these sprawling Xanadus. Captain Kidd would have been at home at those parties. People in Newport have a fondness for sailing ships and for all the things the captain found appealing. Greed is an emotion with which all present would have been familiar.

Near Belcourt Castle, the road turns toward the west, and Bellevue Avenue becomes Ocean Avenue. With a spectacular view of the Atlantic on your left, you'll soon find yourself at Brenton Point State Park. Returning to that map that is large enough to include both New York and Boston, you'll see that in terms of a secluded shore between the two, Brenton Point makes almost as much sense as the mouth of the Sakonnet River. Newport was not Newport then, and Brenton Point would be as safe a place as Sakonnet to stash a whale boat full of sea chests. If sea conditions were not right for a landing at one of these two sites, then the other would have been a reasonable alternative. It is not inconceivable that he might have made a stop at both. On the other hand, if the seas were especially rough, he might have sailed up into Narragansett Bay in search of calmer waters.

The captain might have gone twelve miles up to Hog Island, or he might have found calm waters ten miles closer to the mouth of Narragansett Bay at Conanicut Island. There is, after all, the reputed Pirate's Cave on Conanicut Island. There was also the matter of Mr. Thomas Paine, one of the island's more intriguing residents. Next stop, Conanicut Island.

To reach Conanicut Island from Brenton Point, drive back into Newport and look for signs to the Newport bridge. This four-mile toll bridge crosses the mouth of Narragansett Bay—where the captain would have sailed en route to Hog Island, or to the mysterious "Pirate's Cave." Today there are roads around the entire perimeter of Conanicut Island, so it is not probable that Pirate's Cave has remained undisturbed for three centuries, but there is more than just the cave on Conanicut Island. Unlike many of the other sites, at Conanicut it is virtually certain from documentary evidence that Captain Kidd really did stop here on his way to Boston.

As the story goes, in April 1699 Kidd anchored off Conanicut Island and went ashore to visit an old friend, Thomas Paine (not *the* Thomas Paine), with whom he had sailed in the Caribbean. The visit is confirmed by a deposition taken from Paine by Lord Bellomont, whose own investigation of the missing treasure brought him to Conanicut. Paine told Bellomont's investigators that Kidd had asked him to safeguard the plunder while Kidd went into Boston. Paine claimed he refused.

Was Paine lying? If he was, then the treasure is long gone. If Paine was telling the truth, what did Kidd do next? Did he sail on to Brenton Point or across to Sakonnet?

What we do know is that when Kidd was arrested, his wife contacted Thomas Paine to "provide twenty-four ounces of gold for his comfort while in jail."

Why Paine? What did he have and what did he know?

For many years after Paine passed away—taking the answers to these questions to his grave—a marker at that grave stood in what had been Paine's yard. The words on the marker read "Thomas Paine, Mate to Captain Kidd."

Sometime later, the Thomas Paine place changed hands, and when crews were digging to do some work on the foundation they discovered an ivory elephant's tusk and at least one old gold coin. The tusk was taken to Tufts University, and apparently it is still there. The coin or coins disappeared. Where did the tusk come from? Possibly from the effects of an old buccaneer who did some plundering off India? Where did the gold coin come from, and where did it go? What else may still remain buried?

Leaving Conanicut Island, the Route 138 bridge will take you glancing in your mirror with thoughts of a pirate's cave ivory tusk—back to the mainland. Passing through Allenton, you will rejoin U.S. Highway 1, just six miles from Conanicut Island. Turn left and head south to the town of Narragansett Pier. Here U.S. Highway 1 turns west toward Connecticut, but if you continue driving south on Rhode Island Route 108, it's only about four miles to the town of Galilee and the Block Island ferry, which takes us to the fifth of the six Rhode Island sites—and an interesting sidebar that introduces another intriguing character from buccaneer history.

The Joe Bradish Connection: Too Much of a Coincidence?

Located ten miles offshore, Block Island is a seasonal resort that is sort of analogous to what Nantucket is to Massachusetts—technically part of the state, yet distinct. Block Island is far less remote from the mainland than it was in 1699, but it still is a place apart. When Captain Kidd made his dash to Boston that summer, Block Island would have seemed about as deserted as the dark side of the moon, and that very well may have played into his thinking one night.

At Block Island, when you set foot on the ferry pier and make your way into town, you'll be confronted by the usual gauntlet of tourist shops selling seashell memorabilia and T-shirts with seagulls and sailboats, but if you know where to look, off the beaten track, there will be shops less shrill, where people will be glad to chat for a while. As talk turns to pirate treasure, as it probably will, there will be mention of Captain Kidd and of where and when he may have made landfall on Block Island; and talk will also come around to Captain Joe Bradish.

Bradish was an American-born pirate whose path crossed

that of Captain Kidd in the last year that either of them
breathed air as free men: 1699. Born in Cambridge, Massachusetts, in November 1672, Bradish was just a kid,
barely half Kidd's age, but he already had a reputation that
was well known at the time, even though now it has not
the luster of Captain Kidd's. Bradish was a seaman who
shipped out to the South Pacific aboard the hakeboat *Adventure* bound for the island of Borneo. It was at Polonais
Island, while most of the crew was ashore, that Bradish and
some mates stole the ship and set sail on a career of pirating. Bradish, being a naturally gifted navigator, found himself the new captain.

By March 1699, even as Captain Kidd himself was sailing toward these waters, the *Adventure* arrived off the eastern of Long Island, heavy with loot stolen from ships from
the Atlantic to the South China Sea. According to legend,
Bradish went ashore at Nassau Island with most of this
treasure, but soon traveled to Rhode Island, where after at
least once having been refused because of his shady past,
he finally managed to buy a small sloop. He and ten of his
mates then set sail toward Boston, where, they believed,
they would not be harassed by the law. They were wrong.

Arrested for piracy, Bradish was thrown in jail, but by
happy coincidence, one of the jailers, Caleb Ray, was an
old friend. Elaborate preparations were made for the escape,
and on the morning of June 25 Bradish and the one-eyed
rascal Tee Wetherly were not present for roll call. Lord
Bellomont went berserk and offered a reward of two hundred pieces of eight for the recapture of Bradish and one
hundred pieces of eight for Wetherly.

Bounty hunting often brings curious characters out of the
woodwork; after all, Captain Kidd's venture into that neth-
erworld of the law brought out the greed in several lords
and at least one king. In the case of the Bradish bounty,
one of those stepping up to the plate was the old Native
American medicine man called Essacambuit, who happened
to be in Boston at the time. Somehow he managed to turn
up some information that Lord Bellomont's crime-stoppers
could not, and he nabbed Bradish and Wetherly north of

Saco, Maine, up toward the mouth of the Kennebec River.

Coincidentally, the area around the mouth of the Kennebec River was where—some theorists believe—Captain Kidd was traveling at almost exactly the same time. A month or two earlier they were both in the vicinity of Block Island at the same time as well. This is the sort of coincidence that conspiracy theorists love. Captains Bradish and Kidd on clandestine missions to the same deserted stretches of coastline—first Block Island, then Maine—at exactly the same time. A coincidence?

We do not know whether there was a rendezvous in either place, or if so, why there would have been. We know that Bradish was in both places, and we know that he was in Rhode Island shopping for a sloop. But why did he and the one-eyed Wetherly travel to Maine? How is it that Essacambuit knew where to go to find them? Too much of a coincidence?

If there was no rendezvous in Maine between Captain Bradish and Captain Kidd, there certainly was to be one in Boston. When he was finally returned to the hospitality of Lord Bellomont, Bradish found that he had landed in the same Boston jail as none other than Captain William Kidd. Indeed, in February 1700 the two captains shipped out together—albeit in irons—aboard the man-of-war *Advice*. As with Kidd, this would be the last voyage for both Bradish and Wetherly, who were both hanged at Hope Point in London.

What Did Kidd Really Do with the Treasure?

Captain Kidd did make stops at Clarke's Island and on Gardiner's Island, and he may have made a quick stop in Rhode Island en route to Boston, or he may have landed at a remote island, such as Block Island. Then, too, he may have decided that ill-gotten goods wouldn't have been really safe unless he secreted them on some really remote island, such as Isle au Haut. The romantic streak in all of

us wants to believe such a story as much as the conspiracy
theorists would conjure up links among Bradish, Kidd and
the lordly patrons of Kidd's original scam. After all, who
doesn't love a conspiracy that reaches all the way to the
top? Kidd's reached all the way to His Majesty himself.

As a practical matter, many who fancy themselves as
practical believe that Kidd's secret was buried closer to
New York, where he could get at it easier when that expected pardon was issued by His Lordship on behalf of His
Majesty himself.

This would take us back to the shortest route between
New York and Boston. By sea this would be through Long
Island Sound. The route, of course, is via Block Island, but
if he had wanted it close to New York, it would have been
closer to New York than Block Island. By land the shortest
route is, once again, U.S. Highway 1—the old New York-
to-Boston Post Road.

Traveling west from Galilee, where the Block Island
ferry puts in, the next mainland point—and the sixth Rhode
Island site—that has been celebrated by local legend as a
Captain Kidd treasure site is at Watch Hill, which is located
in that sandy tongue of land that extends along south of
Connecticut below the mouth of the Pawcatuck River. Ni-
antic Native Americans—relatives of the Narragansetts—
lived here before the seventeenth century, and it filled our
criterion of being a very deserted stretch of beach until
the U.S. government built a lighthouse here in 1806. When
the railroad reached nearby Stonington, Connecticut, in the
nineteenth century, developers tried—with moderate success—to turn it into a miniature Newport. Watch Hill
roared with the Roaring Twenties, its summer "cottages"
playing host to the likes of Isadora Duncan, Clark Gable,
Douglas Fairbanks, Jr., Stan Laurel, Mary Pickford, Andrew Mellon, and Henry Ford. However, a hurricane in
1938 wiped out nearly everything. This, of course, brings
to mind the fragility of man-made encumbrances on such
a coastline in the face of nature's fury. If Kidd really hid
something along here, did he take that into mind? He was
a seafaring man. He knew about hurricanes. Would he have

cached his stash far enough above high tide that it would have remained intact even after the miniature Newport was washed away?

Like its neighboring states, Connecticut has a treasure lore that is deeply rooted in both pirate lore and in the eighteenth-century legends surrounding the American Revolution. Whether Captain Kidd did or did not, many pirates once called upon the shores of the Constitution State in the dead of night as the mist scudded across the face of a full moon. Was Kidd one of them?

As one drives west along the ragged Connecticut coastline, there are countless inlets, many of them now choked with modern pleasure craft but some of them associated with that singular sloop of Captain Kidd. Such a place is at Old Lyme, on the eastern side of the mouth of the Connecticut River, thirty-five miles from the Rhode Island state line. There is another site, known to local legend as "Captain Kidd's Cache," in the vicinity of Middletown, twenty-five miles up the Connecticut River from Old Lyme. While the Middletown site would deviate from the theory of a quick stop en route to Boston, it certainly would fit the profile of a place that would be safe from beach erosion. If Kidd had stopped at the mouth of the Connecticut River to put two chests of treasure ashore on Clarke's Island, could he not have landed elsewhere in the area?

Closer to the radius of an easy day's voyage by sloop from New York City, there are alleged Captain Kidd sites near Milford in New Haven County—especially Stratford Point—and at various places in posh Fairfield County, which is, today, possibly the richest suburban county in the United States. Captain Kidd would find himself at home there. Among the places that local legend likes to associate with the captain are Money Island, Pilot Island, and Sheffield Island, all offshore from Norwalk.

In the Empire State itself, there is a school of thought supported by a great deal of local lore—as are most schools of thought having to do with buried treasure—that holds that Captain Kidd sailed more than thirty miles up the Hudson River to cache his sea chest. If one discounts the probability that he took the time to sail up the Kennebec in Maine, the Connecticut in Connecticut, or any number of other rivers in between, then should one necessarily discount the Hudson? Not necessarily. He spent several weeks in and around New York City when he returned from the Caribbean. A trip up the Hudson would have been a Sunday sail for a mariner of Kidd's caliber.

Where, then, are the alleged Hudson River Valley sites? There are several in the vicinity of what later became the U.S. Military Academy at West Point. These include the "Captain Kidd's Crow's Nest" and those at Kidd's Point and at Grassy Point, which is near Stony Point. Considerably farther north is the intriguing Sleepy Hollow treasure, which is associated with Kidd by legend. However, it is in the vicinity of Palenville, a long way upstream from Manhattan.

The coast of New Jersey, like that of neighboring states, is no stranger to tales of pirate treasure. The visitors' bureau brochures love to tout past crimes as much as they wish to convey the impression that crime no longer exists in their locality. As for the theory of the Captain Kidd caches, who is to say that he necessarily hid all his loot *after* he returned to New York? He would have passed the coastlines of all the American colonies on his way north from the Caribbean. He could just as easily have stopped here as in Connecticut, and certainly easier than in Maine. Then, too, there is an interesting political consideration: Lord Bellomont was the governor of everything from New York to what is now Maine. In New Jersey and points south he had no authority. Did Captain Kidd, knowing this, hide a nest egg or two south of his lordship's mandate just to be on the safe side?

South of New York City, U.S. Highway 1 turns inland toward Philadelphia, and the Jersey shore is much better followed by U.S. Highway 9, or by New Jersey Routes 35 and 36. Indeed, the latter two actually ride the crest of New Jersey's barrier islands from Navesink Lighthouse to Barnegat Inlet. Both U.S. Highway 9 and New Jersey Route 35 cross the Raritan River at Perth Amboy, and it is east of here, along the shores of Raritan Bay that several Kidd sites are mentioned in folklore.

It is believed that there are some Captain Kidd sea chests buried at Cliffwood Beach on Raritan Bay near Route 35, and at Sandy Hook, which arches back toward Raritan Bay from Navesink Lighthouse. Today Sandy Hook, along with neighboring Plum Island and Skeleton Hill Island, are part of the Gateway National Recreation Area, some of which is open to the public for recreation and some not.

At the opposite end of the Garden State—reachable by either U.S. Highway 9 or the Garden State Parkway toll road—is Cape May. The cape itself is the southernmost tip of New Jersey and is marked for mariners by the Cape May lighthouse. Nearby is Lilly Pond, another place that Kidd is alleged to have stopped en route to New York City from the Caribbean.

The ferry across Delaware Bay to Lewes, Delaware, departs from the town of North Cape May, which is a couple of miles northwest of Cape May. U.S. Highway 9 ends at North Cape May and resumes ten miles south, at Lewes, so it might be said that this is the only section of a U.S. highway that exists only on the deck of a ferryboat. Traveling by ferry captures a trace of the mood of Captain Kidd's time, for when he crossed the mouth of Delaware Bay—which he did—he sailed these waters. It was a little bit farther out to sea, but it *was* these waters, and he would have been within sight of land.

There is a modicum of belief in Delaware that he did more than simply stay in sight of the shore. Indeed, with a long, sandy, and relatively secluded coastline, Delaware was a favorite place for pirates to put ashore. Not only Captain Kidd but also the notorious James Gillan (or Gillian), a member of Kidd's crew, supposedly buried treasure on Kelly Island in Delaware Bay, thirty miles up from Lewes off of what is now Bombay Hook National Wildlife Refuge. It is not altogether clear whether they both buried treasure here or whether Kidd's name comes up as a means of identifying Gillan. Perhaps Gillan saw Kidd bury his loot at one of those many other sites, then dug it up after Kidd was arrested and brought it to Kelly Island?

To reach Kelly Island after the Cape May car ferry drops you at Lewes, turn north on Delaware Route 1 toward Dover. About four miles north of the idyllic and appropriately named village of Little Heaven, turn right on Delaware Route 9 to Little Creek. At Little Creek take Delaware Route 8 about three miles north to Port Mahon. From here you'll be able to look across a channel in the Leipsic River delta and see Kelly Island. There is no bridge to the island, nor any roads on the island, so you'll need to inquire locally about getting a small boat.

The mudflats of Bombay Hook National Wildlife Refuge have always been a stopping place for migrating birds—red knots, ruddy turnstones, and semipalmated sandpipers—who turn the islands into the second largest concentration of shorebirds in North America during a two-week period in late May. Kidd could have been here in May.

In 1679, exactly two decades before Captain Kidd's last voyage as a free man, Mechacksett, chief of the Kahansink people, traded the Bombay Hook area to a Dutch New Yorker named Peiter Bayard for guns and liquor. Bayard, who called it "Boompijes Hoock" ("little-tree point"), in turn sold it in about 1700 to a Huguenot refugee named Jean Allee. The house built in 1753 by his son, Abraham Allee, still exists.

It is theoretically possible that Kidd knew Bayard during his years in New York and that Bayard had told Kidd about Boompijes Hoock.

South of Delaware, stories of Captain Kidd treasure are far fewer than they are in the area between New York and Boston, where he is known to have sailed on his penultimate voyage. In Baltimore, Maryland, the Druid Hill Park treasure is also known as "Captain Kidd's Cache," and there is a Captain Kidd's treasure associated with Fernandina Beach, near Jacksonville, Florida. These stories may have some basis in fact, but there is much more evidence to support the legends farther north.

Where is Captain's Kidd's true cache? Does it still exist?

Did it ever? Were there, as the multitude of legends suggest, a multitude of caches? There are no definitive answers to these questions. There are only guesses.

The Thomas Paine story sounds convincing, and it did yield some tangible evidence in terms of both gold and ivory, so that would have to rate near the top of a list of probable sites. Then, too, there is the fact that Lord Bellomont sent his own team of investigators to Conanicut Island in 1699, when the trail was still fresh. Block Island is also a strong possibility. Block Island stories have been part of folklore for centuries, and the island is actually closer to the actual route between New York and Boston than is Gardiner's Island, where real treasure was found. Was it too close?

Isle au Haut off Maine is a more remote possibility, just as it is more remote geographically. However, if Joe Bradish and Caleb Ray went to Maine, why not Captain Kidd? And what was it about Maine that drew pirates in the last year of the seventeenth century?

Ultimately, the only man who could provide the elusive answers took it with him when he stepped off Execution Dock in London in 1701. If he was the last man, what about the last woman? Sarah Oort Kidd also was executed. Did she also take the secret to her grave? Did she ever know it? Did James Gillan know, and did he take the secret to the secret place and the treasure itself to Boompjies Hoock?

The questions can only be pondered, but they can be pondered in the face of a fresh breeze in some of the more scenically interesting places on the East Coast of the United States. As we said in the Introduction, this book is about the search as much as it is about the treasure. With Captain Kidd's legacy, there is enough searching to last a lifetime.

Chapter 2

CHARLES WILSON'S ASSATEAGUE ISLAND CACHE

PLACE: *Assateague Island, off the Delmarva (Delaware, Maryland, Virginia) Peninsula*

TIME PERIOD: *Early eighteenth century*

Buried or hidden pirate treasure is elusive because in most cages its true location was deliberately obfuscated by the person or persons who buried or hid it, and because the romantic legends that have swirled around buccaneers and their booty have exaggerated and confused the stories even more. As discussed in the preceding yarn, pirates are so popular in local legend that local visitors and tourist bureaus up and down the eastern seaboard love to make the most of their local pirate. If they didn't have one, they borrow one from somewhere else. This is, I suppose, why there are Captain Kidd treasures in the lore from Maine to the Delaware shore and beyond. Is it really any wonder, then, with so much myth overlaid on reality, that you can dig in sand dunes from Maine to the Gulf Coast and never find a thing?

Indeed, with three centuries of pirate myth obscuring distant pirate reality, why bother? Should we not just give up on wild geese and curl up with an Errol Flynn video or a good pirate novel? Before you say "yes"—or "aye, me hearty"—read on.

Robert Louis Stevenson—the sickly boy turned adventurer who gave us our most enduring pirate archetypes and one of the truly great lost treasure tales of all time—used a treasure map as one of the central features in his 1883 novel *Treasure Island*. And on that treasure map there was an "X," and that X marked a spot.

In fiction, one often reads of treasure maps that lead the protagonists (and often the antagonists as well) to the place where "X marks the spot." In the reality of treasure lore, though, most locations are shrouded in mystery and rumor. Most pirate treasures have no maps, and the maps that do exist are so vague as to be worthless. There are exceptions, however.

On a windswept barrier island off the coasts of Maryland and Virginia that is known as Assateague, there *is* a pirate treasure for which an actual set of directions exists. In the early eighteenth century the buccaneer Charles Wilson roamed these waters, preying on merchantmen from the Carolinas to New England. As was the case with pirates of the day, he would often put in from place to place to stash his plunder for a later day or to lighten his ship for a bout of looting. Among the more attractive places for such an activity were the hundreds of miles of bays and intracoastal waterways that crouch behind the outer banks and barrier islands that run up the East Coast most of the way from Miami to Staten Island. Chincoteague Bay, the thirty-by-ten-mile body of water behind Assateague Island, is such a place, and the complex mass of nooks and inlets on the bay side of Assateague Island, would have provided ideal refuge for a pirate ship—calm waters, shelter, and a haven from the prying eyes of the men-of-war of His Majesty's Navy. Pirates also worked out of Hog Island Bay, twenty miles north of to the south, and there also have been numerous shipwrecks on the shores of Hog Island.

It was to the bay side of Assateague Island that Charles Wilson sailed on at least one occasion, and on this occasion the place where he cached his plunder was memorialized with an "X" that marked a spot. For some reason Wilson made a point of making note of this site, and somehow that information has been preserved. There is an early eighteenth-century manuscript that has been authenticated as having been made by Captain Wilson's own educated

English hand. In it he tells of having buried gold worth an estimated $2 million in current dollars. And he tells us *exactly* where he buried it:

"Ye treasure lies hidden in a clump of trees near three creeks lying 100 paces or more north of the second inlet above Chincoteague Island."

The directions seem simple until one ponders the U.S. Geological Survey topographical map of Assateague Island. North of Chincoteague Island, which fits into Assateague like a ball into a socket, there are dozens of larger inlets, hundreds of smaller inlets, and an uncountable number of often seasonal streams.

Finding the Way to Assateague Island

Assateague Island is off the shore of Delmarva, the mostly rural peninsula that contains all of Delaware as well as parts of Maryland and Virginia. Assateague is not near anywhere. Except for the little-known NASA airfield between U.S. Highway 13 and Chincoteague, the nearest airports are at Salisbury and Ocean City in Maryland, but they are just little general-aviation fields. To get to Assateague Island, the best way is to fly into Washington or Baltimore and take the shortest route to the Delmarva Peninsula, which would be via U.S. Highway 50, which crosses Chesapeake Bay on the five-mile-long William Preston Lane, Jr., Memorial Bridge, which everybody locally calls the "Chesapeake Bay Bridge." Poor William Preston Lane, Jr.

Once across the William Preston Lane, Jr., Memorial Bridge, follow U.S. Highway 50 south and east toward Ocean City, Maryland. Highway 50 is a curious road. It was designed originally as one of the few of the old U.S. highways to actually cross the United States from ocean to ocean. It has one end within sight of the Atlantic breakers at Ocean City; the other end used to share the San Francisco Bay Bridge with U.S. Highway 40 until both roads were superseded by Interstate 80 between Sacramento and the

East Coast. Between the oceans, Highway 50 crosses the emptiest part of Nevada—where it is known as the "loneliest road in the United States"—but, upon reaching Delmarva, it was built to follow the periphery of the state of Delaware, deliberately going out of its way not to leave Maryland.

From Ocean City you can actually see the northern tip of Assateague Island, but there are no roads on this part of the island, and after a very short boat ride to the tip of the island it would be a very long walk to the neck of the woods where old Charles Wilson buried his famous sea chest.

There is no road that runs the thirty-seven mile length of Assateague Island, nor is there even an officially designated hiking trail. Because of its protected status, no such road or trail will ever be built on Assateague Island. The island is now managed by the National Park Service, with the two-thirds of its length that is in Maryland being designated as the Assateague Island National Seashore, and the remainder, which is within Virginia, being set aside as the Chincoteague National Wildlife Refuge. A fence that follows the state line crisply and abruptly separates the two.

Although both sections are administered by the National Park Service, they are administered for distinctly different reasons. The National Seashore is administered for recreation, including—one would suppose—poking around looking for sea chests. The Chincoteague National Wildlife Refuge, on the other hand, is set aside to protect wild animals, including the famous population of wild ponies who have lived on Assateague since their ancestors were abandoned here by the Spanish more than three centuries ago. Countless generations of these animals have lived here in this Delmarvan Galapagos, cut off from the mainland and evolving independent of all horsedom. Like similar populations on the Outer Banks of North Carolina, they are considered by the U.S. National Park Service as being ecologically unique and worthy of preservation. There are, in fact, two separate herds, separated by the state line fence, with the one in the Assateague Island National Seashore being owned by the National Park Service and the one in the Chincoteague National Wildlife Refuge being owned by—of all things—the volunteer fire department of Chincoteague.

There are other differences between the way the Assateague Island National Seashore and the Chincoteague National Wildlife Refuge are administered. The National Seashore is open to off-road vehicles, but the Wildlife Refuge is open mainly for limited hiking access. While the Chincoteague Wildlife Refuge is on Assateague Island, the actual Chincoteague Island is mostly not part of the Wildlife Refuge or the National Seashore, nor does it have wild ponies.

While no paved roads run the length of Assateague Island, there are two such roads that reach portions of the island. About eight miles south of Ocean City, Maryland, Route 611 crosses onto Assateague Island, and there are about three miles of road in and around Assateague State Park. From here a twenty-mile dune-buggy track heads south toward the Wildlife Refuge, where for the sake of the rare ponies, the four-wheeled creatures cannot go. To use the dune-buggy track a permit is required, so while it is physically possible to cross the fence and to walk into Virginia and into ponyland, this is discouraged, and there is no legally designated trail.

To reach the southern (Virginia) end of Assateague Island by road, take U.S. Highway 13 to Pocomoke City, turn east on Virginia Route 175, and follow the signs to Chincoteague. From Ocean City, Maryland, drive west for eight miles on U.S. Highway 50 to Berlin and turn south on U.S. Highway 113. At Snow Hill, Maryland, take Maryland Route 12 south. At the state line, Maryland Route 12 becomes Virginia Route 679, which, in turn, intersects Virginia Route 175 near NASA's Wallops Flight Test Center airfield. Turn east on Virginia Route 175, which crosses a series of bridges across the mouth of Chincoteague Bay, an area famous for its oyster beds and clam shoals.

The town of Chincoteague, which is on the western side of Chincoteague Island, is a picturesque little community that bustles with activity, especially in the summer, when people flock to the shore from the sweltering mid-Atlantic urban areas. It is also a favorite bait and tackle center for fishermen who like to fish the waters of Chincoteague Bay. Just seven miles long, Chincoteague Island is described locally as "Virginia's only resort island . . . and perhaps the most beautiful island on Virginia's Eastern Shore." It does have the distinction of being the home of many of the craftsmen and artists who produce some of the world's finest handcarved duck decoys.

When you pass through Chincoteague, the signs leading to Assateague Island lead you to Maddox Boulevard, and about a mile down the road you reach the bridge that crosses the narrow channel to Assateague. Here you enter the U.S. National Park Service fee area. The rangers will charge you four dollars for a weekly vehicle pass, or two dollars if you are on foot or riding a bicycle.

The old U.S. Coast Guard lighthouse will be on your right and dunes lie ahead as you reach a road junction. To the right, Beach Road leads past Tom's Cove to the Park Service Visitors' Center and the main parking area for beach parking. The Atlantic Ocean is just across the last line of dunes. To the left, at the junction, is Wildlife Loop Road, which encircles Snow Goose Pool. Open only between 3:00 P.M. and dusk, this road is a good deal less traveled than Beach Road. However, at the nine-o'clock position on the loop is the trail head for the trail to Wash Flats, which lie about three miles north of the road and about two miles south of the Maryland state line.

Here your actual search for old Charles Wilson's treasure should begin.

You Need Treasure Maps

Before you go, you need maps. Captain Charles Wilson left no treasure map, but he did leave us with tantalizingly precise directions. They seem, in fact, even better and more precise than a treasure map with an "X" that marks the spot. But don't forget, me hearties, that we are dealing with a shrewd old buccaneer and the passage of three centuries.

You need maps. It is important that you have the most recent U.S. Geological Survey topographical map for the area, because geographical features along these barrier islands are fragile and subject to change. Streams change course. Inlets fill with silt. Fast-moving, seasonal streams carve new inlets in days. The geological features in an area such as the lower third of Assateague Island can remain untouched for a century and change abruptly in the course of a single winter storm. You will want the map that is most likely to show features as they will be when you encounter them.

In this case, for exactly the same reason that you must have the most recent U.S. Geological Survey topographical map for the area, you must have as many old ones as you can as well. Precisely because the terrain on Assateague Island is subject to dramatic changes, it will be very useful to have older maps to compare to the present one so you can see what sort of changes may or may not have taken place over the years. Of course, there was no U.S. Geological Survey at the time Charles Wilson dropped anchor in Assateague Bay, so they produced no topographical maps during that time, but maps have been produced for more than half a century, and these give excellent close-up views of the area in question.

There are, of course, maps of the shoreline of Virginia and Maryland that date back to the days when Captain Wilson plundered merchantmen off these shores. Such maps are still accessible and should be consulted. You should, of course, bear in mind that while U.S. Geological Survey topographical maps are absolutely precise as to the way things are when they were drawn, the older maps may not be exact. However, with your U.S. Geological Survey map in hand you will be able discern any important changes by comparing the two, or possibly three, if you can find a multiple of older maps.

The most recent topographical maps are available from

the U.S. Geological Survey Map Distribution/Map Sales office at Building 810 in Denver, Colorado; the phone number is (800) 872-6277. They will be able to supply you with the current map at a nominal cost, and they will have information on sources of other maps.

For older maps you should go to local sources. Since parts of Assateague Island are in two states, the state archives in both Maryland and Virginia, which have a great deal of excellent material, should be consulted. A visit to one or the other or both will be useful before going to Assateague Island. You may reach the Maryland State Archives in Annapolis at (410) 974-3914, and the Virginia State Archives in Richmond at (804) 367-8506.

Study the directions that Charles Wilson has left for us and plot what you feel to be the probable location or locations on your U.S. Geological Survey topographical map. Then take this map to Annapolis and/or Richmond and compare it with any and all maps that may be available for the area that lies "100 paces or more north of the second inlet above Chincoteague Island." You could write or phone the archives, explain what you are looking for, and ask them to send you good, clear copies, a service for which there will be a charge. Depending on what it is, they may not be willing to copy it, and it is really better to go in person. They will almost certainly let you look at it if you do come in person, and such a visit may be very useful on many levels. It is always good to look at the old maps firsthand, and you will probably meet people who can tell you more about the geography and pirate lore of Assateague Island than you ever knew existed.

Local sources, as always, may be surprisingly helpful. Both of the relevant county seats are less than an hour's drive from Assateague Island, so you could find a place to stay in the area and use this as a base for visiting the county records offices as well as for making your ultimate trip to the island itself. The northern (Maryland) end of Assateague Island is in Worcester County, whose county seat is in Snow Hill, Maryland, just thirty-three miles from Chincoteague. The southern (Virginia) end of Assateague Island is in Accomack County, with the county seat in Accomac—same spelling, except no "k"—in Virginia, twenty-eight miles from Chincoteague.

In the county seats, repeat the process described above for the state archives. Possibly even more than at the state level, you will probably meet people who can tell you a great deal about the geography and pirate lore of Assateague Island. Who knows? You may meet someone who knows someone who has searched for the Charles Wilson treasure.

With maps in hand, or at least with the information gleaned from the maps, you are ready to begin.

Following the Maps

Begin your search from the above-mentioned nine-o'clock position on the Wildlife Loop Road in Chincoteague National Wildlife Refuge. Remember that this loop is open to vehicles only between 3:00 P.M. and dusk, and you will want to get an earlier start, so it is necessary that you park your car at a designated parking area on Beach Road.

Soon after you leave the Wildlife Loop Road and begin hiking toward Wash Flats, you will be able to look off to your left and see Chincoteague Island, only a few dozen yards across a narrow channel from Assateague Island. It is easy to imagine that in a very low tide the two islands could become one. When Charles Wilson sailed into Chincoteague Bay from the Atlantic Ocean three hundred years ago, he would not have sailed through here between Chincoteague Island and Assateague Island. He would have sailed up the western shore of Chincoteague Island, past what is now the waterfront of the town of Chincoteague. Passing through the narrows now crossed by Virginia Route 175, he would have traveled another five miles, generally due north, until he came abreast of the northern tip of Chincoteague Island.

As you are now walking north, you come abreast of the

tip of Chincoteague Island with Wash Flats to your right and the gradually widening channel between the islands to your left. Now is the time to revisit that early eighteenth-century manuscript that has been authenticated as having been made by Captain Wilson's own educated English hand, in which he tells of having buried gold worth an estimated $2 million in current dollars. As the captain wrote, "Ye treasure lies hidden in a clump of trees near three creeks lying 100 paces or more north of the second inlet above Chincoteague Island."

You are there. You are on Assateague Island adjacent to the tip of Chincoteague Island. You are standing on the same dunes, standing in the same bunch grass that the old buccaneer scanned with his telescope. He sailed these waters and he *anchored* in these waters. And he put ashore on these dunes to the squeal of the ancestors of these same herring gulls and under the watchful gaze of the ancestors of these wild ponies. Where exactly did he put ashore? He said the treasure was hidden "in a clump of trees near three creeks lying 100 paces or more north of the second inlet above Chincoteague Island." Here we are. We're almost there!

The second inlet above Chincoteague Island can't be far. All we must do is find the first inlet and look for a second. What constitutes an inlet? As we stand here looking into Chincoteague Bay past the tip of Chincoteague Island, it is easy to imagine that the northern outlet of the channel between the islands would look like an inlet from out in the bay. Even a glance at a U.S. Geological Survey topographical map confirms that the shape of this area could conceivably constitute an inlet. If this is the first, then the second can't be far. But how far?

North of our "first inlet" there is a ragged promontory—you can't really call it a peninsula—that is about a mile wide and that extends about a mile into the bay. On it are about a half dozen bays and inlets. None of these is on the same scale as the feature we have identified as our "first inlet." If it really is the first, none of these would be large enough to constitute the second. On the other hand, if our "first inlet" was too wide to be considered as an inlet, then could two of these smaller inlets be the first and the second?

Immediately north of the promontory there is another major inlet that actually leads into a mile-long pond on Assateague Island that is referred to on the maps as "Old Fields." It is easy to imagine this feature as being one of the two inlets. But is it the first or the second? Did the lay of the terrain appear this way when Charles Wilson made landfall here, or have three hundred years of hurricanes and erosion changed things substantially? Here on the leeward side of Assateague Island, could things have remained much as they were for that long?

To complicate matters, there are two fairly prominent inlets—and a dozen minor ones—within the next three miles. Above that, across the Maryland state line, is Pope Bay and a veritable maze of inlets and small intracoastal waterways.

Charles Wilson described "a clump of trees near three creeks lying 100 paces or more north of the second inlet." There are numerous clumps of trees, but it is extremely unlikely that these have survived exactly as they were some three hundred years ago, so it is probably best to begin looking for places where there are three creeks close together. It is here that your U.S. Geological Survey topographical map—and the other map work you have done— will be essential.

A calculation can now be done like a mathematical equation. There is an "second" inlet, and there is a place with a trio of creeks. In fact, there are many inlets and several places where one might find a trio of creeks. The limiting variable, as explained by Charles Wilson, is that they are separated by a distance of a hundred paces. How far is a hundred paces? This is a question that truly cannot be answered until you get to the area west of Wash Flats, because the length of a pace will always be governed by the terrain. Is the ground hard, or is it drifted sand? You will notice as you walk that your steps will be longer on a hard surface than they will be in sand. Also take into account the length of your legs. Captain Wilson's formula is based on a hundred paces, probably his own. He would have been in good physical condition, and he would have been not much more than five feet tall. For argument's sake, let's say that he was sixty-four inches tall. If this describes you, then your hundred paces in this terrain will be roughly equivalent to his. If you are six feet—seventy-two inches—tall, then his hundred paces will be the rough equivalent of eighty-eight of yours.

Using your topographical map, calculate the distance of a hundred Charles Wilson paces to the scale of the map. Next, identify the two or three best guesses as to the correct "second" inlet north of Chincoteague Island. Using a pencil and a compass (or a ruler or even a blade of dune grass), mark the point a hundred paces north of these inlets. When you find such a point that corresponds—within a margin of error of fifteen paces—to a place where there is (or was, based on old maps) a trio of streams, draw an "X"!

Could this be it? Has anyone figured this out ahead of you? Have the tides shifted the location of Charles Wilson's sea chest? Is there—or could there have been—a clump of trees? Certainly, where there is a stream fed by a freshwater spring, there *could* have been trees.

Now you will have narrowed your search. The use of metal detectors is forbidden on National Park Service land, as is the removal of artifacts, but you have come to within earshot of the place where the old buccaneer buried his treasure, and if you do happen to be digging through the sand when you find something, your name may very well be linked to an archaeological discovery that your new friends in the Virginia State Archives will be telling their grandchildren about. If not, well, there are worse places to spend an afternoon than out here on Assateague Island, in the cool, fresh Atlantic air, "near three creeks lying 100 paces or more north of the second inlet above Chincoteague Island."

Chapter 3

JEAN LAFITTE'S TREASURES

PLACE: *The Bayou Country of the Gulf Coast*

TIME PERIOD: *1812*

The bayou country that runs along the Gulf Coast from the mouth of the Mississippi River as far southwest as Galveston, Texas, was traditionally friendly to the pirates of the Caribbean. Geographically it is unique. The entire eastern seaboard of the United States has a shoreline marked by inlets and intracoastal waterways, but on the Gulf Coast, particularly in the Mississippi Delta region of Louisiana, there is an area roughly the size of the state of Massachusetts (and roughly the *shape* of the state of Massachusetts as well) that is a mass of swampland and intimidating jungle with a veritable maze of interconnecting and dead-end waterways in which even longtime residents can get lost. Roads were virtually nonexistent in the Mississippi Delta and Louisiana bayou country until the twentieth century, and in much of this area, roads are *still* nonexistent. Transportation is by barge or shallow-draft boat, just as it was two and three centuries ago, when it was a pirate haven. In fact, there are still things going on in the bayou country that wouldn't happen in—say—Massachusetts.

The reigning city of the region, New Orleans, the Crescent City, was traditionally a place apart. Even as late as the twentieth century it was justifiably thought of as the least American in character of any major American city.

New Orleans and the surrounding bayou country were physically detached from the rest of the United States until the twentieth century and developed a culture that owed more to Cajun, Creole, and African-Caribbean influences than that of the Anglo-American mainstream. Even today, parts of New Orleans have more of the feel of a Caribbean island city than of typically southern cities such as Baton Rouge and Shreveport, located upstate in Louisiana.

The great city of New Orleans was the gateway to the vast Louisiana Territory, which at the beginning of the twentieth century included all the land drained by the Mississippi and Missouri Rivers, an area roughly equivalent to a quarter of what is now the United States. Spain originally claimed most of it, but ceded Louisiana to France in 1800. Napoleon, who was then at war with Britain, didn't want to divert resources to defending New Orleans from them, so in 1803 he sold Louisiana to the United States at a fire-sale price. This was Thomas Jefferson's famous "Louisiana Purchase," which changed the course of history. Today the state of Louisiana is merely the area surrounding the last two hundred miles of the river, and the bayous of the Mississippi Delta.

At the heart of the Louisiana bayou country due south of the city of New Orleans and west of the mouth of the Mississippi River is a place known as Barataria, with its center around Barataria Bay. The name was derived from the old French word meaning "deception," a description that perfectly describes the complex maze of waterways that were tailor-made for the pirates and smugglers who have always been active there.

It was here in Barataria that the great pirate prince Jean Lafitte had his headquarters, and where he is thought to have hidden much of the vast fortune he stole from British and Spanish freighters and gold ships during the first quarter of the nineteenth century.

The Amazing Prince of Pirates

Jean Lafitte was born in 1780 or 1782—nobody knows for
sure. Nobody knows where he was born. It was probably
in France and surely in some French-speaking place. Maybe
it was a seaport such as Marseilles or Bordeaux, or even
Haiti. The story is that his parents were French aristocracy
who were beheaded during the French Revolution. He certainly had the style and breeding to support the notion of
such a background, but nobody knows. They say that he
died between 1826 and 1829, but, again, nobody knows for
sure. He was like a specter, and the word down around
Barataria is that he is *still* like a specter, that his ghost still
haunts the backyards and the graveyards.

For more than a decade, though, he was a fixture of New
Orleans society, with a barely concealed parallel life in a
compound on Grand Isle (a.k.a. Grande Terre), the island
that guards Barataria Bay from the Gulf of Mexico. He was
the pirate prince of Barataria, which he so aptly described
as the "back door to New Orleans."

Little is known about Jean Lafitte's early days, but records do show that he came to New Orleans in about 1804
as captain of a French privateer—a bounty-hunting private
warship—named *La Soeur Chérie*. The story was that he
was fleeing a slave revolt in Santo Domingo, but nobody
knows for sure. Lafitte dropped anchor for repairs and provisions, but stayed to put down roots in the Crescent City.
By 1809, he and his brother Pierre were listed as being the
owners of a blacksmith shop that is said to have been used
as a warehouse for the transshipment of smuggled goods
that served the needs of the numerous smugglers and pirates
who were based in Barataria. Jean Lafitte was seen as being
the perfect front man for such activities. He was just the
type of man they were looking for, just as they were what
he needed. This was because Lafitte had worked his way
into the upper levels of New Orleans social circles.

Lafitte moved with the best crowd and had business con-
tacts on every level. He was tall, dark, and handsome, and
he fancied himself a gentleman. He was a dashing ladies'

man but also a shrewd businessman. Like a pirate's
cutlass—and like the city that was his adopted home—Jean
Lafitte had his polished side and his rough side. He spoke
four languages—French, Spanish, Italian, and English—
and he operated gambling halls and bordellos. He probably
made a fortune as a broker and fence for the Barataria buccaneers, but he also spent part of that fortune dredging the
waterways and operating a fleet of barges—cut from
hundred-foot cypress trees—that operated continuously between Barataria and New Orleans.

By 1811 Jean Lafitte had become so powerful that he
was literally a prince of thieves. He organized the Barataria
pirates to plunder shipping in the Caribbean and he directed
the operations of as many as a hundred ships that were not
registered in the United States, Britain, France, or Spain
but that sailed under the flag of the infant Republic of Car-
tagena—later part of the Republic of Colombia—which
also had (and has) a reputation for being pirate-friendly. Of
course, such operations were in direct violation of U.S.
laws, but New Orleans and its merchants thrived on the
illicit commerce. His friends in New Orleans society and
in the Crescent City's merchant community knew the nature
of Lafitte's "business activities," and they were pleased. It
was good for their businesses as well.

As noted above, New Orleans and the surrounding area
were a place apart from the United States, both culturally
and economically. In the early years of the nineteenth century, even though there were now more and more Americans living in New Orleans, the majority of the people still
were descendants of the old French or Spanish families and
really did not recognize American sovereignty. People continued to play pretty much by local rules. New Orleans had
been part of the United States for less than a decade at that
time, and the people of the bayou country didn't really
think of themselves as Americans. They had seen both the
French and Spanish flags come and go, and expected that
the Stars and Stripes would soon be gone as well.

New Orleans was like an autonomous city-state, and Jean
Lafitte was like a member of its royalty. His power was

certainly as great as that of a prince. As with the people of
New Orleans, the U.S. government was well aware of La-
fitte, but attempts to curb his operations were fruitless.
When the American governor, William C. C. Claiborne, ac-
cused him of piracy and posted a $500 reward, Lafitte re-
sponded by offering a $1,500 for the arrest of Claiborne.
The whole affair served only to amuse the people of New
Orleans.

When the War of 1812 broke out, however, New Orleans
became a pawn in the superpower conflict, and it was time
for the pirate prince to choose sides. At issue was a struggle
between England and the United States for control of the
Mississippi River. The British approached Lafitte and offered him immunity for his past offenses against British
shipping and even a commission in the Royal Navy if he
would help them evict the Americans from Louisiana. Lafitte agreed or pretended to agree. To this day we don't
know what he had in mind. We know only how it turned
out.

The British briefed the pirate prince thoroughly on their
planned attack on New Orleans, and he promptly took this
information to the Americans. He proposed that he would
put his pirate fleet at the disposal of the U.S. Navy in
exchange for a pardon. Instead, the U.S. Navy attacked
Grande Terre.

The U.S. Army, meanwhile, had different ideas. The
navy was out to destroy British ships, but the army had the
job to assert American control over New Orleans itself.
Army general—later president—Andrew Jackson inter-
vened and got a message through to Lafitte that he would
honor the deal he had asked for.

Jackson once referred to Jean Lafitte and the Baratarians
as "hellish banditti," but "Old Hickory" *hated* the British.
This hatred dated back to the Revolutionary War and the
death of his brother, who was a British prisoner of war.
When Jackson arrived to organize a defense of New Orleans against the redcoats, he was willing to enlist support
from anyone he could. This included the "hellish banditti,"

as long as they were willing to breathe their hellish fire on His Majesty's troops.

Jackson sought out the pirate prince in his favorite watering hole, the Old Absinthe House Bar—which still stands on Bourbon Street—and over their beverages of choice, they cut a deal. Lafitte was willing to supply ammunition as well as the services of his men. In return he asked only for a pardon for all the Baratarians the governor had threatened to throw in jail. Jackson agreed, and the pirates joined the army, which was composed of the general's Tennessee and Kentucky riflemen as well as a group of Cajun, Creole, and Choctaw volunteers.

On January 8, 1815, Jackson's force—along with the Baratarians—defeated a veteran British army two and a half times their size. Ironically, the war was already over—the British had surrendered—but neither side doing battle in New Orleans knew it!

The American victory—though unnecessary in the context of a war already won—was overwhelming, and Lafitte's help is considered to have been pivotal. Indeed, the gunnery of the pirate ships was generally superior to that of U.S. naval ships. The pirate gunners had had more practice.

After the war, President James Madison honored Jackson's promise, and Lafitte's Baratarians were pardoned and given U.S. citizenship. Many stayed to settle down to a somewhat quieter life. Some say that Lafitte turned from pirate to soldier of fortune, running a private privateer navy rather than pirate ships. Then, too, there are those that say he was a privateer all along and *never* a pirate. But, as Lord Byron wrote of Lafitte, "He left a corsair's name to other times, linked one virtue to a thousand crimes."

In September 1819 the U.S. Navy captured eighteen Baratarians—allegedly working for Lafitte—looting a Spanish Ship. They were tried, convicted, and publicly hanged in New Orleans. Because he was implicated—possibly wrongly, but we'll never know—Jean Lafitte shifted his operations center from Grand Isle, Louisiana, to Spanish territory farther west. Specifically, he moved two hundred miles west to the barrier island off the Texas coast that Lafitte called Campeche and that is now known as Galveston Island.

The prince of pirates and his pirates soon constructed a fortress compound at Campeche that rivaled that at Grand Isle, and soon they were up to their old tricks—plundering merchant ships in the Caribbean. He soon accumulated an army—and navy—of pirates, soldiers of fortune, privateers, and adventurers from all over the world, including four hundred officers and men from Napoleon's army that had been defeated at Waterloo. From his combination fortress, warehouse, and home, known as Maison Rouge, Lafitte ruled with a smoking pistol and lived in the elegant manner of a prince. His ships never hesitated to attack any vessels thought to contain rich prizes, including more than a hundred Spanish ships laden with gold.

Through the late teens the pirate prince is thought to have accumulated an immense personal fortune—but he probably already had a sizable nest egg. Although estimates vary widely, it would probably not be an exaggeration to suppose that Lafitte had a net worth—in cash and gold—of about $50 million in today's dollars.

While the Campeche cutthroats concentrated on Spanish shipping—and the occasional British vessel—the thankful Yanks usually turned a blind eye. However, when the pirates started attacking U.S. merchantmen, the U.S. Navy got involved. Despite Lafitte's promises to respect the U.S. flag, the navy threatened brutal retaliation if he did not abandon Campeche and his wicked ways. In 1820 Lafitte loaded his treasure aboard his ship *The Pride* and sailed out of Galveston Bay for the last time. As the story goes, he coasted toward North Padre Island, possibly by way of Espíritu Santo Bay and possibly by way of Aransas Pass. He was in Corpus Christi Bay, possibly anchored near St. Joseph's Island, when he encountered a U.S. Navy frigate.

Lafitte took evasive action, and sailed north through the intracoastal waterway, through San Antonio Bay, back through Espíritu Santo Bay, and into Matagorda Bay with the warship in pursuit. Fifty miles north of Corpus Christi he turned north and began running up the Lavaca River. *The Pride* hit a sandbar and Lafitte ordered that the treasure be taken ashore and the vessel scuttled. On the way across the salt marshes, Lafitte had a hole dug and the treasure buried in it. As the story goes, he took a compass reading of the exact spot and drove a Jacob's staff—a brass rod used by surveyors—into the soft ground exactly above the treasure, so that only the top of the rod was visible. The navy never found the spot, and apparently Jean Lafitte never returned.

The pirate prince was now a man on the run. Where he ran, nobody really knows, but there are several legends that are given varying degrees of credibility. Some people say he fought with the great Simón Bolívar to liberate Spanish provinces in South America; others say he died with ten of his men fighting petty privateers off Isla Contoy, Yucatán. Still others place the scene of his death—of fever—on Isla Mujeres. The year usually stated is 1826, although various stories insist that his death came as late as 1829.

Some of the particularly romantic legends say he went back to Barataria to die and is buried there. Where exactly is hard to pinpoint because the legend in the bayou country is that Lafitte is buried in every backyard. And then there are the ghost stories that say he never died, or that his spirit still walks at night beneath the cypresses hung with moss.

Lafitte's Louisiana Treasures

If the pirate prince accumulated treasure worth $50 million—or even $5 million—we are left to wonder where it went. Did he recover it within his lifetime and spend it or lose it? Was it pilfered by the Baratarians who knew where it was? Is it still hidden somewhere, and if so, where? Has someone stumbled across it by accident? Even to this day, when someone down on the Gulf Coast comes into sudden and unexplainable wealth, it is common to hear it said that the person "found Lafitte's treasure."

If the treasure does remain to be discovered, it remains to narrow down the likely places, and the Louisiana bayou country is still full of Jean Lafitte stories. The place to begin would be in the vicinity of the Crescent City itself. In about 1810 Lafitte often visited d'Estrehan Plantation, which was just up the Mississippi River from New Orleans. The d'Estrehans were influential planters and on friendly terms with the pirate prince. Local stories say that Lafitte took advantage of their hospitality to bury treasure on their property. Years later, the story still circulated among the slaves at d'Estrehan Plantation who knew about Lafitte's cache. It was widely believed locally that the Lafitte's spirit returned for many years to the house on stormy nights and pointed a bony finger at the hearth, which is allegedly where the treasure had been secreted.

So important is the legend of Lafitte to the cultural patrimony of southern Louisiana that in 1978 the U.S. National Park Service established the Jean Lafitte National Historical Park and Preserve to "preserve for present and future generations significant examples of the rich natural and cultural resources of Louisiana's Mississippi Delta region." In addition to its official nod to the pirate prince, the park interprets the influence the many cultures have had on this region's history and development. The park consists of six separate sites in southern Louisiana; specifically in Lafayette, Thibodaux, Eunice, and Charenton, as well as the Barataria Preserve near Crown Point.

Running parallel to and about twenty miles south of the Mississippi River, Bayou Lafourche is one of the longest bayous in the sprawling Mississippi River Delta. It flows out of the Mississippi River at Donaldsville, about twenty miles south of Baton Rouge, and meanders in a southeasterly direction, meeting the Gulf of Mexico at Port Forchon, midway between Timbalier Bay and Barataria Bay and about five miles from Lafitte's old stomping grounds on Grand Isle. Rumor has it that the pirate prince cached some of his treasure on or near Caillou Island, west of Bayou Lafourche. A factor that leads one to suspect that this is more than a theory is that $20,000 in old Spanish and Mexican coins was found on Caillou Island in the early part of the twentieth century.

One of the more intriguing stories takes us to Lake Charles, Louisiana, about three hours west of New Orleans on Interstate 10. While Lake Charles is nearly twenty miles inland from the Gulf of Mexico, one may sail directly into town via Calcasieu Lake and the river of the same name. Jean Lafitte is said to have had a two-room log shack in Lake Charles, specifically adjacent to the Barbe House. The remains of embankments built by pirates—behind which stood mounted guns—can still be seen in Lake Charles, and it is claimed that Lafitte sank a schooner containing part of his treasure in Lake Calcasieu one dark night when pursuers were thought to be near. South of Lake Charles, at the suggestively named Contraband Bayou, there have been a number of searches through the years, but if anyone found anything, he or she is not talking.

A large cache of Mexican gold and silver coins of Lafitte's era was discovered in 1923 at the place known as Jefferson Island. Jefferson Island isn't an island at all, but a salt dome rising from the flat prairie and resembling a tremendous mound. Since for several years before, old coins bearing a 1754 date had frequently found their way into circulation in the area, it was concluded in 1923 that part of Lafitte's treasure had been found at Jefferson Island. How the 1754 dates were linked specifically to Lafitte is a matter to be discovered while perusing microfilmed copies of 1923 newspapers on your research trip to New Orleans or Lake Charles.

In the early part of the twentieth century, hunts were made for Lafitte treasure at Pecan Island, which, like Jefferson Island, isn't an island at all but a long, oak-covered ridge rising abruptly from the surrounding country. Stories that go back to the mid-nineteenth century tell that Pecan Island was once completely covered with pecan trees and the ground was literally covered with human bones. Many explanations of the bones have been suggested; one theory holds that this was the spot where Lafitte had his victims murdered. Treasure hunters have thoroughly dug up the island, and in 1925, not content with digging, they used dynamite and almost blew the place to pieces. Not one old coin was uncovered for the trouble and environmental degradation.

Baton Rouge is about an hour to ninety minutes west of New Orleans on Interstate 10. About the same distance east, one reaches exit 4 and the turnoff for Alabama Route 188. About ten miles south one reaches the town of Bayou La Batre, Alabama. Bayou La Batre is a small community of winding streets and small cottages amid tropical vegetation about twenty miles south of Mobile. It is generally known—or generally taken for fact—that Lafitte and the Baratarians often sailed into the bayou and anchored under the safety of their shore guns while the crew went to Mobile to spend their gold.

Stories that are still told down around Bayou La Batre say that Lafitte buried treasure near here on several occasions, and that this was witnessed by local people. However, they were too afraid of the pirates to dig it up. So greatly was Lafitte feared that the devout Catholic people in the area actually sprinkled holy water in the doorways of their houses to keep him out. Children of later generations were told that Lafitte could reach out of the sea and pull them into the water if they were out too late at night. This was probably not true, but Lafitte's reputation does border on the supernatural.

The Amite River Cache

Today one can drive between New Orleans and the Louisiana state capital at Baton Rouge on Interstate 10—much of the route a causeway—in about an hour, but two centuries ago it was a long trip, not possible in a day, by barge. Traveling overland through the swamps and bayous was a difficult second choice. It was along this route, however, that Lafitte is said to have stashed some loot.

Between New Orleans and Baton Rouge, if one travels

overland and north of where Interstate 10 causeway now runs, one will encounter the Amite River, which flows down from the Mississippi, making a couple of serpentine twists near the eastern side of Baton Rouge before turning east, where it forms the border between Livingston Parish and Ascension Parish.

The mouth of the Amite River is in Lake Maurepas, which, in turn, flows into Lake Pontchartrain. This point, near the border between Ascension Parish and St. John the Baptist Parish, is the site of the little village of Galvez Town, which is now too small to show on most maps but which was an important shipping center when the Spanish were in control of Louisiana. According to local legend, Lafitte once sailed a ship up the mouth of the Amite River end buried a load of gold on the shore opposite Galves Town.

Getting to the mouth of the Amite River is not easy. Whether you travel by land or by water, get an early start, because the daylight can slip through your fingers like sand in an hourglass, and you don't want to be caught in unfamiliar bayou country at night.

By water one can travel across Lake Pontchartrain from New Orleans, beneath the famous Lake Pontchartrain Causeway and west to Manchac Pass, which leads through the Manchac Wildlife Area to Lake Maurepas. The mouth of the Amite River is roughly at the eight-o'clock position on the generally circular Lake Maurepas.

By land one reaches the mouth of the Amite River by way of the tiny town of Brittany, in Ascension Parish. From New Orleans you would take Interstate 10 west to exit 187, which will put you on U.S. Highway 61, the same road that Bob Dylan made famous by "revisiting" it in the 1965 album *Highway 61 Revisited.* (The highway also runs through his hometown of Hibbing, Minnesota, but that is another story for another time.)

On Highway 61 you should travel north (actually northwest, but it is called "north" on the signs) four miles west to Brittany. To reach Brittany from Baton Rouge take In-

terstate 10 east to exit 182, and turn north on Louisiana
Route 22 for two miles.

From Brittany, continue north on Route 22, where you
will actually cross the Amite River. At the point where you
see the Amite River sign, though, you will be more than a
dozen miles from the mouth, and you can get closer. As
the Amite River disappears into the distance on your right,
Route 22 takes you into some of the most remote bayou
country north of New Orleans that is served by a paved
road. The towns of Maurepas and Head-of-Island are on a
trip into a bygone era. A side trip north on Louisiana Route
16 to the town of French Settlement is recommended, but
only on the return trip if you have the time. You don't want
to be traveling in unfamiliar bayou country after dark.

Just north of Maurepas, which is about sixteen miles
north of Brittany on Route 22, watch carefully on your right
for signs indicating Louisiana Route 1039—possibly the
Pelican State's shortest highway—which leads in the direction of Denson, two miles south.

At Denson you are still another two miles from the
mouth of the Amite River, but you are as close as you can
drive on a paved road. Getting to the mouth must be done
on foot through particularly inhospitable terrain. On ancient
maps, inhospitable areas were marked with the phrase
"Here be dragons." A map of the mouth of the Amite
River should be marked with the phrase "Here be snakes."
They *are* here, and they are dangerous. At this point you
should inquire locally about the advisability of going farther. You should also consider the possibility of getting to
the shore of Lake Maurepas—also about two miles away—
and using a boat to circle around to the mouth of the Amite.
Here it will become obvious that your U.S. Geological Survey topographical map will be of vital importance.

Lafitte's Texas Treasures

Jean Lafitte is one of the reigning characters of Louisiana
legend, one of the dark and mysterious characters that a

city like New Orleans loves to claim as its own. While Lafitte is popularly associated with the history of New Orleans and the Louisiana bayou country, it was in Texas that he is last known to have had a permanent home. And the Texas Gulf Coast has embraced him as a local attraction. There is scarcely an island along the vast Texas coast that does not have its favorite tale of buried Lafitte treasure. In 1889 some old Spanish coins and a large chest were found at Virginia Point near Galveston. The chest was empty, but its proximity to the site of Lafitte's old Campeche compound led to the belief that someone had found part of the pirate's treasure.

In the late 1930s some Spanish coins dated 1803 were found on a beach near Anahuac, the county seat of Chambers County, which is at the northern end of Trinity Bay, a spur of Galveston Bay. Then, in 1940, there was considerable excitement in Anahuac when Texas State authorities were asked for permission to salvage a strange ship that could be seen in the glittering sands of a nearby inlet. The vessel was deemed to be one of Lafitte's treasure ships. The state failed to grant salvage rights.

The Sabine River forms the boundary between Texas and Louisiana, and flows into the Gulf of Mexico through a waterway known as Sabine Pass. The town of Sabine Pass, on the Texas side, was a thriving community when the Baratarians ruled the Gulf Coast in the early years of the nineteenth century. Lafitte's fleet of Cartagena-flagged pirate ships frequently sailed through Sabine Pass to drop anchor in Sabine Lake. The surrounding dunes are a treeless expanse of tall salt grass and the kind of place that is often associated in works of fiction with buried treasure and pirate chests, but while there has been a great deal of amateur treasure hunting here, little more than the odd old coin is know to have been found.

If Lafitte was based at the mouth of Galveston Bay, he and his fleet are known to have often used the intracoastal waterways around Corpus Christi as hiding places. Corpus Christi Bay and Nueces Bay behind it were protected from heavy seas that might be encountered out in the Gulf of

Mexico, and as such they offered a safe anchorage, where a pirate crew could drop anchor and put ashore for freshwater and provisions, or to divide their spoils. Because the area was nearly deserted at the dawn of the nineteenth century, this was also a potentially safe place to hide treasure. There is a persistent legend that Lafitte buried three chests of treasure on Liveoak Point near Aransas Pass.

To see for yourself, you can take a boat directly to Aransas Pass from Corpus Christi by simply navigating north from the city, through Corpus Christi Bay, with North Padre Island on your right. By land, from Corpus Christi International Airport, take Texas Route 44—which is also Agnes Street—west to Texas Route 358, which is a freeway also known as Padre Island Drive. Turn right on Texas Route 358 in the direction of North Padre Island. About twenty miles from the airport you will cross onto North Padre Island by way of John F. Kennedy Causeway. Once here, the Gulf of Mexico will be straight ahead, with Padre Island National Seashore to the right. The town of Port Aransas and the actual Aransas Pass are eighteen miles north on Texas Route 361 by way of Mustang Island State Park. The area is much changed since the days when Jean Lafitte and his erstwhile Baratarians made landfall here, but there is a ferry across Aransas Pass that will give you a tiny modicum of the flavor of being on the water in this legendary waterway.

A ferry ride of less than a mile places you in the environs of the community of Aransas Pass, which grew up in the nineteenth century and remained a sleepy fishing village until oil was discovered on the land at the beginning of the twentieth century. Just offshore from Aransas Pass is a long, low island known as St. Joseph's Island. The story locally is that Jean Lafitte had his headquarters here. While he certainly *used* the area as a stopping point through the years, and it is possible that he may have used St. Joseph's Island or the present site of the town of Aransas Pass as a temporary base, there is no evidence that he ever constructed fortifications or buildings around here.

St. Joseph's Island was first settled sometime after Lafitte died, when a coalition of cattlemen and seafarers built a town there they called Aransas Wharves. When or why this town vanished is not known (it may have been a victim of the Civil War), but the island again was uninhabited until the turn of the century, when it was purchased by Colonel E.H.R. Green—the title was fictitious—the only son of famed Hetty Green, one of the richest women in the world. The first actual compound worthy of Jean Lafitte's Grand Isle was built here in the early twentieth century by the great oil tycoon Sid Richardson, who built a large house, wharves, and an airstrip for his guests. In keeping with the Lafitte theme, Mr. Richardson did secure the island with a private guard force.

The Lavaca River Sandbar

What about Lafitte's last known run-in with the U.S. Navy and the treasure he allegedly buried at the Lavaca River? He had been running from a pursuing warship when his ship *The Pride* hit a sandbar. Lafitte had ordered that the treasure be taken ashore and buried. As noted above, he had then driven a brass Jacob's staff into the spongy ground to mark the spot. He probably never returned, but a number of years later, a San Antonio man named J. C. Wise, armed with definite clues obtained from two of the treasure bearers, made repeated searches along the marshy banks of the Lavaca River for the brass rod. These searches were unsuccessful.

Late in the nineteenth century, however, an African-American boy who worked for a horse rancher named Hill was riding near the swampy mouth of the Lavaca River when he stumbled across a brass rod sticking out of the ground. He retrieved the rod and took it to the ranch house with him that night. Several days later, the rancher saw the rod lying near the corral. Recalling the old tales that Jean Lafitte was supposed to have marked the site of his buried treasure with a similar instrument, he asked the boy about where he had found the rod. The boy took the rancher back out into the marshlands where he had been riding, and they thoroughly searched for the matted grass that would indicate the place where the boy had stopped. It had been several days, and a rainstorm had blown through in the meantime, so they were unsuccessful.

Many people have followed in the footsteps of Mr. Hill, and if any have had better luck, they have not shared the news. But you can go to the mouth of the Lavaca River and try *your* luck. From Corpus Christi, take the Nueces Bay Causeway (U.S. Highway 181) to the north. About five miles north of the causeway you will reach a crossroads at which U.S. Highway 181 will veer sharply to the left and Texas Route 35 will go to the right. Take the latter road in the direction of the town of Aransas Pass. From Aransas Pass, Route 35 generally parallels the intracoastal waterway that Jean Lafitte would have taken as he was running from the U.S. Navy gunboat. Follow Route 35 for about sixty-five miles to the town of Port Lavaca, the county seat of Calhoun County. At Port Lavaca there is a large bridge leading across to Point Comfort. Here you should inquire about the best way to reach the mouth of the Lavaca, for you are now only two miles away.

To get here to Point Comfort from Houston, take U.S. Highway 59 south about seventy-five miles to the town of Edna, the county seat of Jackson County. We have identified Port Lavaca and Edna as count seats because it is in these towns where the research that is a prerequisite to finding the Lafitte treasure may be conducted. Our directions will get you to the mouth of the Lavaca River and will position you in a spot from which you can look across the sea of marsh grasses waving in the wind to the general area where the treasure is buried, but without further research you could spend years making the same mistakes that were made by those who came before you—instead of benefiting from those mistakes. Not only that, but also the lore you will discover will make the history of Lafitte's final days as a mortal come alive. You will see twists and turns you cannot now imagine as you immerse yourself in the passion and greed of the treasure hunters who came this way before you.

From Edna, continue south on U.S. Highway 59 four miles to the El Toro exit. As you are leaving Edna you will suddenly find yourself crossing the Lavaca River. Don't bother to stop. You'll be on a freeway where it's illegal, and furthermore, at this point you are about twenty miles upriver from the mouth. At El Toro, turn east toward the Gulf Coast on Texas Route 234 for about ten miles. At the town of Vanderbilt, Route 234 will end, so turn left on Texas Route 616. Once again, you will cross the Lavaca River. Now you may stop. You are on a two-lane road, and it is time to get a feel for the lay of the land—and water. From here you are probably very close to the sandbar where Lafitte's ship *The Pride* went aground.

A couple of miles past your crossing of the Lavaca River you will reach the town of Lolita. If you turn left here on Texas Route 1593 you will be in Point Comfort in about ten minutes. As you will clearly see on your U.S. Geological Survey topographical map, Route 1593 between Lolita and Point Comfort parallels the lower eight miles of the Lavaca River. You can catch glimpses of it as you drive this narrow road, and on the way there will be several side roads that lead out into the marshlands. One of those will place you within a hundred yards of the Lafitte treasure. But remember before you turn off Route 1593 that trespassing is illegal, and trespassing is taken seriously by property owners in these parts. Ask permission first.

If only that young man had not pulled the Jacob's staff out of the ground! A couple of hours with a metal detector and you'd be rich. On the other hand, the fact that he found it is further confirmation of the story.

More than a century has passed since Lafitte ran aground on the Lavaca River, and more than a century has passed since the Jacob's staff was found. The trail is cold, but the treasure *is* here somewhere. Or at least it *was*. The rest is up to you.

Chapter 4

BILLY BOWLEGS'S MANY LOST CACHES

PLACE: *The Shoreline of the Florida Panhandle*

TIME PERIOD: *1830–88*

Curiously, the name "Billy Bowlegs" was shared by two persons who figure in nineteenth-century Florida lore. One or both of them may have been bowlegged, but, as may be obvious, the real name of neither man was "Billy Bowlegs." The first Billy Bowlegs was a noted Seminole leader and raider of the 1840s and 1850s whose real name was Holata Micco and who plundered a great deal of loot from both white settlers and other Seminoles. The second was an English pirate whose real name is said to have been William Rogers (some sources spell it Rodgers), although that is possibly as much an alias as "Billy Bowlegs."

The Seminole Billy Bowlegs, Holata Micco, was born, historians have guessed, in about 1810. He died in about 1864, a date that should be recorded for posterity with more precision—because he was famous by that time—but it is not. Holata Micco was a member of the Royal "Cowkeeper Dynasty" of the Oconee tribe of Seminoles, and he became recognized as a primary leader of the tribe during the Second and Third Seminole Wars—between 1841 and 1858— because of his family connections.

The Seminole Wars were actually a state of prolonged conflict that are seen by some historians as the second-longest continuous war in which the U.S. Government engaged an enemy, second only to the wars with the Sioux that began in 1850 and ended at Wounded Knee in 1891. The origin of the Seminole conflict had its roots in the eighteenth-century white settlement activity in Georgia and the Carolinas, which forced most of the Native American people south into the Gainesville Prairies of Florida. The Seminole people, meanwhile, adapted to farming, which was fine and peaceful until the whites accused them of cattle rustling. This compelled them to move farther south into Spanish Florida, seeking refuge from white interference. Florida became a U.S. territory in 1822, and was earmarked for statehood, but the transition would be delayed for twenty-three years, largely because of the "Seminole problem." In 1823 most—but not all—Seminoles accepted a plan that provided for a reservation along the Apalachicola River. A constant state of hostility led to the Florida Legislative Council urging Congress in 1828 to remove all the Seminoles from Florida Territory. Some Seminoles accepted the bizarre notion of being "removed" to what is now Oklahoma, but others, such as the charismatic young warrior Osceola—known to the U.S. Army as the "Snake of the Everglades"—did not. In December 1835 Osceola ignited what would be known as the Second Seminole War with attacks against both whites and collaborating Seminoles. The defeat—in Florida they still use the word "massacre"—of a contingent of army troops under Major Francis Dade would be the U.S. Army's worst defeat of the Indian Wars until Little Big Horn. In 1837 Osceola was captured while under a white flag and soon died of "natural causes" while in custody.

By 1841 there was increasing white settlement in North Florida, but a guerrilla war still raged in the Everglades. It was now that Billy Bowlegs emerged as the principal leader of the Seminoles. He came to the fore at an auspicious time for his people. As with another unpopular jungle war against an indigenous people some 120 years later—the Vietnam War—there was decreasing enthusiasm in the U.S. Congress to continue what was seen as an expensive and bloody conflict. This was especially true in the context of the rift between the Northerners and the Southerners in Congress. The latter wanted Florida admitted as a state because—as it was in the South—it would be a slave state. The Northerners wanted no more slave states, because that would impinge on their voting majority in Congress. (The Civil War, as we know, was fought for three decades in Congress before the first shot was fired.) In any case, as a by-product of the slave state issue, the Northern Congressional delegation stipulated a curb on expansion of white settlement in Florida and a truce with the Seminoles that would be the price for Florida statehood, which finally occurred in 1845 as James Knox Polk followed John Tyler into the White House. What followed for the next decade was a war of attrition in which white settlers and Seminoles sniped at, and raided, one another at a level that was more nuisance than warfare, although many of the raids conducted by Billy Bowlegs and his associates resulted in what remain as interesting "lost treasure" stories.

On one occasion during the 1840s, Seminole raiders attacked a salvage operation that was recovering gold from sunken ships. The Native Americans lured away the U.S. Army force protecting the salvagers, attacked and killed nearly everyone, and burned the buildings. Some of the salvaged treasure was stolen, some lost, and much was never found.

For the most part, however, the level of pillage that Billy Bowlegs and his cronies committed is illustrated by the occasion of a conference between settlers and Seminoles in which the Seminole leader Coacoochee and his entourage turned up dressed in Shakespearean costumes they had stolen from a theatrical company.

Comedy turned to tragedy in 1855 when, as the story goes, a military surveyor named George Hardstuff trespassed into Billy's banana patch. After leading his people into the disastrous Third Seminole War, which lasted until 1858, Billy Bowlegs finally agreed to take them to Indian Territory in what is now Oklahoma. Three years later, with the start of the Civil War, Billy himself declared war on the Confederacy, because most of the U.S. Army officers with whom he had fought in the Everglades were now Confederate officers. Thus it was that the old part-time bandit from Florida returned to his home state to fight the same foe. This time, however, they were wearing gray, and Billy himself wore the blue of the U.S. Army as a captain in the Union Army's First Indian Regiment. He died in about 1864, the year before the war ended.

Pirate Billy

While the Seminole Billy, Holata Micco, left little to bother with in the buried treasure mythology of the state of Florida, his namesake became the leading figure in that mythology. The pirate Billy Bowlegs, who went by the more conventional alias of William "Billy" Rogers, was born, historians have guessed, in 1795. The place was almost certainly a port city in southern England. They say he was the black sheep of his family and ran away from home to become a pirate. While Holata Micco reputedly died at fifty-four, a relatively young age even for 1864, Billy Rogers died in 1888, having survived to age ninety-three, no small feat for a pirate, although for most of the last half of those ninety-three years he lived not as a swashbuckler but as a hermit.

William Rogers first appears in the history of piracy in about 1810, when he arrived aboard a ship in the port of New Orleans. He was fifteen, and was learning the ropes aboard a sailing ship at the same time that Holata Micco was born in Florida. Rogers is said to have sailed with Jean Lafitte at the Battle of New Orleans in 1814 and to have become a pirate at about the same time. He probably became a Baratarian, and he may very well have been one of those who shipped out aboard one of Lafitte's fleet of Cartagena-flagged ships. He may even have captained one.

When Jean Lafitte and his outlaws from Barataria were pardoned in 1814 after the Battle of New Orleans, many Baratarians settled down to peaceful and relatively law-abiding lives. Not so Lafitte, and not so Billy Bowlegs. As Lafitte departed for the "new Barataria" of Galveston Island, Billy Bowlegs remained in New Orleans and acquired three small vessels.

When his ships were equipped and ready to sail, he recruited a crew from Lafitte's old hands and moved up the Gulf to Santa Rosa Sound near Pensacola, Florida. Here he started a career of smuggling and piracy that was to make him a rich man. At some point, probably in about 1820, Rogers purchased a plantation in Louisiana and married a Choctaw woman. They had six children over the ensuing years, even as pirate Billy pursued his career as a Caribbean buccaneer. Rogers was active through the 1830s, having established his base around Santa Rosa Island, off the sound of the same name.

The stories that are still told along the western coast of the Sunshine State say that Billy Rogers was an especially cruel man. They also say that unlike other pirates who spent their treasure on wine, women, and song—actually more like rum and women without so much of the song—Billy hoarded his blood-stained booty until his dying day. They say he was worth millions and that he could have lived out his later days like a king. Yet, during his later years, he preferred a shack in a mangrove swamp to a fine house with a brace of servants or—for a pirate, all the more possible and preferable—slaves.

It is uncertain how many ships Billy Bowlegs captured through the years—he didn't have to capture many of these to accumulate a great fortune—nor how much treasure he actually salted away. No such records were kept, and the only true measure of a pirate was by how much his name sent chills down the spines of rivals. His name was feared up and down the Gulf Coast, whence he would dart out to seize the Spanish treasure galleons plying the gulf. From them he is said to have stockpiled mountains of gold and silver ingots from the mines of Peru and Mexico, as well as buckets of newly minted coins.

In 1838, as Seminole Billy's political career was on its rise a few dozen miles inland, Pirate Billy also was making a career change. Having apparently decided to put bucca-neering behind him, Rogers dismissed his crew and set about burying what would become Florida's greatest buried treasure.

Rumor has it that he buried most of his gold and silver bars on the northern side of a small, sandy island in Santa Rosa Sound. On the mainland nearby he cached the minted coins. In addition to the Santa Rosa Island area, Rogers is widely believed to have hidden much of his treasure about a hundred miles east, in and around what is now Franklin County, Florida. Among the specific places are Bald Point, south of Ochlockonee Bay; and Dog Island, off the present site of the town of Carrabelle.

The stories say he also kept a million dollars in gold coins aboard his private ship. For the next year or two Rog-ers seemed to have been content to sit back and enjoy the glitter of the Florida sun on his buckets of gold, while his family apparently remained in Louisiana.

In time Rogers grew restless, not so much for his family in Louisiana, apparently, but for his pirate life. He rounded up another crew of Caribbean cutthroats, and in a few short weeks the hold of his ship the *Mysterio* was bulging with gold and silver as well as with the chests of jewels that are popularly featured in Caribbean pirate lore.

This isn't to say, however, that Billy plundered with im-punity. He constantly had to be on the lookout for naval vessels. In one spectacular incident he was spotted by a British man-of-war that was in American waters itself for undisclosed reasons. The British warship gave chase, but Billy outmaneuvered the pursuing ship in the Santa Rosa Island sandbars. He knew that he couldn't outrun the Brit-ish, but he ducked into a small harbor with a sandbar across its entrance. Billy's shallow-draft craft could easily glide across the slightly submerged bar, but the warship could not. Though he scraped bottom several times, Billy Rogers maneuvered his craft to the safety of the lagoon and laughed at the warship riding the heavy seas beyond the bar. The victory was fleeting, however, as the British captain sent several boatloads of armed marines to attack the cornered *Mysterio*.

There was little choice. Billy decided on a radical but very practical move. Gathering some equipment, supplies, and a few bags of coins, he scuttled the *Mysterio* in four fathoms of water. He and his crew then took to the longboat and pulled for the shore and the protective woods. They had too much of a head start for the Royal Marines, and the British were unable to salvage the gold. As they sailed away, having stayed too long in American waters already, Billy Bowlegs was faced with a salvage job of his own. The sunken ship was in relatively shallow water, but the gold in the hold was just deep enough to be unreachable. They could dive and reach it, but no man could lift a gold bar and swim to the surface with it. But the treasure was as safe at the bottom of the lagoon as it would be anyplace. The pirate decided that he'd simply establish a camp here and salvage the gold with deliberation if not speed.

Rogers put his first mate, Pedro Bogue, in charge of building a settlement, while he made his way back to Louisiana to purchase salvage gear and to bring his family back to Florida. It took him several months, but at last Billy returned to the lagoon with equipment and family. What he found upon his return should serve as a reminder to those of us who romanticize the old days in the Caribbean as being particularly romantic. Today, life in the tropics is the stuff of travel brochures, of swaying palms, of tanned supermodels in bikinis, and of icy rum drinks with little paper umbrellas. However, the reality of the tropics until as late as the middle of the twentieth century was tempered by disease. Diseases such as malaria were a fact of life that made the tropics horrible rather than idyllic. Indeed, this was a fact that was to keep Florida so lightly populated until the twentieth century.

When Billy Rogers returned, only four of the twenty-five crewmen remained at the camp. Most had died of "the fever," others had been killed by the Indians, and the remainder had simply wandered away. Billy was short-handed, and all efforts to salvage the treasure ended in failure. When his own wife died of fever, William Rogers gave up trying to recover the gold. He moved across the bay with his children and built a log cabin, where he would live out his remaining years—nearly half a century—within sight of the sunken *Mysterio* and his final plunder.

Meanwhile, he still had immense quantities of wealth buried within reach, not far away. As his children grew to adulthood, they also grew tired of the rustic life around Santa Rosa Island and urged the eccentric ex-pirate to spend some of the hidden hoard to buy a better life for all. The more insistent they became, the more intransigent he became. Finally they gave up and drifted away, never to lay eyes on their father again.

Many years later, after the Civil War, an old friend lived in the cabin with Billy and, as the story goes, one day the pirate actually showed the man where the treasure was buried and promised it to his friend upon Billy's death. In the 1890s the friend finally got around to leading an expedition to the spot, but the area was overgrown, and drifting sand had altered many of the landmarks. They say that the search was unsuccessful, and it probably was.

Billy Rogers died at ninety-three, the last of the old Gulf of Mexico pirates. Apparently he had never touched as much as one piece of eight, although he frequently visited the treasure sites and kept the markers in place. Today his millions are mostly still there under the shifting sands, except today they may be worth hundreds of millions. As for what lay aboard *Mysterio* at the bottom of the lagoon, covered with tons of silt and mud, it was finally located by Bud Worth of Fort Lauderdale and salvaged by him and F. L. Coffman in 1956.

The Pirate Treasures of Florida

There is no dearth of treasure lore along the coast of mainland Florida and in the Florida Keys, where treasure hunting is a major local cottage industry. In the Florida Straits and throughout the Caribbean, the search for sunken Spanish galleons and pirate ships is big business, and a business that often yields big profits. Discovery of such wrecks in the 1980s and 1990s earned millions of dollars, although the expenses in an underwater search can also climb into seven figures.

In addition to the hundreds of Billy Bowlegs's millions, there are Spanish buried treasures and other pirate treasures, as well as fortunes lost or hidden here during the Civil War, or during the Seminole Wars. General Andrew Jackson played an important role in the First Seminole War, and his name comes up in the treasure lore as well. In one instance Jackson hung two traders for selling arms and inciting the Seminoles. Their hoard, which was not recovered—at least at the time—was buried near the junction of two streams at the northern edge of Cross City in Dixie County. On another occasion Jackson and his troops were pursuing a group of Seminoles who hid seven horseloads of gold and silver coins in a swampy area now called "Money Pond" locally and which is near Neal's Landing, southwest of Fernandina Beach, near the Georgia state line in Nassau County.

Besides Billy, one of Florida's most notorious pirates was José Gaspar, known as "Gasparilla the Pirate." It has been estimated that between 1784 and 1821 he plundered more than five million dollars (worth many times that today), of which only about seventeen thousand dollars has been recovered. In one instance, Gasparilla was being chased by several ships when he went ashore on Anastasia Island near St. Augustine and buried a chest containing fifty thousand dollars in gold coins near a large oak tree.

Amelia Island was a notorious pirates' lair, and several small caches of gold doubloons were found in the 1930s. Among those still waiting for a finder are Louis Avery's booty near the southern end of the island, Stede Bonnet's hoard of church plate near Fort Clinch, Blackbeard's chests buried in the vicinity of Fort Clinch, and two large pirate chests buried in a patch of palmettos about a mile and a half from the southern end of the islands and two hundred paces from the beach. Tampa Bay was home to buccaneers long before it was home to the Buccaneers of the National Football League, and with the former came hoards of plunder. Two longboats filled with pirate booty are supposed to be buried close to the airport along Sweetwater Creek near Rocky Point on the eastern side of Tampa Bay. There have been several tales of buried treasure on Christmas Island, near the mouth of Tampa Bay, including the hoards stashed by Gasparilla, the fifty thousand dollars in paper currency buried in the 1920s by a bank robber, and Prohibition-era rum runners' caches.

There are several rumored treasures near the Courtney Campbell Causeway, connecting Tampa and Clearwater across Tampa Bay. A rich farmer buried a treasure chest in the center of the triangle formed by three oak trees on the top of Pierce's Bluff. Nearby Copper's Point, north of the causeway, was a pirates' lair, and the many markings on rocks in the area might be directions to the buried treasures.

Not all the treasures borne to Florida's shores aboard ships were pilfered by pirates. A great deal of it was hidden after being salvaged by sinking or sunken ships. An English ship was wrecked near Mayport in 1784, and the survivors buried four chests of gold coins. When they reached St. Augustine two days later, they were hung as spies by the Spanish, and no one ever found the cache. Many of the caches in the Florida Keys were buried by shipwrecked survivors, but some were also the hiding places of the salvagers sent to recover cargo and treasure. They were putting away a little something for their old age. Treasures have been found on Key Largo, Grassy Key, "Treasure Beach," and elsewhere. There have been literally hundreds of shipwrecks in the Florida Keys through the years, and the island of Indian Key was used as the main salvage area for the Spanish and, after 1810, by American wreckers, all of whom had a habit of burying their hoards. During the nineteenth century several of the richest Indian Key wreckers are known to have had hoards hidden on the island, but these have not been found.

Not all pirate plunder was taken at sea. The John Ashley

Gang were bank robbers who operated in Florida from 1915
to 1926, using Canal Point on the southern tip of Lake
Okeechobee as their base of operations. Supposedly they
buried most of their loot, including $110,000 in gold from
their last bank robbery, at Canal Point.

Sometimes there is treasure that is extraordinarily hard
to find, but when found, it is simply there to be picked up.
And then there are those treasures whose location is known
with absolute precision but that are impossible to get. There
is nothing more frustrating (well, almost nothing) than a
fortune that can be seen but not touched. One such treasure
is in a pool formed by a cold-water spring near Ponce de
Leon Springs in Volusia County. An iron chest lies there,
easy to be seen. The last we heard, divers had been unable
to recover it, and several attempts to use drag lines have
failed.

Then there is the "Mystery Chest," which lies in a
swamp surrounded by quicksand and appearing only during
dry seasons. One attempt at recovery involved a helicopter
and grappling hook, but the downdraft from the copter's
blades made the chest sink out of sight. For those wishing
to try another approach, it is located between the Indian
River and the Atlantic Ocean, close to Florida Route A1A
on the outer bank, eight miles south of Vero Beach.

With the exception of offshore sunken treasure, however,
the name that still inspires the most stories around Florida
is still "Billy Bowlegs."

Searching for Pirate Billy's Stash

In the dive bars and dive shops from Gulf Breeze to Panama City they still talk about the treasures of Billy Bowlegs
and of where they might be found. If Worth and Coffman
were lucky in 1956, why not me? Why not you? Why not
now?

Where, then, might it be? If the man who knew could
not find it in the 1890s, where might it be? Does it wait

beneath the sand to reward the careful search?

Generally speaking, there are two principal areas where the stories seem to crop up most often. One, of course, is the area around Santa Rosa Island, while the other is south of Panama City, down around Apalachicola in Franklin County. Our suggested starting point for a Franklin treasure hunt is through Tallahassee, Florida's state capital. If you are coming from out of state to chase the ghost of Billy Bowlegs, you may wish to fly into Jacksonville International Airport and take Interstate 10 to Tallahassee, or fly into Tallahassee Municipal Airport, but since the easiest way to Franklin County is through the state capital, we will begin there.

Another reason for beginning your search in Tallahassee is to visit the Florida State Archives, which contain as much detailed information on buried treasure and treasure recovery as can be found anywhere in the state. Also contained in the collection will be old maps that will be useful in fine-tuning your research. In addition to its collection of state and local government records, the archives have a manuscript collection that includes correspondence, diaries, journals, maps, and photographs.

The Florida State Archives are on the first floor of the R. A. Gray Building, at 500 South Bronough Street in Tallahassee, just two blocks west of the State Capitol building. The public research facilities are open regular business hours Monday through Friday but close early on Saturday. The archives recommend that people intending to do research here phone in advance to (850) 487-2073. Some types of research can be conducted by mail, but we recommend that you go in person, since we are leading you through Tallahassee anyway.

To get into Tallahassee from Interstate 10, take exit 29 within the city limits. This exit is at U.S. Highway 27 in both directions but is a bit confusing because it has two *names* depending on direction. To the north it is the Old Quincy Highway, but you should take the southbound direction, which is Monroe Street, and which leads toward the center of the city, where the Florida State Archives are located.

About two miles south of downtown Tallahassee, as you are driving away from the archives, you will reach a fork in the road. Take the right fork, which is a one o'clock right. This is Florida Route 61, also known as Crawfordville Road, because it will take you to the city of Crawfordville.

If you are arriving through Tallahassee Municipal Airport, pick up your rental car and turn right. Take Southwest Capital Circle—which is also marked as Florida State Route 263—to the east for about five miles to Crawfordville Road. At this point turn right toward the city of Crawfordville. To avoid confusion, note that at the point where Southwest Capital Circle intersects Crawfordville Road, the latter changes from Florida Route 61 to U.S. Highway 319.

In any case, you should be on Crawfordville Road, headed south toward the town of the same name. Crawfordville is the county seat of Wakulla County, which is separated from Franklin County by the Ochlockonee River, which flows into the bay of the same name. It was around Ochlockonee Bay that Billy Bowlegs is believed to have stashed many of his plunders. Six miles south of Crawfordville, U.S. Highway 319 intersects U.S. Highway 98, which leads due south, about seven miles, to a wide, four-lane bridge that crosses Ochlockonee Bay.

Before or after crossing the bridge, it is worthwhile to stop to ponder the bay, and the Ochlockonee River upstream. It will become obvious, even after two centuries, why this place was a favorite with pirates. The river itself is a maze of sandbars and snag-choked channels, while cypress swamps and quiet sloughs surround the bay. Even with the encroaching Gulf Coast development and the myriad of motorboats buzzing about, the river area is a scenically underdeveloped place.

Immediately across the Ochlockonee Bay bridge, begin watching for the turnoff to County Road 370, which will be on your left. Three miles ahead on Road 370, you will reach Alligator Point and an excellent view of the Gulf of

Mexico. Turning left for two miles from Alligator Point will take you to Bald Point, where Billy Bowlegs is said to have buried some of his plunder. Armed with information you may have gleaned from the Florida State Archives, you should be able to narrow your search.

Moving on to the next Billy Bowlegs site, rejoin U.S. Highway 98 in the direction of Carrabelle, about twenty miles away. This small resort town—which boasts a telephone booth that is billed as ''The World's Smallest Police Station''—and its adjacent sister city, Carrabelle Beach, face south across St. George Sound toward Dog Island, another of Billy Bowlegs's alleged treasure sites. A ferry now operates between Carrabelle and Dog Island, and in about fifteen minutes this ferry service can place you ashore on the same dunes on which the old pirate came ashore nearly two centuries ago.

The Billy Bowlegs treasure sites around Santa Rosa Island can be reached either by flying to Pensacola, or by driving in from Tallahassee on Interstate 10, or from Carrabelle by continuing on U.S. Highway 98. Part of the Gulf Islands National Seashore, Santa Rosa Island is a barrier island that is more than forty miles long and less than a mile wide and that stretches from the mouth of Pensacola Bay near Pensacola Naval Air Station to the mouth of Chochtawhatchee Bay adjacent to Fort Walton Beach.

Once it was forty miles of drifting sand, isolated from the Florida mainland and deserted. Today it is forty miles of drifting sand connected to the Florida mainland by two toll bridges and crowded with hundreds to thousands of beachgoers, sun worshipers, and fishermen. If Billy Bowlegs's Santa Rosa Island treasures have not been uncovered yet, it will take more than some casual beachcombing.

To reach Santa Rosa Island from Tallahassee by way of Pensacola, take Interstate 10 to exit 4, then Interstate 110 toward downtown Pensacola and exit at Gregory Street, which is U.S. Highway 98. At this point follow the signs to the bridge that leads across Pensacola Bay to the town of Gulf Breeze.

Among its other attributes, Gulf Breeze has been popular

for its UFO sightings, which generated a lot of attention between November 1987 and May 1988 and which are still being reported today. The fact that Gulf Breeze is about five minutes' flying time from the U.S. Air Force Developmental Test Center at nearby Eglin Air Force Base may have something to do with these sightings, but those who want there to be an extraterrestrial connection are undeterred.

From Gulf Breeze, go south to State Highway 399, which is Pensacola Beach Boulevard. From here, Santa Rosa Island is reached by crossing the short toll bridge that spans Santa Rosa Sound. Once on the island, Via de Luna, on your left, leads to Navarre Beach and a second toll bridge to the mainland. To your right, at the Gulf Breeze crossing, is the road to old Fort Pickens. The fort was built in the early nineteenth century to protect Pensacola Harbor and saw limited action during the Civil War as Confederates tried to capture it. Later it used as a military prison whose most notable inmate was the Apache leader Geronimo.

Beyond Navarre Beach is about fifteen miles of Santa Rosa Island that has no roads, though it is far from deserted. It is perhaps here, and here alone on this island, that you can get a feel for what it must have been like when William ''Billy'' Rogers—or whoever he was—made landfall here, his whaleboat heavy with plundered gold he would never spend.

Chapter 5

KARL STEINHEIMER'S OAK TREE CACHE

PLACE: *Near the Little River in Texas*

TIME PERIOD: *About 1836*

Another name well known to treasure hunters is that of Karl Steinheimer, a former German merchant seaman and sometime pirate. Steinheimer was not much more than eleven when he ran away from home and found his way to the lewd and lively North German port city of Hamburg. Here he found exactly what he was looking for: a chance to see the world. He shipped out with a merchant ship and grew up following the life of a rough and roving sailor, carousing in ports all over the world and rubbing elbows or fists with men in all walks of life.

It was at about the time of the War of 1812—or possibly five or so years earlier—that Steinheimer found himself in the Gulf of Mexico, where he happened to fall in with a bunch of smugglers, slave traders, and pirates based on Galveston Island, off the coast of Texas. It will be remembered that it was here, just a few years later, that Jean Lafitte and his renegade Baratarians would establish their own bastion of buccaneering. Whether Steinheimer was involved with the Baratarians, the legend does not say, but the time and the place are close enough to raise the possibility.

What the legend does say about Karl Steinheimer's days as a pirate is that they were short-lived and that they ended in his losing a power struggle with another man for leadership of the gang. It may have been Jean Lafitte, but one cannot imagine that Lafitte would have let him walk away, and Steinheimer *did* walk away. As he walked, he probably made his way to New Orleans, and he probably got a job working on one of the Mississippi River boats, for he soon found himself in St. Louis, Missouri. Here he met and courted the girl who turned out to be the girl of his dreams. When he got around to asking her to marry him, she balked. She probably hesitated at the thought of settling down with an ex-pirate and probably at the thought of an ex-pirate settling down at all. Finally she accepted his proposal, and Steinheimer made plans to put down roots. At the last minute, however, she backed out and announced that she had found the man of *her* dreams, and that man was *not* Karl Steinheimer.

The jilted German then pulled up stakes and headed south, not back to the Gulf Coast, but to Mexico, from which stories were emanating about various promising gold discoveries. The luck that had eluded Steinheimer in Galveston and St. Louis crossed his path at last in Mexico. Starting out as a prospector, he soon became a mine owner in the state of Nuevo León, and he amassed considerable wealth over the next two decades.

One day in about 1835, some twenty years after going to Mexico, Karl Steinheimer happened to be drinking in a Monterrey cantina when he got to talking with an American. In a scenario befitting an old romantic movie, the stranger happened to mention that he had recently come from St. Louis. Karl Steinheimer was filled with memories. Hesitatingly, he asked whether the American might know a certain lady. Yes, indeed, the stranger *did* know her— very well. Further conversation brought out the fact that Karl's former sweetheart had *not* married the other man after all. In fact, she had never married anyone. With all the wealth he now possessed, Steinheimer wondered if he might not at last win the girl of his dreams.

It is well known that men will do crazy things for gold and that they will do crazy things for women. Whether it was crazy or calculated, Karl Steinheimer decided to sell

everything and return to St. Louis. Having reduced twenty
years of his life to its value in gold coinage, Steinheimer
hired a group of Mexicans, formed a pack train, and headed
north. Before him lay Texas and trouble. Mexico had become independent of Spain in 1821, but Texas, which had
become a Mexican state, was populated largely by Americans, and they generally favored independence. In 1836, as
Karl Steinheimer was beginning to make his way north, the
Texans were on the verge of launching their war of independence. The Mexican government, which had largely ig-
nored Texas since 1821, was indignant at the loss of
territory and sent its army to put the Texans in line.

In 1836 Texas was extremely dangerous country to be
traveling through and, to make matters worse, Steinheimer
was neither Mexican nor Texan. Steinheimer's pack train
reached Matamoros safely and joined with a Mexican military detachment. The two groups rode together almost to
San Antonio.

Realizing that the conflict was about to turn into open
warfare, Steinheimer decided to put as much space between
himself and the Mexican troops as he could. As the latter
went north along the old road to San Antonio, Steinheimer
and his ten muleloads of treasure set out across country.

A few miles north of Austin he met a party of Mexicans
fleeing south toward the border, who warned him that the
Texans were driving all Mexicans out of Texas and that
many Indians were supporting them. Steinheimer looked
around. His entire party, except himself, were Mexicans,
and even he was arguably a Mexican citizen after having
lived there so long. He was certainly not a Texan. Under
these very precarious conditions he decided that it would
be safest to bury his treasure, leave the country by the shortest possible route, and return to recover his wealth after
things had quieted down.

With this in mind, the German dismissed all the Mexicans in the train except two whom he thought he could
trust, and started watching for a spot that would be easy to
remember. A hilly, wooded area near the junction of two
streams appeared to be just what he was looking for. They

buried the entire multimillion-dollar treasure under a tree (some stories say it was an oak) a few miles south of Temple, at a place where the Leon and Lampasas Rivers join to form the Little River. Steinheimer and the two Mexicans dug a large pit into which they lowered the treasure. They then filled in the hole and carefully tamped down and replanted the surface of the ground to avoid discovery. To make sure he'd know which tree, Steinheimer pounded a brass spike into the trunk.

When the treasure was sufficiently obscured, the three men rode east, intending to get out of Texas as soon as possible. Barely three hours later, they were attacked by Indians. Forced to dismount and find cover, they hid behind a small hill and attempted to defend themselves from the attackers. After a brief spate of gunfire, the two Mexicans were dead and Steinheimer was wounded. Somehow he managed to get into a ravine, where the Indians were unable to locate him.

When the Indians finally rode away, Steinheimer took stock of his pitiful situation. He was wounded and alone without a horse in hostile territory. At least he still had a gun and some ammunition. He buried a small bag of gold he'd been carrying and set out on foot. Steinheimer had nearly starved to death when he was discovered several days later by some Texans. They gave him some food, but by now his bullet wound was so badly infected that he had little chance of surviving long enough to reach a doctor.

As he lay dying, Steinheimer drew a crude map of the area where the treasure was buried and wrote a long letter to the woman in St. Louis. He explained to her that his love still burned strong after the many years they'd been apart, and he told her about the gold, which would be hers if he did not reach St. Louis in three months. He sealed the letter and somehow managed to convince the Texans that the letter was a last farewell to his sister. He asked them to mail it from the first town they came to.

The Texans agreed to this, a dying man's last wish, and rode away, leaving the pirate turned millionaire mine owner to die alone on the prairie.

It was several weeks later when the letter was at last delivered to the woman in St. Louis. What went through her mind can only be imagined. The man she had jilted had remained in love with her for twenty years, but he had died on his way to rejoin her with ten wagons filled with gold. After she reacted in the sort of emotional way one might expect after having read such a letter, the woman thought about the gold. She and her relatives decided that with the Texas War of Independence raging, it would be a bad time to try to make a search.

The war was short-lived, however. The Mexican Army, under Santa Ana, overwhelmed the Texas defensive position in San Antonio—the Alamo—on March 2, 1836, killing every man. This victory only served to intensify the resolve of the Texans, who defeated the Mexicans decisively at the Battle of San Jacinto on April 21. Texas would remain independent for nine years before joining the United States in 1845.

As for the St. Louis woman, time simply slipped away, and it was to be many years before some men whom she hired went back to look for Karl Steinheimer's gold. They found the junction of the two streams as he had described them, but an oak tree with the brass spike has never been found.

Finding Karl Steinheimer's Millions

The oak tree—if it was an oak—is probably long gone but a few miles south of the town of Temple, in central Texas, the Leon and Lampasas Rivers still unite to form the Little River. The brass spike, though badly corroded by now, may also still be there. So, too, may be as many as ten pack muleloads of gold. While the spike corrodes, the gold could survive there for centuries. Today such a treasure is probably worth millions. How many millions? Many.

To look for Karl Steinheimer's millions, start in Austin. You could fly into San Antonio or Dallas/Fort Worth, but

begin your search in Austin and arrive with the junction of
the Leon and Lampasas Rivers marked on your U.S. Geological Survey topographical map. This is an excellent
start, but you will need more information of the kind available at the Texas State Archives in Austin. It is here that
Karl Steinheimer's story—and the stories of those who
have come looking for the treasure he wanted to give to
the love of his life—will come to life.

In Austin make your way to the Texas State Library offices and collections, in the Lorenzo de Zavala State Archives and Library Building at 1201 Brazos Street, directly
east of the Texas State Capitol in downtown Austin. If you
are arriving by car from Interstate 35, take the 15th Street
exit and head west on 15th Street. From Texas Loop 1 take
the Enfield Road exit and head east. Enfield Road turns
into 15th Street, and from 15th Street take San Jacinto
Street south, and the Lorenzo de Zavala State Archives and
Library Building will be on the right between 13th and 12th
Streets. Look for the six seals of Texas government along
the back of the building.

Search for all the information there is on the treasure.
Look at old maps and documents, scouring them for any
data that either confirm or conflict with the notion that the
Leon and Lampasas Rivers are the "two streams." Then,
using your topographical map and state or local records,
ascertain who owns the land at that junction, for you will
need their permission to dig.

Of the fifty states we contacted for clarification of laws
governing treasure hunting, Texas was one of eleven that
supplied useful information. We contacted the Texas attorney general's office for information and were referred to
the Texas Historical Commission, the agency responsible
for administration of antiquities in the state. The Texas
Historical Commission has published many informative
booklets and circulars dealing with antiquities conservation
and legislation in Texas, and these may be obtained by
contacting the Department of Antiquities Protection at the
Texas Historical Commission—also in Austin—at (512)
463-6096.

In general two fundamental requirements must be met prior to treasure hunting on any state-owned lands in Texas: (1) securing an antiquities permit from the Texas Historical Commission and (2) securing a permit or other access agreement from the agency that controls the land.

In general the Texas Historical Commission considers unregulated treasure hunting as inimical to the best interests and stated policy of the state, because of its potential for adversely affecting significant cultural resource sites. Such activities on the 20.5 million acres of state-owned lands are covered by the declared policy of the state, found in the Texas Natural Resources Code, Chapter 191, whose purpose is to protect and preserve significant cultural resources.

In Texas, according to Chapter 191, "It is the public policy and in the public interest of the State of Texas to locate, protect, and preserve all sites, objects, buildings, pre-twentieth-century shipwrecks, and locations of historical, archaeological, educational, or scientific interest, including, but not limited to, prehistoric and historical American Indian or aboriginal camp sites, dwellings and habitation sites, archaeological sites of every character, treasure embedded in the earth, sunken or abandoned ships and wrecks of the sea or any part of their contents, maps, records, documents, books, artifacts, and implements of culture in any way related to the inhabitants, prehistory, history, natural history, government, or culture in, on, or under any of the land in the State of Texas, including the tidelands, submerged land, and the bed of the sea within the jurisdiction of the State of Texas. . . . Sites, objects, buildings, artifacts, implements, and locations of historical, archaeological, scientific, or educational interest, including those pertaining to prehistoric and historical American Indians or aboriginal campsites, dwellings and habitation sites, their artifacts and implements of culture, as well as archaeological sites of every character that are located in, on, or under the surface of any land belonging to the State of Texas or to any county, city, or political subdivision of the state are state archaeological landmarks and are eligible for designation."

In Texas it is, as usual, also illegal to dig for anything on someone else's land without that person's express permission.

The Spike Is Still There

Having finished in Austin, it is time to head north, as Karl Steinheimer did so long ago. In 1836 there was a wagon road between Austin and the present site of Temple. Later there was U.S. Highway 81, and today there is Interstate 35. The wagon road is virtually nonexistent now, and there are only remnants of U.S. Highway 81 to form bits of Frontage Road. That's how long it has been.

Take exit 285 off Interstate 35—the first of two Salado exits—about a half hour north of Austin. Drive east on County Road 2268 toward Holland, a distance of about 10 miles. At Holland turn north on Texas Highway 95. A few minutes later you will cross the Little River, a few miles downriver from the place where the Leon and Lampasas Rivers come together. This is as close as you can get on a public road. Stop and look to the left. The spike is still there.

Imagine Karl Steinheimer and his ten wagons in an era when paved roads were nonexistent. Imagine what must have been going through his mind when he reached these prairies and these rivers. Maybe he is still out here, haunting these hills and still trying to get back to St. Louis.

Chapter 6

THE LOST BREYFOGLE MINE

PLACE: *Death Valley, California*

TIME PERIOD: *1864*

One of the most desolate stretches of "nowhere" in the United States is the Mojave Desert of California, which stretches from Death Valley in Inyo County to the Mexican border, encompassing San Bernardino, Riverside, and Imperial Counties. It is a desolate wilderness larger than the Netherlands and is as hospitable to human life as the dark side of the moon.

The centerpiece of this wilderness is Death Valley National Park (formerly Death Valley National Monument), which boasts more than 3.3 million acres of undisturbed wilderness, spectacular desert scenery, and interesting and rare desert wildlife as well as historical sites. It also boasts the lowest point in the Western Hemisphere—near a place called Badwater—that is 282 feet below sea level. Death Valley National Park also can pride itself—if "pride" can be the word—on being the hottest place in the Western Hemisphere and one of the hottest places on earth. A temperature of 134 degrees Fahrenheit was recorded here in 1913, and it is frequently above 120 degrees.

Even Native Americans avoided Death Valley much of the time, although they did venture into most of the Mojave to hunt. The first non-Indian people to come here were almost certainly lost. They may have been prospectors who took a wrong turn chasing the 1849 gold rush, or settlers headed for southern California who got lost. There is a story of a wagon train that arrived in Death Valley on Christmas Day in 1849 and *most* of the people died. In July they would probably not have been so lucky!

Death Valley has had some very rich mines through the years. Some were gold mines, but most of them were borax mines. They used to call the white powder "the White Gold of the Desert." Beginning in 1884, there were twenty-four-ton wagons pulled by twenty-mule teams hauling borax from the old Harmony Borax Mining Company works in Death Valley to the Southern Pacific Railroad loading dock in Mojave, California, more than 165 miles away through mountains, deserts, and blistering heat. A round trip required twenty days. New borax discoveries near Barstow ended the Mojave shipments in 1889, and the Harmony Borax works closed in 1890 when the operation was transferred to Daggett in the Calico Mountains, which was closer to the railroad. The mule teams were a thing of the past, but the "20-Mule-Team" brand name survives on borax products for sale in supermarkets today. In the 1950s and 1960s the product was the sponsor of a Western television series called *Death Valley Days,* which starred such young actors as Clint Eastwood, James Caan, and Carroll O'Connor, and was hosted by an older actor named Ronald Reagan.

Even before the heyday of the borax operations, evidence of gold and silver, such as the long-rumored Lost Gunsight Silver Lode, brought many prospectors into the Mojave Desert in the middle years of the nineteenth century. A few of the prospectors who came in search of gold and silver were rewarded beyond their wildest dreams, but many went crazy from heat and loneliness or ended up as bones bleached by an unrelenting sun.

Of the "lost" and abandoned mines in the area, few have had fired imaginations more than the Lost Breyfogle Mine—which is probably more of an outcropping or "ledge" than a mine. The story began—or climaxed—in 1864, when a man named Breyfogle staggered into an Inyo

County trading post—some stories say that he was found near Big Smoky Valley, Nevada—shoeless, with his clothes in shreds and a sunburn on his bald head so severe that people thought he'd been scalped. Nevertheless, his pockets were filled with the richest gold ore anyone had ever seen.

Who Was This Man Named Breyfogle?

Most of the stories that have been told about Breyfogle describe him as the archetypical crazy old prospector and give his first name as "Jacob" or "Jake," a name that is common—for some reason—in many "lost treasure" yarns in the Southwest. Maybe it has something to do with the perennially popular Lost Dutchman tale, in which the Dutchman and his partner both really were named "Jake." But Breyfogle really was neither a "Jake" nor a crazy old prospector. He was a slightly crooked politician named Charles C. Breyfogle, who was both greedy and lucky but not crazy—at least not until after he got lucky.

Breyfogle arrived in California from Ohio in 1849 as part of that massive migration of people that constituted the California gold rush. Amazingly, there were few disappointments in the gold rush of 1849, and there really was so much gold that until 1852, most prospectors went away satisfied, if not rich. Breyfogle was one of those who arrived early and probably went away at least satisfied. By 1852 he had left the gold fields of the Sierra Nevada to settle in Oakland, the quiet and comfortable railhead city that was established across the bay from the bustling city of San Francisco.

In 1854 Charles Breyfogle ran for Alameda County assessor, and he had served three years when he decided to run for county treasurer in 1857. Elected to this office, he was accused two years later of misuse of public funds, a charge that is often leveled at politicians but that seldom sticks. In Breyfogle's case it did, although he seems to have been guilty more of negligence than of criminal malfeasance. He was forced out of office, but apparently he did no jail time for his misdeeds.

Despite his Ohio roots, Breyfogle became a Confederate sympathizer during the Civil War and ended up in Arizona leading a band of Confederate partisans. In 1863 or possibly 1864 he happened to be in Los Angeles for some reason—possibly related to his rebel activities—when he happened to start hearing stories about the gold being found in Death Valley. A number of people he met were organizing prospecting ventures. Charles Breyfogle remembered the thrill of fifteen years earlier, and the gold fever washed away his Confederate idealism.

He met and joined forces with two other prospectors, known as O'Bannion and McLeod. Their first names are not known to the legend, so one would suppose that we could call each of them "Jake." In the late summer of 1864 the three headed out of Los Angeles rode through Mint Canyon, out past the present site of Ridgecrest, California, and through the southern foothills of the Argus Range past the present site of the town of Trona. Several days after leaving Los Angeles they crossed the Panamint Range somewhere around the 7,196-foot Manly Peak and dropped down into Death Valley through Warm Springs Canyon or Johnson Canyon.

Having crossed the Panamints, they camped near a water hole. Because of the steep terrain, they wound up unrolling their bedrolls in widely separated places, with Breyfogle a considerable distance from O'Bannion and McLeod. In the middle of the night Breyfogle awoke suddenly to the blood-chilling sounds of screams. The two "Jakes" were being butchered by Indians. He grabbed his shoes—he was fully clothed—and ran barefoot as fast as he could through the flesh-ripping rock and cactus.

Gold!

By morning Charles Breyfogle was at the base of the mountains, somewhere in Death Valley, with the fiery desert sun blistering him relentlessly. He trudged on, hoping the Indians would not catch up with him. Desperately thirsty, he drank from an alkali wash, but the brackish water only made him vomit his guts out. He struggled on through the afternoon, finally spotting what appeared like a patch of green vegetation on a side hill. Believing that there would have to be a spring to support greenery, he made his way toward the spot.

On his way he started noticing light-colored rock that he recognized as pink feldspar. Despite his thirst, he paused to examine it and discovered that the pieces contained wide veins of solid gold. He wrapped several of the nuggets in a bandanna and struggled on toward the green patch. It turned out to be just a bush covered with bright green seedpods. There was no spring.

Over the ensuing days, Breyfogle went mad, and he staggered through Death Valley aimlessly. When he finally reached civilization—whether it was in Inyo County or over at Big Smoky Valley, Nevada—he had no memory of anything that had happened to him since the first day, and he had no idea how many days it had been. Given the distance traveled, it would have had to have been at least three, but he couldn't have survived much longer than that.

After he regained his strength, Breyfogle took his gold nuggets to Austin, Nevada, where an old friend named Jake Gooding operated a quartz mill. Gooding examined the feldspar and calculated that it was the richest ore ever discovered in that part of the country. They organized a small expedition and went back toward Death Valley in the fall of 1864. However, as they were about to cross the Funeral Mountains, they ran into a Shoshone raiding party, and they decided to turn back and try again. The next try came the following spring. Breyfogle was able to find the alkali sink, but try as he might, he could not seem to find the place on the hillside where he had seen the patch of green. After several days the water was running low and the rest of the party turned back, leaving Breyfogle to search on in vain. Finally he, too, returned empty-handed.

Well into the 1870s, Charles Breyfogle continued to re-

turn to Death Valley, to scour the hillsides for a ledge of pink
feldspar. He made dozens of trips, sometimes with others
and often alone, but he always came back empty-handed.
One time he just did not return. Nobody ever saw him again.

Did Breyfogle find the lost ledge and retire in style to
San Francisco, New York, or Paris? Did the Indians who
killed O'Bannion and McLeod finally catch him? Did his
horse spook at the sight of a rattlesnake and throw him?
Did he break his leg and starve to death, unable to get out?

Nobody ever found any sign of Breyfogle and nobody
ever found his lost ledge, although during the late nineteenth century there were several gold discoveries in Death
Valley. One of these might have been it, except that the
ore was not as rich as that which Breyfogle had with him
when he stumbled out of the valley back in 1864.

For more than a century there have been many attempts—throughout Death Valley—to find the Lost Breyfogle Mine. There have been so many that by the beginning
of the twentieth century the word "breyfogling" became
synonymous with looking for lost mines.

Going Breyfogling

Breyfogling in Death Valley is not recommended for the
faint of heart. For those who are unprepared, the Mojave
is a cruel, inhospitable, and potentially deadly place. While
the mother lode country of northern California is a land of
wooded hillsides and meadows bisected by streams, the
Mojave is dry, desolate, and often hot. Remember that
Death Valley has the hottest recorded temperatures in the
Western Hemisphere. They don't call it "Death" Valley
for naught. The sands still blow across the bleached bones
of travelers and prospectors whose luck ran out here.

Death Valley is sunny, dry, and clear throughout the
year, and while the winters can be mild, summer temperatures commonly run above 120 degrees Fahrenheit. Sun
protection and a broad-brimmed hat are essential in the
summer and recommended even in the winter. Sturdy walk-

ing shoes are important year-round. Some experience with hiking in the desert is mandatory. The heat does more than dehydrate you, and desert mirages can be more than reflective ripples. Desert heat can disorient you and confuse your distance perception, as it almost certainly did with Charles Breyfogle.

If you are planning to be traveling out of sight of paved roads and familiar landmarks in Death Valley, either on foot or in a vehicle, always carry your topographic map and a compass. Also carry adequate food and water—especially water. Remember Charles Breyfogle. Imagine how thirsty he was. A cup a mile—both coming and going—may be excessive if you are strolling in the park back home, but in Death Valley in the summer, you will find it to be the minimum.

In areas where it is specifically required, stay on marked trails and/or roads. When hiking in Death Valley or when driving on unpaved roads or off-road areas, always carry a watch, and allow plenty of time for your trip. Consider distance, elevation, weight being carried, physical condition (of yourself, your traveling companions, and your vehicle), weather, and hours of daylight. Even if it is not particularly "hot," people can be subject to heat exhaustion. In the summer try not to stray too far from civilization between noon and 4:00 P.M.

When you turn off a paved road, or if you are driving on an especially remote paved road, always start your drive with a full tank of gas, and turn back when your gas gauge has reached the "half full" mark. You should also carry both a properly inflated spare tire and a flashlight.

Also of consideration are federal restrictions on what sort of excavation and treasure hunting may be done in Death Valley. Since the valley itself is a national park, you simply may not disturb or remove anything, whether it be a naturally occurring feature—such as a gold nugget or worthless rock—or an archaeological artifact. Today the entire area around the park is under the jurisdiction of the Defense Department or the U.S. Department of the Interior through the California Desert Protection Act. This law, passed by Congress and signed into law on October 31, 1994, created the 1.4 million-acre Mojave National Preserve. It also expanded Death Valley and Joshua Tree National Monuments by 1.3 million and 234,000 acres, respectively, and redesignated them as national parks. The act also designated 57 million acres of land as wilderness, the largest in the nation. As such, the strictest rules that apply in Department of the Interior areas—National Park Service rules—apply in most of the Mojave Desert.

Getting to Death Valley

In 1864, when O'Bannion, McLeod, and Breyfogle headed out from Los Angeles, they traveled east to Death Valley along the route followed by the modern-day Interstate Highway 15. Today, if you are traveling *east* from Los Angeles, this highway is the fastest first leg. If you are traveling from Las Vegas, Nevada, which actually has the nearest major airport, Interstate 15 *westbound* is the fastest first leg. In 1864, when O'Bannion, McLeod, and Breyfogle traveled this route, they would have come as far as Barstow and then turned north past Coyote Lake and through the Granite Mountains. Today this area is the U.S. Army's Fort Irwin Training Center and hence is off-limits to travel. However, sixty miles east of Barstow you should turn north on California Highway 127 at the town of Baker. From Las Vegas, simply drive west ninety miles to Baker.

You should plan adequate time to explore Death Valley, meaning that you plan to stay on-site, because driving time to get there is so long. Death Valley is a two-and-a-half-hour drive from Las Vegas by automobile and as much as twice that from Los Angeles, depending on traffic conditions on the freeways as you are leaving the City of Angels. Because a four-wheel-drive vehicle is recommended for back-country travel, the driving time will be greater. You could plan to camp in one of the National Park Service campgrounds in the valley, or call ahead to the Furnace

Creek Inn at (760) 786-2311 and book motel accommodations within Death Valley.

Driving north on California Highway 127, the Avawatz Mountains will be on your left for about 30 miles before giving way to the Ibex Hills, which rise above the foot of Death Valley National Park. Two miles north of the little town of Shoshone and fifty-eight miles north of Baker you will reach the turnoff to your left that will put you on California Highway 178, which in turn takes you into the lower end of Death Valley. Don't be tempted by a gravel road that goes off to the left twenty miles south of Shoshone. When you leave Shoshone, be advised that there is no gas or water for seventy-five miles. Be prepared. There is, however, nonpotable radiator water available at the ruins of Ashford Mill, twenty-five miles from Shoshone, but you'll be doing some serious climbing in those twenty-five miles, so it is best to check your radiator in Shoshone.

On Highway 178 you cross through 3,315-foot Salsberry Pass and 1,290-foot Jubilee Pass—which cut across the Black Mountains—and descend into the below-sea-level terrain of Death Valley. From Jubilee Pass you will see the valley spread before you ahead and to the right. It was directly across the valley that Breyfogle first entered Death Valley, coming through a pass in the Panamint Range, which lies before you.

Five miles from Jubilee Pass, near the ruins of Ashford Mill, Highway 178 dips below sea level, and five miles beyond that you will reach a junction in the road. Highway 178 continues north along the eastern side of Death Valley at roughly the sea level line, while an unpaved gravel road, cleverly designated as "West Side Road," follows the west sea level line. The two roads run parallel, with about five miles—all beneath sea level—between them, and come together again about forty miles north.

As noted above, there is no drinking water on either road, and the paved Highway 178 is obviously the faster road. If you forgot to fill your canteen in Shoshone, or if you have drunk it all, take Highway 178. West Side Road, however, is important because this is the side of Death Valley from which Breyfogle arrived, and it more closely follows the route he probably took than does Highway 178.

Also on West Side Road, there are five rugged gravel roads, recommended only for four-wheel-drive vehicles, that lead off to the left up into the Panamint Range. The first of these, only about a mile from the junction, is Warm Springs Canyon Road, which leads up into Butte Valley and across the Panamint Range to the paved Panamint Valley Road. This excruciating, seventy-five-mile drive is really more like a mule track, but people do cross with four-wheel-drive vehicles. Warm Springs Canyon is important because it is the leading candidate for being the route taken in 1864 by O'Bannion, McLeod, and Breyfogle when they entered Death Valley from this direction.

Somewhere up there, probably seven to ten miles from West Side Road, is the place where the three men were attacked. As he made his escape, Breyfogle would have run north, probably along the face of the Panamints. He probably would have stayed at a constant elevation as he made his initial escape, because to have dropped down toward the valley would have relinquished the high ground, and climbing higher would have slowed him.

Only after he was out of earshot of the massacre—and possibly not until first light—would he have descended into the valley. There are a number of dry "washes" or creekbeds that fork off from Warm Springs Canyon and lead to the northeast into the valley. One of these, Galena Canyon, does not actually intersect Warm Springs Canyon, but it does come close, and its head would be easily reachable in an hour or so by a man moving quickly at night. Galena Canyon is conveniently the next such canyon served by a four-wheel-drive road. Breyfogle may have taken either of these two named canyons, or he may have taken one of the nameless washes that seemed less likely to be a route the Indians would take.

The foot of Galena Canyon is about five miles north of Warm Springs Canyon, and between them one can make out numerous dry washes that come down out of the mountains, cross the road, and disappear into a twisted maze at the bottom of the valley. It was into this maze that Charles Breyfogle stumbled that morning. It is easy to see, when contemplating Death Valley from West Side Road, why he was never able to find his way back. Somewhere out there is the pond that held the brackish water that sickened Breyfogle, but features such as that change from week to week, year to year, and certainly century to century. The one you may find today may not be the same one.

The terrain for hundreds of square miles is a confused mass of canyons that intersect other canyons, and canyons that lead nowhere. It is a place where the form of everything changes constantly with the harsh light and the razor-sharp shadow lines. The view at noon is not same view in morning light or at the end of the day.

West Side Road continues on, past Johnson Canyon, Hanaupah Canyon, and Trail Canyon, all of which may be explored with a vehicle. You rejoin Highway 178 just six miles south of Furnace Creek, where accommodations, food, water, and gas are all available. North of Furnace Creek, Death Valley continues for another sixty miles, and the desert continues for hundreds of miles, through Nevada and deep into Oregon. It is possible that Breyfogle continued in Death Valley past Furnace Creek, but we don't know and neither did he, for he had no memory of where he went after he found the gold. He may have wandered out through Grapevine Canyon, at the northern end of the valley, or he may have crossed one of the passes such as Daylight Pass, which leads over to Beatty, Nevada, past the old mining town of Rhyolite.

It is hard to retrace the steps of a man who had no memory of his own steps. Indeed, in this desert, it is often hard to retrace your own steps from earlier in the same day.

Many breyfoglers have tried to retrace those steps. Many have wandered these canyons and washes, their throats aching from thirst, their skin roasting slowly in the sun. There are stories that are told—and stories that are whispered—of people who think they may have found Breyfogle's El Dorado. This writer remembers one man who was so sure he knew where it was that he wouldn't even share his snap-shots.

As with many treasures in the lost treasure lore of the United States, it probably is really out there—somewhere.

Chapter 7

THE CONFEDERATE TREASURY

PLACE: *Wilkes County, Georgia*

TIME PERIOD: *1864–65*

To describe the Civil War as the defining moment in American history is an understatement. It was a crossroads from which the United States might have become two nations. The course of world history flows from this moment, and it could very easily have been a much different course. From the point of view of the victorious Union, it was a turning point when the existence of the United States as a unified nation was called into question, threatened, and saved. From the defeated and discredited Confederate point of view it was a tragedy that resulted in the destruction of a nation and a way of life.

The Civil War was the bloodiest war ever fought in the Western Hemisphere, and it likely will remain so. A larger proportion of the population of the United States fought and died in that war than in any other.

Today we take it for granted that the Union won, but for several years in the 1860s the issue was in doubt. During 1861 and 1862 the Union armies flubbed and faltered and very nearly lost the war. By 1863 the Confederate armies were ready to invade the North. If Gettysburg had gone the other way, today's history books might tell a very different story. But the Union won. President Abraham Lincoln of the United States saved the Union and was revered for the better part of a century as a hero, if not a saint. President Jefferson Davis of the Confederacy was reviled as a criminal and thrown in jail.

In 1861 the Confederate States of America issued its Declaration of Independence, just as the United States of America had done in 1776. For four years—from 1861 to 1865—the Confederate States of America was an independent nation with a constitution, a currency, a capital city, and a Treasury.

The United States of America had responded to that 1861 Declaration of Independence with a declaration of war. There would be no independence. There would be no new nation. The United States of America did not recognize the Confederacy as a sovereign nation, but rather as a group of rebellious U.S. citizens who were breaking the law. The U.S. government responded with force in 1861, just as it has in more recent times when bands of zealots have barricaded themselves in a compound and declared themselves not subject to U.S. law. It was just that in 1861, but it happened on a very much larger scale.

It was an uneven fight. On one side was an agrarian nation built on a class system that condoned and defended institutional slavery. On the other side was one of the world's greatest industrial powers, with thundering factories, a world-class navy and merchant marine, one of the largest railroad networks on earth, and its own army of slaves arriving every day on immigrant ships from Europe.

When the war was over, the United States of America prevailed. There was no new independent nation. The Confederate constitution was just a worthless piece of paper. The currency was just a bunch of worthless paper. The Confederate capital city—Richmond, Virginia—was just a bombed-out hulk. But the Confederate Treasury was as good as gold, because it *was* gold. In the war's final year the Union armies seized the initiative and burned, blasted, and seized nearly everything of value in the Confederacy, but they never got the Confederate Treasury.

What happened?

The Setting of the Confederate Sun

The turning point came in 1863. Robert E. Lee's defeat at Gettysburg was the end of Confederate hopes for victory in the war, while Ulysses S. Grant's Union triumphs at Vicksburg and Chattanooga sealed the fate of the Confederacy. From there, the Civil War was a Wagnerian tragedy.

Lincoln elevated Grant to the top job of supreme commander of the Army of the Potomac, and in the spring of 1864 Grant gave General William Tecumseh Sherman command of Union armies in the West with a mandate to "cut the South in half." What followed was Sherman's hellish "March to the Sea," the campaign that was the war's bloodiest—especially in terms of civilian casualties. Today, more than a half century after it was adapted as the backdrop to *Gone With the Wind,* Sherman's campaign has taken on a sort of melodramatic quality, but in 1864 it was anything but.

While the war's most visible theater was obviously the northern Virginia front, Atlanta and northern Georgia would be important, both in the context of Sherman's offensive and in the coming drama that would surround the disappearance of the Confederate Treasury.

On May 4, 1864, Sherman marched toward Atlanta with 98,797 troops, 254 cannons, and a mandate to break the back of southern resistance forever. Indeed, the mandate given to Grant by the declaration of war, and by Grant to Sherman by direct order, was to render null and void the Declaration of Independence the Confederate States of America had issued in 1861. Sherman met blistering resistance from the Confederate forces under General Joe Johnston, who beat the Yankees at the Battle of Kennesaw Mountain on June 27, 1864, but he was forced to fall back. The Confederacy was exhausted. It was no match for the industrial and transportation might of the United States, with its tidal wave of Irish, Italian, and German cannon fodder.

Sherman took Atlanta on September 1, 1864, and in November, as he prepared to march to the Atlantic to complete the process of cutting the Confederacy in half, he torched the city. Sherman's intention was to destroy factories and everything else that could be of any remote strategic value, but he wound up burning nearly the whole city of Atlanta.

Sherman continued his brutal scorched-earth March to the Sea, destroying everything in a path sixty miles wide from the Georgia capital to the port of Savannah. By spring it was all over.

Dixie Götterdämmerung

The last days of the Confederacy were a time of chaos. Sherman had burned Atlanta, and Grant was on Richmond's doorstep. Robert E. Lee surrendered to Sam Grant on April 9, 1865, at Appomattox Courthouse in Virginia and General Joe Johnston surrendered to Sherman on April 17, 1865, at Raleigh, North Carolina. The war was effectively over, although the Confederacy would continue to exist for about three weeks.

The rebel nation finally ceased to exist on May 5, 1865, when President Jefferson Davis met with his Confederate cabinet for the last time to officially vote themselves out of business. This momentous event occurred not in the capital at Richmond, but four hundred miles south, in the small hamlet of Washington, the county seat of Wilkes County, Georgia, a day's ride east of the still-smoldering Atlanta. The Confederate States of America were officially dissolved in a town named for the same Virginia war hero as the capital of the United States of America.

It is ironic that the cabinets of both nations met that day in towns named Washington, and it is ironic, too, that Jeff Davis met with his cabinet for the last time at the Heard house, the Georgia Branch Bank Building, in the town that was the last place that anyone ever saw the Confederate Treasury.

To this day there is a great deal of mystery surrounding

the arrival of the Confederate Treasury in Washington. Why it was picked for both the last cabinet meeting and the Treasury is uncertain, although, by May 1865, Richmond was in Union hands, and northern Georgia—the Union mauling of Atlanta notwithstanding—was probably perceived as being a safe distance away.

The most important question left shrouded in mystery is, of course: What happened to the treasure when it left Washington?

However, there are some corollary questions that are also important, such as: How many treasures were there? To whom did they really belong?

A Tale of Three Treasures

In April 1865, on the eve Lee's surrender at Appomattox Courthouse, legend holds that what was left of the Confederate Treasury, estimated at $450,000 to $500,000—or roughly $10 million today—in gold, started out under heavy guard from Richmond, Virginia. For more than a month, as the Confederacy fell apart, boxes and chests of bullion and gold coins were moved from one Southern town to another to pretext it from being intercepted by the Yankee cavalry, which was roaming at will throughout the states of the imploding Confederacy. As gold that was being claimed as part of the Confederate Treasury, it was subject of seizure and confiscation by the U.S. government, which recognized the Confederacy not as a sovereign nation but as a gaggle of rebels behaving illegally.

Of course, we are not altogether certain why the Confederacy was going to all this trouble when it was about to put itself out of business. The plan for squirreling it away had to have presupposed either a revival of the Confederacy, or the personal greed of certain individuals. For more than a hundred years, the phrase "the South shall rise again" would echo throughout the states of the former Confederacy, but there was never a serious scheme to reestablish the Confederacy. Or was there?

Where the final destination was supposed to have been for these wagons loaded with gold, no one seems to know. Maybe those guarding the gold didn't know where they were going or what they were doing. Maybe it was an elaborate shell game.

As the story goes, the treasure was taken through Washington, Georgia, twice before it came back for a final visit. Apparently Washington was the last town to shelter the intact fortune, and Union troops did seize $100,000 of the original amount hidden in a Washington bank. Some of the gold was captured with Jefferson Davis himself when he was taken into custody in Irwinville, Georgia, about a hundred miles west of Savannah, but to this day the legend persists that the balance of the Confederate Treasury is buried somewhere in different locations in and around Wilkes County and neighboring Lincoln County. Some of the paper currency (which is of no current value except as a novelty) and a few gold coins have been found, but the gold bullion is still missing.

But was the gold bullion that arrived in Wilkes County entirely Confederate Treasury gold? Supposedly part of what was on those wagons was the property of several Virginia banks, although it may have been gold owned by a third party that had been left on deposit in Virginia banks. Either way, it was subject to seizure, but whereas the U.S. government had grounds upon which to claim ownership of "Confederate Treasury" gold, third-party gold could be argued to belong to that third party, no matter whether it was a bank or an individual.

Under this legal theory, it is possible that actual Confederate Treasury gold might have been identified as belonging to a bank to keep it from being confiscated, but as a practical matter, the Union troops were really not paying too much attention to proper legal procedure when it came to confiscations of property in Georgia in the late spring of 1865.

However, it may have mattered who exactly the "third

party" was. One particularly intriguing "third party" story tells that the gold that rolled into Wilkes County had been part of what was loaned to the Confederacy by Napoleon III, the emperor of France, to help support the war effort. The story says that Jefferson Davis had given his word to Louis Napoleon that the gold would be returned—regardless of the outcome of the war. As the outcome became clear, Davis ordered the gold returned, and it was a Confederate naval officer known as Captain Parker who drew the task of getting it back to France.

The "French gold" scenario holds that Parker and a team of volunteers undertook the task of getting the gold to Savannah, where it would be loaded on a waiting ship and taken to France. As a first stage of this task, they took the gold from Richmond to Anderson, South Carolina, by train. It was here, in this town near the Savannah River, about fifty miles due north of Washington, Georgia, that Sherman's mischief of a year earlier had destroyed the railroad tracks. This forced the Parker project to unload the treasure from the train and reload it aboard the wagons. Like a chapter from a Robert Ludlum novel, legend has it that Parker had been briefed to travel to Wilkes County and to camp near Washington. It was here that Jefferson Davis himself would materialize and provide further instructions. However, Parker reached Wilkes County up to three weeks after May 5. Jeff Davis had gone, and there were no further instructions.

It is not entirely clear what happened next. If Napoleon III really expected to get the gold back, he never said. Nor are we clear how much gold was involved. One of the more interesting mysteries is: Why, with everything else he had on his mind at the time, was Jeff Davis so obsessed with the idea of getting the gold to France? And why, if he was so obsessed with the idea of getting the gold to France, did he not make more of an effort to meet it in Washington?

Maybe he did. Maybe he had some of this gold with him when he was captured in Irwinville. Or maybe the gold never made it to Washington. Maybe something happened on the way.

There are a number of theorized "on the way" scenarios that deal not only with the French gold but with the Confederate Treasury as well, and the lines of many of these scenarios seem to cross at a place called Chennault Crossroads. In 1865 Chennault Crossroads was little more than literally a crossroads, and it is little more than that today. The roads were hardly more than tracks then, and they are hardly more than tracks today. But the stories they tell about the places!

Chennault Crossroads is fifteen miles from Washington and about a stone's throw from the Wilkes County line in Lincoln County. It is only about five miles from the Savannah River, which forms the border between Georgia and South Carolina, and which would have had to have been crossed by anyone coming into Georgia from South Carolina or from Virginia. Even by the most direct route, Chennault Crossroads would have been arguably on the way from Anderson, South Carolina, if one were taking the back roads from Anderson, as Captain Parker would have been.

Under the scenario in which the Confederate Treasury was being moved from place to place in Wilkes and Lincoln Counties, Chennault Crossroads certainly could have been one of those places.

One story that has a great deal of credibility locally tells that on the night of May 24, 1865, between two and five wagons filled with gold were hijacked at Chennault Crossroads, about a hundred yards from the front porch of the main house of the Chennault plantation. The plantation was owned at the time by Dionysius Chennault, an elderly planter who also happened to be a Methodist minister and who was one of the key witnesses to the hijacking.

Though the date and place are generally agreed, the source of the gold, and even the direction in which it was traveling, are subject to disagreement. In one variation, the wagons were southbound, with one or more of them carrying the gold from the Confederate Treasury and one or more others with money from the Virginia banks.

Another variation tells that the wagons were filled with the French gold and manned by Captain Parker and his volunteers. They were actually headed *north* after reaching Washington because Parker couldn't find Davis and because Parker's scouts had encountered Union troops on the way to Augusta. Ralph Hobbs, from Winnsboro, South Carolina, who researched the hijacking for many years, believes that it was the Virginia bank gold and that it was actually on its way *back* to Richmond when the hijacking occurred.

There is even a theory that says the hijacking didn't happen at Chennault Crossroads.

While legend generally does agree that the hijacking took place at Chennault Crossroads, it is worthwhile to note that some versions of the story tell that the gold was hijacked on the same night in Lincolnton, the county seat of Lincoln County and a town that is fourteen miles south of Chennault Crossroads and twenty miles east of Washington. Under this scenario the hijacked gold was taken to Chennault Crossroads by the hijackers.

In any case, the teamsters driving the wagons arrived at Reverend Chennault's home late on the evening of May 24 and asked his permission to park their wagons and spend the night in his corral. Permission was granted, but during the night, persons unknown struck and took much—but not all—of the gold. As witnesses, apparently including Reverend Chennault, told it, there were remaining gold coins in piles that were ankle deep.

As to the identity of the perpetrators, there are a number of theories. Two leading contenders are Union troops and Confederate troops. They would have been sufficiently well armed to pull off such a raid, and they would have had horses, including pack animals, for a fast getaway. Union troops would have been obliged to confiscate the gold and turn it in, but marauding, victorious troops don't always follow the letter of the law when it comes to spoils of war. For Confederate troops, stealing Confederate property would have been treasonous, but it certainly could be rationalized that one cannot commit treason against a country that no longer existed, nor against a lost cause.

While a case could be made to indict either side in the

recently concluded conflict, one interesting theory that is often discussed on warm summer evenings on the broad front porches down around Wilkes County is that it was the Virginia bankers stealing their own property to keep it from falling into Union hands.

Union troops did arrive eventually, and they did know about the gold. The fact that the Yankees devoted so much attention to the Chennault plantation in 1865 clearly indicates that the preponderance of evidence at the time supported the theory that the something very big happened to a very large quantity of gold at the plantation on the night of May 24. As the story goes, the Union troops tortured the people at the plantation to try to get them to talk, and took the Chennaults to Washington for interrogation. Reverend Chennault and his family had nothing to add, and they were eventually released and sent home.

Apparently the gold was gone and apparently the Yankees never found it.

What Happened to the Confederate Treasury?

What, then, happened to the gold? Maybe the U.S. government learned enough from the Chennaults to locate it. Probably not.

Conventional wisdom holds that there is $10 million from the Confederate Treasury, the Virginia banks, and/or the French loan buried somewhere in Wilkes County and/or Lincoln County. The disagreement comes in narrowing it down beyond that.

There are any number of stories that the gold is buried within a five- or ten-mile radius of Washington, but an unusually large number of gold coins have turned up through the years around the Chennault plantation itself. Those could be the remnants of the ankle-deep leftovers of the hijacking, or they could be confirmation of the often-advanced theory that the whole stash was buried on the Chennault plantation after the raid. You can't go down there now without running into somebody with a metal detector.

You'll hear all sorts of rumors about people finding bars of gold in streambeds around these parts, and some folks will emphatically specify that it was buried at the place where the Apalachee and Oconee Rivers flow together. Then there are stories that it was thrown into the Savannah River (with or without wagons and/or horses). The problem with that idea is that after the construction of the J. Strom Thurmond Dam down by Pollard's Corner, the Savannah River had become the J. Strom Thurmond Lake, and every bit of the 1865 shoreline is under hundreds of feet of water. In fact, about half of what was dry land Lincoln County in 1865 is now lake bottom. If it was thrown into the Savannah River, or buried anywhere near the Savannah or upstream ten miles on the Little River, you'll need a wet suit and scuba tanks to look for it and a great deal of patience to find it.

The Consolation Prize?

If the Confederate Treasury is lost for all time at the bottom of the J. Strom Thurmond Lake, or if it was discovered and quietly taken away from the Chennault plantation sixty years ago, there are still plenty of wild geese to chase in Georgia.

As with the other states of the former Confederacy, Georgia's hills still hold many treasures that date back to the Civil War. For example, in 1864, during Sherman's sacking of Atlanta, some Union soldiers made off with close to $6 million in gold, silver, jewelry, and other valuables that are still hidden—so the story goes—near the state capital.

There is another rumor that will not die that tells of about $3 million in gold that was hidden by a man named Guy Rivers and several slaves as Union forces were approaching Dahlonega in 1864. Rivers died of a heart attack before the gold was recovered, but legend tells that the gold was hidden either in what is now known as Guy Rivers Cave on the Josephine Mine property, or somewhere along Rocky Etowah River Bluff in Lumpkin County.

Gold coins and family silver were also said to have been buried during the Civil War on the Brock homesite, four miles northeast of Clermont, close to Route 129 between Gainesville and Cleveland near the Chattahoochee National Forest.

What may be the best tale of all—the Confederate Treasury excepted, of course—takes us back to the vicinity of Wilkes County, specifically to Crawfordville, which is about fifteen miles south of Washington in Taliaferro County. It seems that on the night of May 24, 1865—"coincidentally" the same night that all the excitement was happening up at Chennault Crossroads—the prize hunting dog belonging to Alexander H. Stephens of Crawfordville passed away. The poor cur was buried promptly beneath a large stone marker. The whispers still say that the dog did not go under the earth alone that night.

Could it have been that some hard-riding Confederate troops arrived in Crawfordville that night with pack animals foaming with sweat?

Alexander H. Stephens was the vice president of the Confederate States of America.

Following the Ghosts of Confederate Gold

The Confederate Treasury may be lost, but the road to Wilkes County is easy to follow. Start with a flight to Atlanta. Just as the Lost Dutchman Mine is probably fewer than a hundred miles east of Arizona's largest city and state capital, the Confederate Treasury is probably fewer than a hundred miles east of Georgia's largest city and state capital. In both cases, that's the easy part.

Hartsfield Atlanta International Airport is on the south side of town, so you don't even have to set foot in Atlanta itself to be on your way to Wilkes County. You will come out of the rental car maze with a choice of north or south on Interstate 85. Do as Jeff Davis or Alex Stephens would have done and pick the south—but only for about two miles. When you come to Interstate 285, which is Atlanta's beltway, head east toward Mountain View and Jonesboro Road.

As you go east on Interstate 285, you'll be going around the beltway counterclockwise, and the exit numbers will be diminishing. Exit 36 will be Flat Shoals Parkway, and exit 35 is Interstate 20. Take Interstate 20 east in the direction of Augusta, and settle back for about a sixty- to ninety-minute drive—depending on traffic.

Near Greensboro, exit 53 off Interstate 20 will put you eastbound on Georgia Route 44, which leads directly into Washington, but if you are in the mood, you could cruise on to exit 55. If you get off here and drive north for two miles on Georgia Route 22, you'll find yourself in Craw-fordville, where you can visit Alex Stephens State Historical Park and try to find the stone marker that marks the place where he buried his dog. When you finish with this stroll down the history trails of the Peach State, continue north on Route 22 for about nine miles and you'll find Route 44 and a road sign pointing right, toward Washington, Georgia.

Almost immediately after you pass the place where Routes 22 and 44 come together, you will cross the Wilkes County line. It is really pretty quiet out here on this little two-lane road, so it doesn't take much of a stretch of the imagination to hear the wheezing of tired cavalry horses in the woods or the clank of ghostly spurs up around the next bend.

Washington is only about twelve miles northeast of the Wilkes County line. To say that Washington hasn't changed in the years since the Civil War would be very wrong but still can get something of a feel for the old days. William Tecumseh Sherman burned Atlanta, not Washington. You can even walk over to the Washington city library, where they have an old battered chest whose battering dates to a night in May 1865. It is empty of all but the memories.

Washington still has a lot of history that predates that night in 1865. Even before they settled Savannah, traders and trappers passed this way. In 1773, after the area was "ceded" by the Creek and Cherokee Nations, Royal Governor Jim Wright sent flyers out to the Carolinas, Virginia, and Pennsylvania offering the rich, deep-loamed, well-watered hills of northeastern Georgia for headright settlement, and farmers and families with English, Scotch-Irish, and German surnames came in to start working the land. Four years later, and a year after the Declaration of Independence, Wilkes County—named for John Wilkes, a Colonial supporter in the British House of Commons—became one of the eight original counties of the new state of Georgia. In 1779 the patriots beat the British in the Battle of Kettle Creek, about eight miles west of where Washington has stood since 1780, when it was established as the first town in the United States named for George Washington.

Washington is a good place to catch up on Confederate Treasury lore. Most people around here will have something to say on the matter, and if anyone sees you getting a metal detector out of the trunk of your rental car, they'll probably smile and nod. Strangers with metal detectors, like theories about where the gold actually is, come and go, but, just as the gold crisscrossed the back roads of Wilkes County, so all the stories seem to cross through that place up the road called Chennault Crossroads.

It is only fifteen miles from Washington. Take Georgia Route 17 north and watch attentively for the signs. If you blink you'll miss it. Better still, ask directions at one of the gas stations on U.S. Highway 78.

Highway 78 is a narrow, winding road where the hiss of your tires on the asphalt seems to whisper, "They came this way. . . . They passed this way. . . . They brought that gold right this way on this road."

When you get to the place where the road from Washington crosses Georgia Route 79, you're there. If you've driven in from Atlanta, it may be getting dark. As you ponder this gathering dusk, you may remember the wagons that drove in here from Washington at dusk on May 24, 1865, filled with gold. The Confederate troopers stopped right here in this place. The officer in charge went up the front steps, walked across the front porch of the main house of the Chennault plantation, and inquired with the Reverend Dionysius Chennault as to whether they could spend the night. Before the morning sun again touched the eaves of the main house, the Confederate Treasury had disappeared into the mists of history.

Tonight you drive in from Atlanta by way of Washington with your mind filled with thoughts of wagons filled with gold. You stop right here in this place and go up the front steps. You walk across the front porch of the main house of the Chennault plantation and ask whether you might spend the night.

Today the main house is the Chennault Plantation Bed & Breakfast, and they may tell you that you could have called ahead. You have that luxury—which the teamsters of 1865 did not have. You could have dialed (706) 359-3039 and made a reservation to spend the night here in that same house.

Before the morning sun has again touched the eaves of the main house, you will have sat on the porch of the Chennault plantation, and you will have slept with an ear open for a rebel yell, and in your dreams you will have pondered the fate of the Confederate Treasury, which disappeared into the mists of history only a hundred yards from here.

Chapter 8

CONFEDERATE GOLD

PLACE: *Between Richmond and Williamsburg, Virginia*

TIME PERIOD: *1863–65*

Virginia has had a rich and turbulent history. Through it all, there were fortunes made and fortunes lost. The end of the Civil War provided a great many of the latter. For instance, Captain John Mosbey, a Confederate guerrilla, is said to have buried a treasure in gold and silver worth millions—from coins to church plate—as well as weapons, between two large pine trees between Culpeper and Norman. Other Civil War–era treasures are supposed to be buried on the grounds of the Carter's Grove plantation, six miles southeast of Williamsburg.

Perhaps the most intriguing Virginia Civil War treasure story involves the case of $10 million in gold coins and bullion that the British government loaned to the Confederacy in 1863. As the Confederate government began to accept defeat as a possible conclusion to the war in 1864 or early 1865, this gold was buried on the Virginia Peninsula, along the banks of the James River, and never reclaimed.

The long stretch of land known as the Virginia Peninsula stretches from Richmond east to Hampton Roads and the Atlantic Ocean. It is defined geographically by the York River and its broad estuary to the north, and the James River and its estuary to the south. It was the scene of the

"Peninsula Campaigns" during the Civil War, as the Union forces attempted to gain a foothold here to flank Confederate forces protecting the Confederate capital at Richmond. In 1862 U.S. Army general George McClellan began the first Peninsula Campaign by ferrying a one-hundred-thousand-troop force down the Potomac River from Washington, D.C., into the Chesapeake Bay and on to Hampton, where he began a move west toward Richmond. In seven days of fighting that left thirty-five thousand casualties writhing in pain or lying still on the battlefield, McClellan was forced into retreat by Confederate general Robert E. Lee.

Two years later, as the fortunes of the Confederacy were in decline, it was U.S. Army general Ulysses S. Grant who led the Union forces in the final offensive against Richmond. Following his own maxim that "Lee's troops and not Richmond" were his battlefield objective, Grant engaged the Confederates in a bloody war of attrition, pushing south and east from Fredericksburg, eventually flanking Richmond, and pushing south across the James River to Petersburg. This cut Richmond off from the sea and put Grant in control of the Virginia Peninsula.

In the meantime, the $10 million in gold was buried on the peninsula, reportedly on or near the three thousand acres of the famous Berkeley plantation, which is east of Hopewell in Prince George County.

Known officially as the "Berkeley Hundred Plantation," the Berkeley plantation still stands, a popular tourist attraction on Virginia Route 5 near Charles City along the James River between Richmond and Williamsburg. The mansion, a three-story brick house that dates to 1726, was built by Benjamin Harrison IV and his wife, Anne. Benjamin Harrison V, son of the builder of Berkeley, was a signer of the Declaration of Independence and a three-time governor of Virginia. His third son, William Henry Harrison, was born at Berkeley and later became the ninth U.S. president. In turn, William Henry's grandson, Benjamin Harrison, was a Union officer and later the twenty-third president of the United States. Indeed, all of the first ten U.S. presidents visited Berkeley. During the Civil War it was occupied by Union Army units during both Peninsula Campaigns, and it is known that U.S. Army general Daniel Butterfield composed ''Taps'' while encamped with McClellan's troops at the Berkeley plantation in 1862.

Today there is hardly a more genteel buried treasure site in the United States than the Berkeley plantation, with its thoroughly restored mansion and its meticulously manicured grounds, but somewhere out there is a treasure that is possibly worth billions.

Where on the James?

The Berkeley plantation is easy to find, but that's just the beginning. So, starting at the beginning takes us to Richmond, capital of Virginia and capital of the late Confederacy. The city can be reached by air directly, or by way of the airports in and near Washington, D.C.—the capital of the *other* side during the late Civil War.

Because it will be vitally necessary to fine-tune your search before trying to find the missing British loan, you should absolutely make the beginning point at the Virginia State Archives, which are conveniently located in Richmond and reachable by telephone at (804) 367-8506. Research all you can about missing and lost Confederate gold in the Richmond and peninsula areas. There will be a great deal of overlap, but keep your eyes on the ball and plot everything on your U.S. Geological Survey topographical map with the same meticulous attention that they give to dusting these old plantation houses they keep open for tourists (you'll see what I mean when you get out to Berkeley).

Fortunately, because of the military cartography done during the Civil War—especially during the Peninsula Campaigns—there will be very detailed 1862–65 maps of the James River area. Comparing these to your current U.S. Geological Survey topographical map will reveal any changes that have occurred to the exact shoreline—both

north and south—of the James River and its tributary
creeks.

With your research completed, it is time to go into the
field to explore the banks of the James River and the Berkeley plantation. As you come out of the Virginia State Archives, you will see the dome of the Virginia State Capitol
building. The street to the south of the capitol is Main
Street, which is also—as the signs will show—Virginia
Route 5. Outside of downtown Richmond, Main Street becomes New Market Road, but it will remain Route 5. If in
doubt, follow the signs to Richmond National Battlefield.
After that, following Route 5 should be easy.

The drive from the state capitol to the Berkeley plantation is about twenty-five miles, and it is about another
twenty-five miles to Williamsburg. As you drive south on
Route 5, you will be able to see the James River on your
right much of the way. Indeed, Route 5 will be parallel to
the northern shore of the James River all the way to Williamsburg. You may be driving this far, but you won't
know for sure until you finish at the archives.

On the southern shore of the James River there is no
road that follows the shore as Route 5 does on the north.
There is Virginia Route 10, which roughly parallels the
river, but it is generally between five and ten miles away.

In the fifty-mile section of the James River where the
treasure is thought to be located, you will note that there
are two places to cross. About five miles west of the Berkeley plantation there is the Virginia Route 156 bridge, which
links Route 5 to Route 10 at Hopewell. This is really the
only bridge across the James River between Richmond and
Norfolk, but there is a ferry that operates across the river
between Jamestown on the north and the small Surry
County town of Scotland on the south.

These directions describe the perimeters of the search
area. Somewhere out there is the treasure, but as you will
soon realize as you drive these roads to get a sense of the
lay of the land, the shoreline is very remote from paved
roads, and renting a boat may be the best way to do your
exploring.

As with most of the treasures described in this book, the passage of more than a century will have taken its toll on terrain features. If subsequent floodwaters have eaten into the bank where it was buried, the coins could have been swept downstream and/or buried under many yards of silt. The bullion probably will be at the original location, but if the original bank was eroded, then the shoreline probably will not be in its original Civil War–era location. Even if the bullion has not moved laterally, it is likely to have sunk and/or have been covered by silt and mud. It is now well away from the present shore, and salvage may be virtually impossible or extremely expensive because of river currents.

Finally, there is the issue of ownership. Most of the shoreline of the James River—both north and south—is in private hands. To conduct salvage operations you would have to enter into a negotiated agreement with the owner. An exception is that the area around Jamestown is federally owned and managed by the U.S. National Park Service, who might be convinced that a salvage operation on their turf would benefit the historic-interpretation aspect of their mandate, but it would have to be done under the watchful eye of Park Service archaeologists.

As for the gold itself, you would certainly have to share some of the profit with the owner of the land, and there may be nineteenth-century claimants who will reach out from the past with bony fingers. With the Confederacy long since gone, one wonders who would be responsible for the interest on the original loan, and whether the U.S. government would recognize any claim on the treasure by the British government since the Confederacy was a national entity never recognized by the United States.

Chapter 9

THE LOST ADAMS DIGGINGS

PLACE: *Northwestern New Mexico*

TIME PERIOD: *1864*

There are many treasures to be found on the back roads of New Mexico, treasures that range from gold and silver to magnificent vistas and captivating legends. One of the most amazing stories in American treasure lore involves the "Lost Adams Diggings," a placer so rich that gold could be picked up by the fistful. While such hyperbole is certainly not uncommon, especially in tales originating in the Southwest, the Adams site is either more widely corroborated or is a rumor more consistently and more widely spread than most fabrications. It is either the subject of the tallest of tales, or one of the richest unexploited placers in the world. It is named for Adams, not because he found it first or profited most, but because of those who were there, he was the one to survive and to tell the tale.

Adams, who like Liberace, Cher, and Madonna, went by a single name, once earned his living running freight wagons between Tucson and California. He was born in Rochester, New York, in 1829 and came west in 1861 to get into the freight business, or out of fighting in the Civil War, or both.

In August 1864 Adams was heading west out of Tucson with two wagons led by a twelve-horse team. He was breaking camp one morning near Gila Bend, Arizona, when he was attacked by a group of Apaches set on stealing his horses. Grabbing his rifle, he fought back and managed to kill one of the intruders before the others escaped with two of his team. He spent the morning rounding up the remaining ten animals, only to return to his camp to find his wagons burned. His provisions and the bankroll he kept under his wagon seat had been stolen, so he set out for a Pima village he knew was located on the Gila River about a day's ride to the north, hoping to get some food.

Arriving there, he was surprised to find that the Pimas had other visitors, a group of prospectors—several Americans and a German whose name was Emil Schaeffer. For some reason there seems to be a German associated with many of the treasure legends of the Southwest, and he is almost invariably referred to as "the Dutchman," a bastardization of *Deutsche* man.

With the Americans and "the Dutchman" was a young Mexican man with a deformed ear who told a story of he and his brother having been kidnapped by Apaches when they were boys. They had grown up as Apache slaves. His brother had been killed in a fight with an Apache, and the young man had retaliated by killing the Apache. Knowing that a slave accused of murder, no matter how justified, is in a hopeless situation, the young man decided to run. He headed south toward Mexico and had stumbled into the prospectors' camp just before Adams.

In conversations with Adams and the prospectors, the young Mexican was amazed to hear them say that the shiny yellow metal called gold could be traded for things of "real value," such as guns and horses. Having been raised beyond the fringes of "civilization," he had no concept of lumps of this yellow metal being worth the same or more than tools that could actually perform a function. When he discovered this, he had told the prospectors that he knew of a canyon where the ground was littered with gold nuggets ranging in size from that of acorns to that of turkey eggs. He told them that in one day a man could load his saddlebags with as much gold as his horse could carry.

Naturally, this got the attention of the prospectors, who

wanted to know where this canyon might be. As the story goes, the boy with the shriveled ear gestured to the northeast, toward Apache country, and indicated that the place was in that direction, about "ten sleeps" distant, meaning ten days' ride, or a hundred to two hundred miles, depending on the terrain. He added that the canyon was *bien escondido* (well hidden) and let that phrase hang for a moment. He hadn't known the full value of the shiny yellow stuff that these men prized, but he knew intuitively how to bargain. He knew that they wanted the yellow stuff, and he knew that they needed him to get there. In the space of a few days the kid with the shriveled ear had gone from slave to wanted fugitive to the most important person in a crowd of about a dozen people. His life, which was previously worth nothing or less, was now extremely valuable to a whole crowd of men.

When asked politely but urgently whether he could take them to this *bien escondido* canyon, the boy thought for a minute and promised to help them in exchange for items of real value: a horse, a saddle, a gun, and some ammunition. Apparently he had now learned the value of gold, for he also readily asked for two $50 gold pieces. He told them that he was so sure they would be happy with what they found that he would gladly allow them to defer payment until they reached the *bien escondido* canyon, and that if he didn't take them there, they could shoot him. Apparently he trusted them sufficiently to believe that they would not just shoot him anyway.

As the plan was hatched to go to the *bien escondido* canyon to gather up the gold nuggets ranging in size from that of acorns to that of turkey eggs, Adams himself took on an important and mutually fortuitous role in this expedition. This was because the prospectors were short of horses, and Adams had ten. Horses were vitally important. Ahead of them lay rugged country with little water and no settlements that were populated either by white people or by Native Americans who could be regarded as "friendly." It was country about which the old-timers used to say that "a man without a horse was no man at all."

With horses for everyone to ride, and a dozen pack animals, the party of twenty-two men set out for the ride of ten sleeps. As anyone who has traveled long distances in the West on horseback knows, the speed of a large group is governed by the slowest horse. In this case, the slowest horse was one that was used as a packhorse to carry a large supply of provisions.

How long they traveled is not known. While legend holds that the Mexican boy said "ten sleeps," other stories claim eight days, and still others suggest that it was longer than two weeks. While we know that they generally traveled to the northeast, it is hard to know exactly where or how far. Without knowing how long they took to get where they were going, time cannot be used to judge distance. It seems that in his retellings, Adams himself was inconsistent in regard to time, as though it did not really matter. It fact, for identifying their destination, it doesn't matter. It would if we knew how fast they traveled or how many hours a day they rode, but we don't. Unless one makes notes, such data are easily forgotten.

As for landmarks, the stories say that the young Mexican took Adams and the others to the top of a mountain—identified in some accounts as being Mount Ord—and showed them a pair of mountains near which was the entrance to the canyon. Their route—which would have taken them through what is now Navajo and Apache Counties in Arizona, and McKinley and Cibola Counties in New Mexico—is mesa country, and they would have seen many pairs of mountains. One of them may have been the prominent El Morro mesa (now El Morro National Monument), on what is now New Mexico Route 53, about forty miles east of the Arizona state line.

One important clue is that at some point—a half day's ride from a place where they filled their canteens in a stream that flowed through a cottonwood grove—they crossed a wagon trail that the Mexican identified as leading to "the fort in [or near] *el malpais*." This fort was almost certainly Fort Wingate, about twelve miles east of Gallup, New Mexico, and fifty miles from El Malpais lava beds (mostly now contained within El Malpais National Monument and Cibola National Forest and Wilderness Area). The term *malpais,* which is the Spanish word for "badlands," occurs frequently in the stories about the "Diggings," and there is little doubt that the lava beds of today's El Malpais National Monument would be a likely place for the *bien escondido* canyon.

El Malpais is also surrounded by miles of sandstone cliffs, another geologic feature that figures into the legend. Even today these lava beds are an almost impenetrable labyrinth, with only a couple of unpaved roads that probe them tentatively from the edges. The lava beds are very difficult to cross. The jagged rock can severely injure the hooves of a horse—even with horseshoes—and can tear tires or hiking boots to shreds. This writer has seen it happen.

The night of the day they crossed the wagon trail, the young Mexican indicated that they should camp near a spring that was surrounded by an area where Native Americans had apparently once cultivated squash. From this place, which the stories sometimes refer to as "the pumpkin patch," the boy led them for two hours through an extremely narrow canyon to a lava-covered plateau from which the two haystack-shaped buttes could easily be seen to the northeast. The young Mexican indicated that the gold was now between them and the buttes.

As the story continues, the expedition was riding parallel to a line of high, steep cliffs until about noon, when the Mexican led them behind a boulder that appeared to be part of the wall. Here they found a virtually invisible "hidden door" that led to a narrow Z-shaped canyon. Nobody in the party had noticed the entrance until the boy rode into it. The portal was naturally camouflaged, and apparently it was so well camouflaged that it was virtually invisible. It appeared when he first rode into it that he was disappearing into the rock face of the cliff itself.

The idea of a "secret door" is present in many folk legends from throughout the world. Rife with subconscious or deliberate symbolism, secret doors have been used as metaphors for everything from rites of passage to mysteries that really should be kept secret. For those twenty-two men who rode through that secret door in the New Mexico badlands on that fateful September day, nothing would ever be the same.

Riding through this steep, narrow canyon beyond the secret door was extremely difficult, the trail twisted and turned as it led steeply downhill. At the bottom, they found a flat, open area with a small stream running through it. In the gravel bars at the side of this small stream the ground really *was* littered with gold nuggets ranging in size from that of acorns to that of "turkey eggs." Even more of it was found to be buried just under the surface. The more one dug, the more gold there was to be found. It was unlike anything any of the prospectors had ever seen.

The Mexican boy was paid off as promised and even given a second horse. He left immediately and was never seen again. It is not known whether he reached Mexico, or crossed the path of the Apaches who wanted him dead. There were stories of someone having seen Apaches riding the horses he had taken, but nothing is for sure.

In any case, Adams and his group then set up camp and began collecting piles of gold. A day or two after they arrived, they also began construction of a small cabin, cutting down some of the trees in the area and using logs that were present in the stream. This cabin was built over an ancient Native American grinding rock that was located near a small falls in the stream, and it was agreed that everyone would pool the gold they found, that it would all be placed in the hollowed-out part of the grinding rock and covered with a flat stone for safekeeping. Everyone but Schaeffer, the German, participated in this plan. He worked alone, distant from the others, and kept his gold to himself.

After ten days of digging, food was running low, so it was decided that a man named John Brewer, along with several others, would leave the canyon, find the wagon trail, and go up to the trading post at Fort Wingate for supplies. It was estimated that a round trip would take about a week.

By this time—according to the story—the weather was getting cooler, the days shorter, and there was probably some thought of the coming winter. If they had started out at the end of August and traveled for two weeks before starting a ten-day dig, it would probably have been close to the end of September. Winter can often come early in the mountains of New Mexico, and there would have been discussions of increasing the amount of gold that could be taken out before the snows came. Better tools would certainly help in that process. Since there was now plenty of gold, Brewer and the party heading out to Fort Wingate could buy plenty of additional equipment and mining tools as well as necessities such as food and tobacco.

In the meantime, the men had also made contact with a group of Chiricahua Apaches. This group, including Chief Nana, were camped above a falls in the stream in another part of the same canyon, which Nana called Sno-ta-hay. Nana had agreed that the Apaches would not bother the prospectors if they stayed below the falls and away from his camp. He was quite adamant—in the way that a nineteenth-century Apache leader could be adamant—about not being disturbed.

Schaeffer would recall later that he sensed the inevitability of trouble between the Apaches and the ever more greedy prospectors. He whispered to Adams that he was planning to ride out with Brewer's supply party—taking his gold with him—and that he would not be coming back.

The *Deutsche* man's premonition proved to be correct, although it was more than a week after he left for Fort Wingate when the tensions bubbling in the little canyon finally boiled over. This issue was the ledge, or vein of gold, from which all the nuggets came. It extended above the falls and reached far up into the portion of the canyon that Nana had designated as being off-limits. It was potentially far richer than anything that lay on the ground or under the sand in and around the streambed in the prospectors' end of the canyon.

One day, a man who was ostensibly—and possibly innocently—trailing stray horses up above the falls, came back with an enormous nugget, which he showed to Adams. The story of Adams became like the story of Adam in the

Book of Genesis. Just as Adam and his companions were tempted to eat the forbidden fruit from the forbidden tree, so Adams and his companions were being tempted to take forbidden gold from the forbidden end of Sno-ta-hay. Adam balked and urged her not to, but Eve ate. Adams balked, but despite his admonishments to the contrary, the men started sneaking into Nana's territory.

The huge nuggets they brought back only encouraged further, more reckless, transgressions.

Meanwhile, a week had come and gone with no word from Brewer's supply party. Growing nervous, Adams and another man, named Davidson, decided to go out of the canyon and search for them. They saddled up and rode back out through the Z-shaped, zigzag canyon and passed through the ''secret door.'' To their horror, they almost immediately stumbled over the bodies of five men amid scattered tools and broken flour sacks. John Brewer's mortal remains, however, were not be found.

Quickly placing the five bodies in rock crevices and covering them with packsaddles to preserve them from coyotes until they could be properly buried, Adams and Davidson hurried back to tell the others. As they reached the bottom of the canyon, they heard a commotion up ahead. The Book of Genesis analogy here suddenly changed to that of the B-grade Western movie. Adams and Davidson heard the popping sound of gunshots and screams of frightened, injured men coming from the direction of the log cabin.

They crept to a vantage point from which they could observe what was going on and, as they hid themselves among the boulders, they looked on aghast as their friends were slain and mutilated by a group of Apaches. Adams and Davidson assumed correctly that the Apaches would make a head count of the deceased prospectors and discover that two were missing, so they released their horses, hoping the animals would divert the Apache search parties long enough for the two men to make their escape.

After dark, the two survivors sneaked into the camp to get a drink of water and hopefully to grab some of their gold. The cabin, which had been burned by the Apaches, still smoldered and was too hot to touch so they couldn't get to the gold in the grinding rock. They were afraid to splash water on it for fear of alerting the Apaches, but fortunately Adams had hidden one or more large nuggets outside the cabin and was able to recover it. Unfortunately, however, they were able to find only two canteens in the dark. Filling those, they escaped from Sno-ta-hay Canyon before dawn.

As it turned out, John Brewer had survived the ambush at the "secret door," and he also sneaked back into the canyon that night. He saw Adams and Davidson creeping through the shadows and mistook them for Apaches, but they did not see him. Apparently he crept out of the canyon before they did and was long gone when they emerged.

Traveling only by night for fear of being found by the Apaches, Adams and Davidson hiked southwest, back toward Arizona. They decided to keep to the hills in the hope of not leaving a trace that the Apaches would find. Finally they crossed the wagon trail and followed it as best they could while keeping out of sight. It was very difficult going, traveling in the dark and without horses or adequate food. It was a classic Old West "lost in the wilderness" scenario—two men, running scared and tearing their boots to shreds on rocks and lava outcroppings as they stumbled through the cold October nights. They lost their way, found it, lost it again, and trudged on. Days melted into a week as they fretted with the coming of the frost and the first light snows.

The gold that Adams carried had great value anywhere but the mess in which they found themselves. It was a bitter irony after they had chided the young Mexican for not realizing that gold had "real" value. They had both guns and gold, but they had no soles left on their shoes and very little to eat. They survived on acorns and piñon nuts, but finally, when he could stand it no longer, Adams decided to try to shoot some game. He was desperate, and besides, he probably figured that if the Apaches had followed them, they wouldn't need an excuse such as one stray gunshot to swoop down and kill the two haggard fortune hunters.

When he took aim at his quarry—a rabbit—Adams did wrap a piece of his shirt around the barrel of his revolver in an effort to muffle the sound. At last they had fresh meat. To cook their meal, Adams and Davidson made their first fire since leaving the canyon, using aspen, which doesn't smoke as much as other woods.

As they were cooking their food, they were spotted by a group of riders. Fortunately, these men turned out to be American Cavalry troopers, who took them to Fort Apache, which is on present-day Arizona Route 55 at the southern tip of Navajo County.

Meanwhile, Brewer had staggered to the east, hoping to reach one of the Mexican trading posts along the Rio Grande. After several days he passed out from sunstroke and exhaustion, but he was discovered by a group of Native Americans—not Apaches—who lived in one of the Rio Grande pueblos north of Socorro, possibly near Las Lunas or Belen. After having recuperated, he joined a pack train headed for Santa Fe and eventually worked his way back to Missouri over the Santa Fe Trail. He probably didn't know for years that he had not been the only survivor.

As Adams and Davidson were recovering at Fort Apache, a group of Apaches came in under a flag of truce. Adams saw them, and recognizing one of them as a member of Nana's group in the canyon, he went berserk. Taking out his revolver, he opened fire, killing two of the Apaches before the troopers could stop him. Since the U.S. Army and the Apaches were technically at peace at that time, Adams was arrested for murder and thrown into the guardhouse.

In the Old West of myth and legend, killing a Native American was usually acceptable and often encouraged, but in fact, killing Native Americans while they were under the protection of the U.S. Army was a punishable offense, and military justice was often swift. The man who had staggered through the desert for many difficult days to escape being killed by the Apaches was about to be hanged by his rescuers for killing Apaches.

It was here that the legend of the Lost Adams Diggings

may have been lost forever, but it was at this point that its life as a legend really began.

As the story goes, Adams stole a horse, and he was on the run again. Well fed and equipped with a horse, he made better time than he had on his earlier odyssey with Davidson. Somehow he found his way to Los Angeles, got married, and settled down to raise a family. There is also an alternate story that tells of him showing up in Tucson at some point with $22,000 in gold nuggets.

Davidson was not so lucky. Whereas Adams was only thirty-five, Davidson was a somewhat older man, and he never really recovered from the ordeal in the desert after the massacre. The legend tells that he died soon after, without ever having revealed the location of the diggings.

Of those who had actually been there, the only survivors were Adams, Schaeffer—who'd returned to Germany—and Brewer, who had gone on to Missouri. Schaeffer left the United States vowing not to return, and he kept his promise. John Brewer would not return to New Mexico for a quarter of a century. And being wanted by the U.S. Army, Adams was in no hurry to go back in search of the gold.

In Search of the Lost and Elusive Adams Diggings

As Adams established his new life in the relatively sophisticated Golden State, Arizona Territory and New Mexico Territory remained as they had been since long before he had first crossed their dangerous deserts. They were truly a time capsule of a life and a culture that had faded from most of the West and certainly from most of the United States.

These were the 1860s. The West was still wild, and the Apaches would rule the rugged hills of Arizona and New Mexico for most of the next two decades the same way they had for the previous two centuries. It would be 1886 before Geronimo, the last Apache warrior chief, would surrender the last Apache war party to the authority of the

U.S. Army. It would be a half century before Arizona and New Mexico were tame enough for statehood. Beyond the towns, roads, and rail lines, little had changed for centuries, and the Apaches ruled their turf with irrefutable authority. Until the 1880s, Nana's rules for Sno-ta-hay Canyon applied throughout the Southwest, wherever an Apache leader said they would apply. This curbed any desire that anyone would have had for a return to Sno-ta-hay Canyon. Nevertheless, the man who would become the new namesake of the place couldn't resist spinning yarns of the lost riches whenever a glass of whiskey loosened his tongue. He told of the gold, the Apaches, and the human bones hidden in the rocks and covered with packsaddles, and Sno-ta-hay Canyon officially became the Lost Adams Diggings.

The story, when overheard in the relative comfort of a Los Angeles saloon or card room, was enough to make the mild-mannered become greedy and to make the greedy decide to ride out at sunup. It was in 1874 that an old Canadian mariner known as Captain C. A. Shaw paid Adams $500 to stop talking and start walking. The captain had amassed a substantial nest egg that he planned to invest in a treasure hunt he was betting would net him enough to retire in luxury to Guam, an island he had visited during his years at sea and that was the end of his rainbow.

Adams took Shaw and a party of sixteen to Arizona, where he attempted to reconstruct the original trip from the Pima village on the Gila River. They rode northwest across the desert, with Adams trying to recall landmarks from a decade before. They followed the San Francisco River into New Mexico, crossing the territorial border south of the present route of U.S. Highway 60 and about 50 miles southwest of El Malpais.

By 1874, however, relations between the Apaches and the whites had become even more violent than in the 1860s, and the threat of hostile action by the Apaches made Adams nervous. He led Shaw and his party aimlessly through the wilderness of dusty hillsides and pine forests, scratching his beard and shaking his head with a sense of confusion about him. Finally, he simply gave up. When pressed to explain what had happened, he just shrugged and explained: "The Apaches made me forget."

What exactly did he mean? Was it the shock and the ordeal of the massacre and the escape, or was it a panicked fear of facing the same fate in 1874 that he had escaped in 1864? The specter of Nana and his firm warning still cast a long and distinct shadow across the hopes and dreams of the aging prospector.

At one point during the expedition, Shaw and Adams were sitting on the porch at a trading post near the San Carlos Indian Reservation when a group of Apaches passed by. Among them was—as the story goes—Nana himself. The chief was talkative at first, but when Adams asked him if he'd been back to Sno-ta-hay Canyon, he just glowered and turned away. According to the historical record, Nana did in fact go onto the San Carlos Reservation in 1874, so that may confirm the truth of the tale of him bumping into Adams and Shaw.

Maybe it was Nana's expression, or the hard, cold glint in his eye that froze Adams's spine and make him eventually admit "The Apaches made me forget."

When Adams gave up, most of those in the expedition turned back to California, but Captain Shaw stayed on in New Mexico to do a little detective work. He sought out those he could find who had claimed to have something to say about Adams's tale. The captain visited Fort Wingate and was able to confirm that in 1864 six men had in fact come into the fort's trading post to buy—using gold nuggets—supplies for a small placer mining activity they claimed was in El Malpais. Shaw also apparently met a clerk named Chase at a trading post at the Warm Springs Agency who had discussed gold with Nana and who had written the name "Sno-ta-hay" in his ledger.

These clues convinced Shaw of the veracity of Adams's story. The captain became like a man possessed. The Lost Adams Diggings became his personal obsession. He shoveled his entire nest egg into his quixotic quest, and he never again laid eyes on the ocean, much less his beloved Guam. Year after year, until his death in 1917, Shaw rode the hills and canyons of western New Mexico, following leads and extrapolating what he could from every shred of evidence. Shaw probably never actually found the Lost Adams Diggings, but what he did find helped to corroborate Adams's tale and to add fuel and substance to the legend.

As for the man himself, Adams seems to have spent a good deal of time in New Mexico during his later years, but apparently he did a lot more talking about the diggings than looking for them. In September 1886 he had a heart attack while on a hunting trip and was taken back to Los Angeles on the Atchison, Topeka & Santa Fe. Soon after, he died, taking the truth about Sno-ta-hay to his grave.

Adams and Shaw may not have ridden together again in the years after 1874, but there were many who did ride with Shaw, and the stories that these men told continued to expand the legend into the early years of the twentieth century. One of them was a businessman named John F. Dowling, who had been in the mining industry for many years. He was not given to idle barroom chatter and did not tell his Lost Adams tale until just before he died in El Paso in about 1927.

In 1881 Dowling was a barely out of his teens and working as a miner out around Socorro, New Mexico, when a man named Dr. Spurgeon tired him to help find the Lost Adams Diggings. Spurgeon claimed to have been the post physician at Fort Apache in 1864 when Adams and Davidson were brought in. He had heard their story firsthand and had seen Adams's gigantic nugget or nuggets. He wanted to go back immediately to look for the gold, but army officers and doctors are typically disciplined not to abandon their posts, and the years slipped away from Spurgeon. The doctor went home to practice in Toledo, Ohio, after his hitch was up in the army, but finally returned to New Mexico in 1880.

Apparently most of the city slickers Spurgeon enticed to join him on the expedition had become disillusioned during the brutal New Mexico winter of 1880–81 and had gone home. This left the good doctor and a young fellow named Moore. After meeting John Dowling and offering him a share in the diggings, Spurgeon decided that he, too, would go back east.

According to Dowling's story, he and Moore, along with two cowboys Dowling knew, headed north toward the West Fork of the Gila River. Their trip was characterized primarily by a feud between Moore—who refused to do any work around their campsites—and the others. Apparently this ultimately led to the expedition turning back in disgust, but not before Dowling had recognized the landmarks—the burned cabin and the waterfall—to make him realize that they had actually reached Sno-ta-hay Canyon.

Dowling said nothing, but turned back with the others, hoping to come back on his own someday. He never did. After he returned to Socorro, he took a job in Mexico, and the years got away from him. Eventually he went blind, and this ended any chance of his ever getting back to El Malpais. In 1907, however, he gave detailed directions to a friend who did ride into El Malpais and who did find the wreckage of a burned-out cabin along a streambed. Dowling's friend claimed that he searched the area and found no evidence of gold nuggets the size of acorns or turkey eggs.

What did he really find, this friend of John F. Dowling? Did he find a burned cabin and nothing more shiny than quartz? Did he find incalculable riches about which he did not tell?

Did Dowling's friend find the wrong *bien escondido* canyon—one that had never held gold—or the right *bien escondido* canyon, but only after it had been plundered of everything of value by a faceless stranger who had sat at a barroom table in 1874 drinking in details as Adams and Captain Shaw drank themselves into hyperbole? Perhaps we'll never know. Certainly Dowling never knew for sure.

At about the same time that a blind John Dowling was dreaming his last dreams of Lost Adams gold, stories were going around southern New Mexico about an old cowboy named Aamon Tenney who had his own stories about meeting up with the only other surviving American to have actually been in Sno-ta-hay Canyon during those fateful weeks in the fall of 1864. As Adams went west toward

Arizona—thinking he and Davidson were the only survivors—John Brewer of the supply party had staggered toward the Rio Grande Valley, thinking that he alone had survived. He went back to Missouri, and for the next twenty-four years the back of his mind simmered with the belief that he and only he had a memory of the secret door and the magic canyon.

In the summer of 1888 Brewer and his Indian wife rode into the St. John's country of Arizona to search for the gold, unaware that Adams had spun out the legend in those same parts for a dozen years before he took his last ride home in 1886.

Aamon Tenney was just a boy at the time—growing up on his father's Windmill Ranch—when he met up with Brewer and tagged along with him on some of his rides in search of lost wagon tracks, a lost pumpkin patch, and a secret door. The old man filled the kid's head with the same stories that had haunted his own for a quarter century. He could remember the details—such as the feel of the egg-sized nuggets in the palm of his hand and the terror of watching men hacked to death—that made the story exciting for a boy and memorable for an old prospector, but he could not remember details such as the shape of the rock that hid the secret door. Apparently Brewer died disappointed and Aamon Tenney grew up and grew old with his own unique take on the Lost Adams Diggings legend, which he was only too glad to share with later generations of impressionable youngsters.

With Brewer's passing there was only one white man left who had been there, and the only one who had the good sense to get out in time. What, you may ask, became of the "Dutchman"? In 1900 Emil Schaeffer was actually tracked down, in Heidelberg. He confirmed the story of the canyon and the nuggets and told how he had managed to get to Hamburg with $10,000 worth of gold. That had been enough to live comfortably, and he had no interest in traveling halfway around the world to return to El Malpais after thirty-six years. He was insistent about wanting nothing more to do with finding the diggings again, and his memory of landmarks and details was no better than either Adams's or Brewer's.

The man who tracked down the Dutchman was a relatively resourceful prospector named "Doc" Young, who figures in a lot of early twentieth-century Lost Adams lore. His level of commitment is clearly evidenced by his sailing all the way to Germany. This was no small undertaking in 1900, when just getting to an Atlantic seaport was a major accomplishment for a man from the mountains of New Mexico. Like Aamon Tenney, Doc Young was a colorful character in his own right, and something of an icon of local folklore. He lived in the Mogollon (pronounced "Muggy-own") Mountains of western New Mexico, prospecting and wandering and telling tall tales. There is no record of when he was born, but apparently he was ageless, for all through the 1920s and the 1930s he regularly claimed to be ninety-two years old.

Two generations before Carlos Casteneda had his series of best-sellers about the mythical "Don Juan," Doc Young was a devotee of Indian herbology, which he claimed had made him ageless, psychic, and able to fly with eagles. Doc Young claimed that he had met old Captain Shaw and that he saved the old sailor's life. All through the 1920s and the 1930s he regularly claimed he knew exactly where the Lost Adams Diggings were and that he would be going there "next summer." Like both Adams and Shaw, the ninety-two-year-old doctor ran out of next summers long ago and long before he passed through the secret door. Or did he? Perhaps he is soaring out there now. Eagles have little need for gold.

Another captain whose name is listed among those of men for whom the Diggings became an almost irrational obsession was Captain Michael Cooney, who may not actually have been a captain but who *was,* for a time, a territorial legislator in Santa Fe. Captain Cooney had come out to the mining boomtown of Silver City, New Mexico, from Louisiana in 1880 to handle the affairs of his late brother Jim, who had been killed by a band of Mescalero Apaches associated with the notorious warlord Victorio. If

Adams had been made to forget by the Apaches, then Captain Cooney was a man whom the Apaches inadvertently introduced to the legend.

When Captain Cooney's eyes and ears had a taste of the treasure tales in the barrooms of Silver City, his brief stay in New Mexico became permanent. Like many before and since, he looked at the wealth being dug from the mines around Silver City and decided that the "wealth of the world" was somewhere up in the Mogollons, which lay just to the north.

Apparently his attention span was somewhat fickle in those days. After prospecting awhile in the Mogollons, he learned of the Lost Adams Diggings, and these captured his interest for a year or so until he went on to the legislature. However, while he was in Santa Fe he heard the tale that made him devote the remainder of his life to an obsession with the place called Sno-ta-hay.

It was in Santa Fe in 1892 that Captain Cooney—now Legislator Cooney—met a printer from Kansas City with a ten-year-old letter from his nephew. A few years before the letter was written, the boy—who had been scarcely older than ten at the time—was riding with surveyors working on the border of Socorro County. He got into a fight with some men in the survey party and took off on his own, deciding he would rather be in Silver City. Stumbling through the badlands, the boy got thirsty and paused to drink from a waterfall, under which was a ledge filled with large nuggets of gold. Captain Cooney immediately recalled that Sno-ta-hay Canyon had a waterfall, under which was a ledge filled with large nuggets of gold.

As the letter explained, the boy got through to Silver City with a pocketful of nuggets, where he had them assayed by a mining engineer named Burbank. The boy wanted to go right back to the waterfall, but Burbank talked him out of this because of fear of the Apaches, who still controlled the hills and backcountry of New Mexico.

The boy went home to St. Louis for a couple of years, but he returned to Silver City in his late teens. He headed into the Mogollons, where he is known to have camped for a time between Turkey Creek and Sycamore Creek. He showed up in Silver City at least one more time, and this was to mail the letter to his uncle. He described the mine in words that echoed Captain Cooney's own from almost the same era, saying it was the "richest mine in the world." He promised that he had blazed a trail from his camp to the ledge, so that his Kansas City uncle could find the place if something happened. Something did. The boy, now a young man, disappeared without a trace.

Armed with this information, Captain Cooney dropped everything, and like all those before and since, he devoted the rest of his life to his magnificent obsession. He is said to have found traces of a camp between Turkey Creek and Sycamore Creek, and he found blazed trees. However, he did not—so the story goes—ever find the waterfall, although he would search for years.

Like the perpetually ninety-two-year-old Doc Young, Captain Cooney became a hermit and a recluse, haunting the Mogollons like a specter. And, like Doc Young, he became the subject of discussions around schooners of beer from El Paso to Flagstaff, and especially around Silver City and Las Cruces. The one mystery that was most often mentioned but never explained was one of geography. If the Lost Adams Diggings were up north in El Malpais, why did Captain Cooney haunt the Mogollons? Turkey Creek and Sycamore Creek were a hundred miles from El Malpais. Could it be that there were two diggings—the Lost Adams, and another that had been discovered by the kid from Missouri?

All lost-treasure legends are populated with strange casts of characters, and among the most intriguing are those who know where it is—or, of course, *claim* to know—and profess no interest in having it. In the Lost Adams lore, this latter role fell to an El Paso photographer named James B. Gray. In the 1930s, when he was interviewed on the subject by folklorist and author J. Frank Dobie, Gray claimed to know where to find Sno-ta-hay Canyon, but had no interest in it because, being a Rosicrucian, he had "sworn off money."

Gray had been an army scout on the Chiricahua Apache Reservation in the 1880s, worked on the 3H Ranch in Arizona, and had ridden with Teddy Roosevelt's Rough Riders in Cuba. He had worked in North Africa and the Middle East and had fought as a soldier of fortune in China and with the French Army during World War I. Looking for lost mines had apparently been a hobby of his, and he said he discovered the Lost Adams Diggings while he was riding as a scout on the Chiricahua Reservation. He found it, but like Emil Schaeffer, he did not want to go there again.

There are a lot of similar stories that tell of people who made one or two attempts to find Adams's diggings, or who stumbled on the place and never found their way back. Then, of course, there are those for whom it became a life's obsession. There were, of course, the doctor and the two captains. And then there was Langford Johnston. Before he died in 1917, Captain Cooney passed the baton handed to him by Adams himself to Langford Johnston.

In 1886 Shaw met Johnston, who was running cattle down around New Mexico's San Francisco River. Johnston had a reputation as an expert tracker and a good shot, and Shaw said he needed a partner. As the story goes, Shaw told Johnston that Adams had told him a secret about the location that nobody else knew. Whatever it was, they both took the secret to their graves, and whatever it was, apparently it wasn't enough.

For forty-three years, until he was eighty-four, Johnston abandoned his family for weeks or months at a time to scour the hills between the Mogollons and El Malpais. Whenever he left home on one of his quixotic expeditions, his wife would ask her Ouija board when her husband would find the Lost Adams Diggings. The answer was always the same: "He's almost at it now."

And so it goes with the never-ending story of elusive Sno-ta-hay Canyon and the Lost Adams Diggings. So close, but so far. Who will find them? Will it be you?

Traveling to El Malpais

Over the past century, the story of the Lost Adams Diggings has inspired numerous active search attempts, and an even greater number of long nights of spirited speculation.

Nobody knows where it is or whether it was found and plundered long ago. How much would it be worth if it were found intact? The stories with dollar values attached say that Adams traded his gold for $22,000 and that the Dutchman got home with $10,000. This was at a time when gold was valued at $20 an ounce in 1860s dollars. With a pinch of the twentieth-century inflation that mauled the dollar, that $32,000—even when discounted for probable exaggeration—would now have at least a couple of extra goose eggs and would be a healthy nest egg for nearly any treasure hunter.

Fly to Albuquerque and read everything you can on the legend in the University of New Mexico Library. From Albuquerque you can drive to the north end of El Malpais in fewer than two hours if you take Interstate 40 west, or a little longer if you treat yourself to a drive on "historic" U.S. Route 66, which parallels the interstate highway as a frontage road. Leave early in the morning.

Take exit 89 off the Interstate and turn south on New Mexico Route 117. From here you'll start to get an idea of the lay of the land. After having read about the Adams Diggings, you'll swear that you recognize the place. Route 117 takes you along the sandstone bluffs that rim the eastern edge of the lava beds. About twelve miles south of the highways, still on Route 117, stop at the El Malpais National Monument ranger station and pick up a free trail map. A quarter of a mile farther, take the turnoff for a spectacular overview of El Malpais from the sandstone cliffs.

You will now be circling El Malpais on paved roads to get oriented. As you go, make a log of all the trails and unpaved roads that enter the lava beds from the paved roads. There are no paved roads into El Malpais. About fifty miles southwest of the ranger station, Route 117 will intersect with Route 36. At this point you'll be able to look directly northeast toward the lava beds. Look for the twin buttes. You are standing on the Continental Divide, and you are on a direct line between Gila Bend, Arizona, and El Malpais. Adams, Davidson, Schaeffer, Brewer, and their ill-fated colleagues passed this way, or very nearly this way. Fort Wingate is due north, while the Mogollon Mountains and the San Francisco Mountains are due south.

Take New Mexico Route 36 to the north and it will meet New Mexico Route 53 after fifty-three miles. You should now turn east on Route 53, but the Zuni Pueblo is only nine miles west and worth a visit if you have gotten an early start from Albuquerque.

Driving east on Route 53 you'll reach the tiny town of Ramah, New Mexico, about eighteen miles from the Route 36 intersection. From Ramah, New Mexico Route 400 is a dirt road that heads pretty much due north, winding through Cibola National Forest to Fort Wingate, about thirty miles away. On this road you'll almost certainly be following the route of the old wagon trail that John Brewer and the guys took when they went to the trading post at Fort Wingate for supplies. In terms of riding time Ramah is almost exactly halfway between the fort and the edge of El Malpais.

From Ramah your drive east by southeast to the lava beds takes you past El Morro National Monument, a mesa that is, as you'll soon see, a major landmark in these parts. You'll reach the edge of El Malpais about fifteen minutes later, near the road to the Cerro Bandera Ice Caves. However, watch for New Mexico Route 42, an extremely difficult unpaved road—recommended only for four-wheel-drive vehicles—that will take you as deep into El Malpais as you can go without going on foot, and it will take you on a nearly all-day tour of the entire western side of El Malpais. Riding in from Arizona, Adams and his party bisected the route of this road at some point. Keep your eyes peeled. Remember the boulder that appeared to be part of the wall and the virtually invisible "hidden door" that led to a narrow, Z-shaped canyon.

A spur off Route 42 leads to the El Malpais National

Monument's "Big Tubes" area and beyond to Cerro En-
ciero. From here it's a five-mile hike to the "Hole in the
Wall," an area where you can almost smell the sweat of
the men who worked the Lost Adams Diggings.

Back on Route 53, you head north to Route 66 at Grants,
New Mexico. Here you return to Interstate 40, only five
minutes from exit 89, where your clockwise encirclement
of El Malpais began. You now know as much about the
lay of the land as all but a handful of those who dreamed
of the Lost Adams Diggings. The next step is up to you.

Reflecting on El Malpais and the Lost Adams Diggings

In your circumnavigation of the lava beds you've experienced a stunning wonderland of light and shadow, where
the colors of the mesas drift from fiery red to deep purple
in moments. You have also seen that this beautiful landscape is also a place where a person can die of thirst, and
his bones be bleached by the sun before he is found.

Yet, out in that wonderland of light and shadow, where
the colors of the mesas drift from fiery red to deep purple,
there are lost riches waiting to be found. If you cock your
ear you can almost hear the wind telling you where it was
hidden.

There is the tale of the man who found an inscription on
an aspen tree high in the Mogollons that read: "The Adams
Diggings are a shadowy naught; and they lie in the Valley
of Fanciful Thought."

Chapter 10

MAXIMILIAN'S LOST TREASURE

PLACE: *At Castle Gap in West Texas*

TIME PERIOD: *1866*

For the years 1861 to 1865, students of North American history tend to focus their attention on the Civil War in the United States. However, in terms of global politics, the events going on at the same time south of the border were also of interest and importance.

In France, meanwhile, the greedy and ambitious Charles Louis Napoleon Bonaparte—the son of *the* Napoleon Bonaparte's brother Louis—was on the throne under the title Emperor Napoleon III. He chose the moment of America's preoccupation with the Civil War to seize control of Mexico's government. He declared Mexico to be an "empire" allied with France, and in 1864 he installed an Austrian archduke named Ferdinand Maximilian to be "emperor" of Mexico. The farce would be one of the more intriguing footnotes in North American history, and it would provide one of the more intriguing buried-treasure tales.

Louis Napoleon's "Mexican Empire"

After having been involved in several schemes to get the family back in power, Louis Napoleon had been elected president of France's Second Republic in December 1851. A year later he declared the Second *Empire* and made himself emperor as Napoleon III. It was an empire in name only, for France no longer had the vast conquests of Napoleon Bonaparte. An emperor without empire is a greedy man, and Louis Napoleon set out to resolve that problem. To his credit, his grandiose vision of imperial France did result in massive public works programs, including a national railway network, but his greed was ultimately his downfall. In 1859, in cooperation with Britain, he defeated Russia—something at which his uncle failed—in the Crimean War. He also gained concessions in Italy against the interests of Austria. His ultimate undoing was, of course, his declaring war on Prussia in 1870.

When France was decisively defeated in the Franco-Prussian War, Louis himself was captured, and republicans in Paris proclaimed the Third Republic. It was the end of the monarchy in France.

Louis Napoleon's Mexican adventure was part of his scheme aimed at creating a global empire to rival that being assembled by Britain. His idea was to invade Mexico with French troops and establish a "Mexican Empire" that would essentially be a wholly owned subsidiary of the French Empire. With this idea fully formed in his creative mind, Louis Napoleon started thinking about whom he could get to play the role of "emperor of Mexico." In those days, royalty was traded back and forth across national boundaries with little regard to their nation of origin, so it probably never occurred to Louis Napoleon to pick a *Mexican* to be his puppet emperor. (Louis Napoleon himself was descended from Corsicans and was married to a Spanish woman, while across the English Channel, in Britain, Queen Victoria's mother was a German and her children became royalty in Prussia, Russia, England, Battenberg, Hesse, Waldeck, Argyll, Saxe-Coburg, and Schleswig-Holstein.)

The man whom Louis Napoleon picked to rule Mexico— before Mexico even knew that the French emperor was picking its ruler—was Ferdinand Josef Maximilian, an

Austrian archduke who was married to Charlotte, the daughter of Leopold I, the king of the Belgians and who was born a German prince. Maximilian's own résumé included having served his family's empire as a naval officer and governor of Lombardy-Venetia in *Italy* from 1857 to 1859.

Neither Maximilian nor Charlotte had ever been to Mexico, and it was once suggested that Mexico's new empress couldn't even pick out the country on a map. None of this bothered Louis Napoleon. It mattered more to him that he was building alliances with Max's bother Franz Josef, the emperor of Austria, and with Leopold, Belgium's German king. As for Maximilian, he saw it as an opportunity to be the emperor of someplace. Princes and archdukes were a dime a dozen, but to be able to add "emperor" to his résumé appealed to Maximilian.

Because Mexico had defaulted on its foreign debts, Louis Napoleon was able to get Britain and Spain to acquiesce to an invasion of Mexico in 1862. The United States, of course, was deeply embroiled in the Civil War and chose not to intervene. However, even against only Mexican troops; it took French forces the better part of a year to fight their way from the port of Veracruz to Mexico City and overthrow the Mexican Republic. Nearly a year later, in May 1864, Max and Charlotte—she would be known as Carlota in Mexico—finally arrived to be crowned, and to take their places on their newly established thrones. Supported by Mexico's upper crust, the new emperor and empress demonstrated a voracious appetite for riches, and incredible quantities of gold and silver flowed into his palace from Mexico's rich and profitable mines.

Carlota, merely twenty-four years old, relished in her role as empress of a land she had not known existed just a few years earlier. Eventually she would be the subject of a grand opera with a libretto by Norma Carrillo and Robert Avalon, music by Robert Avalon, and based on the poetry of Senora Juana Ines de la Cruz.

As a ruler, Maximilian pleased nobody. The well-heeled landowners who supported him initially, were dismayed by his refusal to rescind the liberal reforms of the Benito Juárez republican government, and the republicans resented the idea of an Austrian backed by French troops ruling their country. Within two years Max could see that his position was degrading from tenuous to untenable.

In 1866 the United States was flush with victory in the Civil War and making noises about wanting French troops out of Mexico. Maximilian knew that his time as emperor was running out, and he started to prepare for his future life as a gentleman ex-emperor in his castle back in Austria. To make this a happy life, he wanted to take with him as much of his mountains of gold and silver as possible. To get it there, he could not ship it out directly through the port of Veracruz, because that would arouse suspicion. Therefore he decided to send his treasure home secretly, by way of a port in Texas, such as Galveston of Corpus Christi.

The Wagons of Flour

One day in 1866, fifteen wagonloads of gold and silver coins—as well as jewels, plate, and other treasure—disguised as barrels of flour, were sent north clandestinely, where they successfully crossed into West Texas near Presidio.

Soon after crossing the Rio Grande, the four Austrians guarding the wagon train met a group of Confederate soldiers from Missouri who were escaping to Mexico. The six Confederates reported Indians and bandits on the road ahead, and the Austrians hired them to help protect the valuable load of ''flour'' they were anxious to get to San Antonio. The finicky way that the Austrians guarded their ''flour'' struck the Missouri men as a bit odd. It seemed that they were treating it as though the cargo was more valuable than flour. No doubt it had to have seemed odd that four Austrian soldiers were escorting flour across West

Texas. Finally, the Missourians' curiosity reached the point where they had to find out.

At camp one night, while five of the Confederates lured the Austrian guards away from the wagons, the sixth lifted the canvas on some of the carts and pried open a few of the barrels. When he reported that he had found them full of gold and silver and jewels, it was decided that the Austrians should not be allowed to keep it. The following night, as the caravan was camped at a place called Castle Gap, fifteen miles east of the Horse Head Crossing of the Pecos River and with two Austrians standing guard, the Missouri men struck. The Austrians were all killed before the fifteen Mexican teamsters were aware of what was going on. Then the Missourians turned their attention to them, gunning them down one by one as they slept or as they were attempting to escape. When the slaughter was over, nineteen dead men lay on the ground, and the treasure belonged to the Confederate soldiers.

They were now faced with the problem of what to do with their fifteen wagons of loot, a treasure conservatively valued at millions. It had to have occurred to them that killing the Mexicans was a really bad idea, since it would be very hard for six men to drive fifteen wagons *and* act as outriders to keep watch for Indians. After a heated debate over their fortune and future, the men concluded that it would be unsafe and unwise to try to move the treasure across the Plains. They then decided to bury it and return when things quieted down—whenever that would be.

The hiding of such a load so it would be reasonably safe from being discovered had to have been a daunting prospect. It wasn't like burying a strongbox or a suitcase. They had before them, fifteen huge wooden freight wagons, fifteen *teams* of oxen, and nineteen dead bodies, which were slowly ripening in the West Texas sun. They also had fifteen tons of treasure to hide. After setting aside all the coins each man could carry, they dug a hole or holes in the sandy floor of the canyon and buried Maximilian's gold and silver and the many chests of jewels. They also threw in the nineteen rotting corpses.

Having buried the "evidence," they broke up the wagons and burned them on top of the site, believing the result would be something that resembled nothing more than a burned-out campfire. The oxen were turned loose to shift for themselves. With their saddlebags heavy with Mexican coins, the six murderers headed toward San Antonio to spend some it and to make plans to come back. Why they changed their minds about escaping to Mexico, we simply do not know.

Two days later, one of the men said he was becoming sick, and he dropped out for a rest. The others decided that he might be planning to sneak back to Castle Gap to get more for himself, so they decided to just kill him so there would be more for each of them. They simply shot him off his horse and rode away, each assuming he was dead. But he was not.

A few days later, the wounded man recovered sufficiently to be able to walk, and he continued on, heading toward San Antonio. He soon came upon the bodies of the other five Missouri men. Ironically, a short time after shooting him and leaving him for dead, they had themselves been ambushed by someone—possibly a Comanche raiding party—and killed. Their empty saddlebags were scattered around, and it was obvious they had been robbed.

Of the twenty-five men—Austrians, Mexicans, and Missourians—who had camped that last fateful night at Castle Gap, only one now survived, and he was badly wounded. He could do nothing but struggle forward, trying to make the miles and to keep from being spotted by Indians. Finally, one evening, he spotted a campfire and struggled toward it. What turned out to be a group of horse thieves took him in and gave him something to eat. He bedded down with them that night, but before dawn, a sheriff's posse that had been trailing the men surrounded the camp. The Missouri man was naturally assumed to be one of them, and he was taken to jail with them.

By the time he was able to get someone to believe that he was not a horse thief, to get a lawyer, to get out of jail, and to get to the attention of a doctor, the Missouri man's gunshot wounds were so badly infected that he really did not stand a chance. His condition went from bad to worse no matter what the doctor did, and finally, just before he died, he told the whole story related here, and he drew a treasure map and gave it to the doctor.

Several years later, when the Indian wars in West Texas had subsided, the doctor and the attorney took the treasure map and went to Castle Gap. They were able to find none of the landmarks on the map, and they found no evidence of freight wagons having been burned. Was the Missouri man lying? Had someone gotten there first?

Meanwhile, at the "gentle" urging of the United States, Louis Napoleon withdrew the French Army from Mexico in 1867. Charlotte—who was reportedly beginning to show signs of mental illness—left, ostensibly to go to Europe to beg for aid from Louis Napoleon. Maximilian stayed on, having been convinced by supporters that he could retain the throne. In fact, he had virtually no support, and without the French Army, no protection. He was snatched by republicans and executed at Cerro de las Campanas. Benito Juárez was promptly elected president, and Mexico has been a republic ever since. Charlotte died in a mental institution in Austria in 1927 at the age eighty-seven. Only a few odds and ends of their great wealth were discovered in their palace in Mexico. The rest had disappeared.

The Curse of Castle Gap

As with many of the many lost treasures in the West, the treasure at Castle Gap—or *near* Castle Gap or at someplace that *looked like* Castle Gap—is not known to have been found. However, from time to time one runs across a reference to remnants of burned-out wagons and attempts to dig beneath them. If fact, there were probably dozens, if not hundreds, of burned wagon trains in West Texas.

Where is the lost wagon train of Castle Gap? Somewhere

under a foot or two of sand in a canyon southwest of Odessa and about thirteen miles east of the Pecos River. To specifically search for Maximilian's lost loot, begin with the U.S. Geological Survey topographical map that is specifically called "Castle Gap" and numbered TTX0663-607502541.

The site is, like so many in this book, pretty far from major population centers. The two most convenient major airports—El Paso and San Antonio—are several hours' drive away. There are closer, smaller airports at Midland and San Angelo, but the extra time you'd have to spend changing planes would offset the distance advantage. From El Paso take Interstate 10 east. From San Antonio take Interstate 10 west. Exit at Fort Stockton, the county seat of sprawling Pecos County. A bit of research time in Fort Stockton might be surprisingly useful. When you are ready to move on, take Texas Highway 18 due north. Virtually the next landmark you see—twenty miles up the road—will be the Pecos River bridge. It was very near here, back in 1866, that those fifteen freight wagons forded the Pecos River, and there is still evidence around here of the many fords that were used by wagon trains in the nineteenth century.

Two miles north of the Pecos River is the town of Grandfalls. Turning right here onto Texas Route 329 will take you along the eastern side of the Pecos River, bisecting the route taken by the fifteen wagons. At this point it will be time to triangulate any anecdotal information you may have gleaned in the county seat with the precision of your topographical map.

Parenthetically, for more anecdotal information drive up to Odessa, which is the county seat of nearby Ector County, or to Crane, the county seat of Crane County. Odessa is quite a large city, while Crane is a very small town. Both characteristics will prove to have advantages for a researcher working the library or county record room. Crane is about thirty miles east of Grandfalls, on Highway 329. Odessa is, in turn, about thirty-two miles north of Crane, on U.S. Highway 385.

In both towns you will probably find someone willing to talk at length about the Maximilian gold and about the irony of what happened to everyone who touched it: Maximilian was killed, Charlotte went mad, and twenty-five men in Texas died violently. There have even been some thoughts of a curse, but most people don't take those thoughts seriously.

The treasure at Castle Gap is not the only lost treasure in the American West whose only witnesses died violently and soon after it was hidden. But it *is* the only lost treasure in the American West that is virtually an entire imperial treasury. If found today, its value would certainly exceed $10 million, and it may be greater than that. The historic and archaeological value would make it priceless.

Chapter 11

THE LOST DUTCHMAN MINE

PLACE: *The Superstition Mountains of Arizona*

TIME PERIOD: *1870–91*

Perhaps the most famous "lost treasure" story in American folklore is that of the Lost Dutchman Mine. A source of incomparably pure gold ore in staggering quantities, this mine has been the subject of several dozen books, countless articles in various periodicals, and it has served as the general prototype for dozens of grade B Western movies, including one that starred Glenn Ford as the Dutchman himself.

There are lost Dutchman mines throughout the West—and there is *the* Lost Dutchman Mine. The treasure lore of the Old West is filled with lost Dutchman mines because wherever stories of lost mines are told, retold, and wondered about, there often seems to be a Dutchman. It seems that many mines in the West have been lost and/or found by Dutchmen. Of course, in most cases the "Dutchman" is not Dutch but rather *Deutsche,* meaning German, just as the famous Pennsylvania Dutch are not necessarily descended from people from the Netherlands.

Why there are so many "Dutchmen" in these stories is probably because there were a great many Germans among the westward immigrants of the nineteenth century. Why their names come up so often in the lost, buried, and found treasure stories is anyone's guess, and it certainly has been the subject of more than a few conversations at out-of-the-way saloons on the two-lane back roads from New Mexico to the Idaho Panhandle.

And then there is *the* Lost Dutchman Mine. And, of course, there was *the* Dutchman. Actually there were two. *The* Dutchman was a German immigrant named Jacob Walz, although in some tailings his surname is spelled Waltz, which is probably a phonetic misspelling. The Indians called him "Snowbeard," a name that indicates that his appearance was archetypal of the pop culture/B-movie image of the grizzled old prospector. The other Dutchman was a German named Jacob Weiser, who met Jake Walz in Arizona in or about 1870. Both men had come into Arizona to look for gold, and legend has it that they met while working at the legendary Vulture Mine, which was founded by Henry Wickenberg—another "Dutchman"—whose name is still known as the appellation of a modest-sized town on U.S. Highway 93 northwest of Phoenix.

According to the legends concerning the origins of Jake Walz, the Dutchman was born at the end of the first decade of the nineteenth century in or near the town of Oberschwandorf in the German state of Württemberg. He landed in New York in about 1845 in the midst of the first major wave of German immigration to the United States. He was in his midthirties and anxious for adventure and his share of those riches that European immigrants were supposed to find in the New World.

The Dutchman found the streets of New York not to be paved with gold, but he heard stories of the big gold strike down in North Carolina, so he headed south to the Meadow Creek country. As almost invariably happens in most gold strike stories, the facts were but a ghostly shadow of reality, and most of the Meadow Creek sites had either been worked to death already or had been claimed. Instead of heading back north, Walz followed the gold strike stories south into Georgia, where he apparently spent a year or so.

By the autumn of 1848 Walz was in Natchez, Mississippi, that riverboat town on the Mississippi River. According to courthouse records that have been linked to *our*

Jake Walz, it was here on November 12 that the Dutchman filed papers expressing his intent to become an American citizen, although he would not actually get his citizenship for more than a decade. Why he chose citizenship and why he chose Natchez are questions open to conjecture, although it has been suggested that it had to do with needing to be a citizen to stake a claim on a mine. If Walz had a claim somewhere near Natchez we don't know where, but that really doesn't matter. He was the Dutchman and, as we know in hindsight, his fortune lay farther down the dusty road to the Golden West.

The year of 1848 that found Jake Walz in Natchez was also the year that gold was discovered on the American River in California. The following year, 49ers by the tens of thousands swarmed west in the great California gold rush. There were no doubt thousands of Dutchmen among them, and among these was the Dutchman.

Jake Walz worked the gold fields of the Sierra Nevada foothills for more than ten years. These were fabulous years when incredible amounts of gold were found. In the early days much of it was placer gold—just lying on sandbars waiting to be picked up. Nuggets weighing up to a hundred pounds were found, and for several years more than half of the world's total gold production came from the goldfields of what became known as "mother lode" country. The mother lode was that fantastic, albeit theoretical, vein of gold from which all the fabulous nuggets came. It has never been found, but not for want of trying. However, that, as they say, is another story.

Within a few years, the placer gold that could be picked up was gone. The smaller nuggets that could be swirled in a gold pan were reduced to a trickle, and most of the hard-rock mines had either become unprofitable or were in the hands of big investors. The prospectors and 49ers had started to drift away. Some went home and settled down, and others settled in the cities and rich farm country of California. The hard-core ones—those who could not rid themselves of the gold fever and that faraway look in their eyes—followed the 1858 Colorado gold rush or news of the gold being found in the San Gabriel Mountains of Southern California. Jake Walz was one of the latter. It was while working in the San Gabriels that the Dutchman finally got around to becoming an American. Los Angeles County records show that on July 19, 1861, Walz became a naturalized citizen of the United States.

Sometime over the next two years, the faraway look in the Dutchman's eyes took him from the more and more crowded Golden State to the rugged mountains and deserts of Arizona Territory. There is a record that a Jacob Walz filed a claim in Prescott on September 21, 1863, for a site in the Bradshaw Mountains. Over the next four years Jacob Walz is also noted on claim forms filed for the Big Rebel and General Grant Mines in the same area. This probably was *the* Jake Walz, but it is not known what he actually found on these claims.

In 1868 Walz, now nearing sixty—and probably wearing the whiskers that earned him the name "Snowbeard"—arrived in the proximity of *the* legendary mine. It is known that in that year he homesteaded in the Rio Saltillo (Salt River) Valley on the northern side of the Superstition Mountains.

The same Pima Indians who called the Dutchman Snowbeard called the mountains Ka-atak-tami, which meant—as deciphered by the Anglos—that some serious supernatural stuff went on up there. So the Anglos called this forbidding wilderness the Superstition Mountains, and that name still applies.

Long before any Dutchman ever dreamed of this place—indeed, long before the Pima people ever dreamed of this place—the prehistoric Mogollon people lived here. A few of their cliff dwellings are here, but no one remembers what they called the Superstition Mountains.

Most stories about the Dutchman agree that he spent most of the next twenty years prospecting in the Superstitions, although he also may have traveled seasonally around Arizona Territory working for wages to support himself while searching for the fortune that history tells us he eventually found. During one of these sojourns he met Jacob Weiser, probably while working at Henry Wickenberg's Vulture Mine in 1870.

A version of the Dutchman legend holds that Jake Walz was fired from the Vulture for stealing gold, but at some point the two Jakes left Wickenberg's employ and struck out on their own. Somehow, somewhere, they soon struck it rich in the Superstitions and were seen around Phoenix, paying for drinks and dry goods with bags of nuggets. Some historians have suggested that the gold was part of what had been stolen, although there seems to be a consensus that it was of higher grade than had been found at the Vulture, and Jake Walz would continue to spend nuggets in Phoenix for the next two decades.

Various stories have circulated that tell about how they found the mine. One has it that they shot and killed two Mexican miners whom they mistook for Indians and discovered they'd been digging gold. Another tale, and the one most often accepted, is that they were told about the mine by a Mexican don whose life they saved.

The don in question is believed to have been Don Miguel Peralta, an adventurer and prospector who was the son of a rich landowner in Mexico. According to stories that are reportedly corroborated by evidence that is independent of the Dutchman legend, apparently he had found an unusually rich gold deposit in the Superstition Mountains in about 1845, the same year that Jake Walz arrived in the United States, and three years before this part of Arizona was transferred from Mexican to American sovereignty. In retrospect this writer wonders whether it might be possible that Peralta—and those who relate his part of the story—may have used the 1845 date to establish that the mine was found when the Superstitions were still in Mexico and therefore subject to Mexican law in terms of original claims of ownership.

Other questions of detail also remain. For example, was Peralta's find a naturally occurring vein or a mine being worked by the Indians? The latter seems to be the most probable, but in any case the site soon became a mine that would be known as "the Peralta Mine," for the young don returned to Mexico and came back with a large crew of miners and enough pack animals to take a small fortune in gold back to Mexico during the next two or three years.

There are also variations on the story that tell of as many as two dozen "Spanish" mines having been operated in and around the Superstitions through the seventeenth and eighteenth centuries—many of those mines owned by the Peralta family.

As for Don Miguel's mine, however, the Apaches were getting restless at the intrusion into land that was important to them. In 1847, according to some accounts, the colorful Chiricahua Apache warlord Mangus Colorado assembled a band of warriors to chase the Mexican miners out of the Superstitions, but somehow Don Miguel found out about Colorado's plan and decided to break camp and head south before the Apaches could attack. As the story goes, Peralta's men disguised the entrance to the mine, buried their equipment, and started out of the mountains with as much gold ore as they could carry.

However, the Peralta pack train was ambushed. The burros carrying the gold scattered through the box canyons and arroyos, where they were killed by the Apaches, who apparently did not recover the gold ore. Most of the Mexicans were killed. Some stories say that only two men escaped and that Don Miguel was one of them. Through the rest of the century people would tell of finding piles of animal bones mixed with pieces of ore.

Don Miguel Peralta kept the map he had made of the route to his mine, and, as the story goes, in about 1870 he crossed the path of the two Jakes. This chance meeting may have taken place in Arizona, but some versions say it happened in Mexico. In any case, the two Jakes saved Don Miguel from certain death in a saloon knife fight and were rewarded with a look at the treasure map.

The trio are said to have become partners and to have gone back to the Superstitions to work the mine. After they had taken out a great deal more of the gold, the two Dutchmen bought their partner's interest in the mine.

Another version of the story is that Don Miguel did not survive and that the Mexicans the two Jakes killed were members of the Peralta expedition that had been ambushed two decades earlier. They had come back for the gold and had hit really bad luck instead.

Sometime over the years, Jake Weiser disappeared. Some say he was killed by Apaches, but others say it was Jake Walz who did him in. Jake Walz remained in view, at least periodically. Long periods of time would go by with no one seeing him, and then he would be around Phoenix paying for drinks with gold nuggets again. The story is that the stuff the Dutchman had in his saddlebags was the richest gold ore local assayers had ever seen. For the rest of his life Jake Walz commuted between the mine and Phoenix, where he gave often contradictory hints to his drinking buddies about the mine's location. He never filed a claim, as he probably figured it was ultimately more dangerous to tell the location on a claim form than to just protect the claim with obfuscation and deception.

The winter of 1890–91 found an aging Jake Walz befriending Julia Elena Thomas, an old Mexican widow who owned a small bakery in Phoenix. There was talk of a romance, and most versions of the tale report that he told her the whole story of the mine. Late in the summer of 1891 he promised to take her there "in the spring."

But for the Dutchman, the spring would never come. He died at Julia Elena's home on October 25, 1891. They found a sack of rich gold ore beneath his deathbed.

Immediately after Jake Walz slipped out of Phoenix that last time, a number of men who knew the bits and pieces of the story rode into the hills to find the elusive secret. Among the first was another pair of "Dutchmen," Rhinehart Petrasch and his brother Hermann, who spent many years searching with clues given them by Julia Elena Thomas. Two prospectors named Sims Ely and Jim Bark spent the next quarter century searching in vain for what they dubbed as "the Lost Dutchman Mine."

Within two years of the Dutchman's last ride, there were major gold discoveries just west of the Superstitions on the way to Phoenix. They were near the present site of the aptly named "ghost town" of Goldfield. The strike that would become the Black Queen occurred in November 1892, and within four years of its discovery on April 13, 1893, the legendary Mammoth Mine gave up three million dollars' worth of ore.

As this activity was keeping the local treasure hunters busy, the Petrasch brothers drifted away, and Julia Elena told what she knew to Pierpont Constable Bicknell, a newspaper writer from San Francisco who researched much of the story of the Peraltas and the two Jakes for a story published in 1895.

The secret the Dutchman did not leave behind has fueled more than a century of speculation. Hundreds of prospectors have searched the vast and rugged Superstition Mountains country, and hundreds have come home with little more than sunburns and tales of close encounters with rattlers and gila monsters. The various theories have filled dozens of books and pamphlets and have fueled countless late-night debates around campfires and in Phoenix hotel bars.

Despite the fact that they are within twenty miles of the edge of the Phoenix metropolitan area, the Superstition Mountains are an almost hopeless labyrinth of dead-end gullies and box canyons in which the entrance to a cave might easily be concealed against even the most exhaustive search. Bark and Ely never did find Walz's claim, but their search helped to establish the legend.

In 1929 an American veterinarian named Erwin Ruth helped smuggle a Mexican family into the United States, one step ahead of the Mexican Revolution. These people, as the story goes, were Peraltas related to the original partner of the two Jakes. For his trouble these Mexicans gave Erwin Ruth a copy of the original map. Ruth gave it to his father, Adolph Ruth, a federal clerk in Washington, D.C.

In 1931 Adolph Ruth retired and went to Arizona to find the treasure. He hired a pair of cowboys to take him into the mountains. Several days later, Tex Barkley, the rancher for whom the cowboys worked, began to worry about the elderly city slicker out in the hills in the summer heat, so he went to look for him. Barkley found Ruth's camp but not the man. A six-week search turned up nothing. In December a skull was found in West Boulder Canyon, five miles from where he'd made camp. It had what looked like two bullet holes in it. It was identified as Ruth's.

Ruth's death attracted national media attention to the Lost Dutchman Mine and led to numerous attempts, especially during the 1950s and early 1960s, to find it. Yet it remains hidden, along with perhaps as many as 160 other treasures, in the canyons and mesas of the forty-eighth state.

Traveling to the Superstition Mountains

The Superstitions are not hard to find. On a clear day, a million people can see them from Phoenix, Scottsdale, and Mesa. They're almost within spitting distance of one of North America's fastest-growing metropolitan areas. Getting *to* the Superstition Mountains is easy. Getting *into* the Superstitions is another matter. The best way to get started is to take a little drive around the periphery of the Superstitions. Actually, it's a rather long drive—120 miles of slow going—so it's best to start early.

Take a flight to Phoenix, check into a motel, and get a good night's sleep. As you leave Sky Harbor Airport, you'll cross the Salt River. Yes, this is *the* Salt River—Rio Saltillo—the one on which the Dutchman had his homestead, but that was up the river many miles. At least you're getting close. When the place names start getting familiar, the adrenaline kicks in and the thrill is on.

After crossing the Salt River, take either Apache Boulevard or U.S. Highway 60—the Superstition Freeway—east to Apache Junction; take the exit marked "Apache Trail, Salt River Lakes, State Highway 88." This will put you in Apache Junction, a moderately sized town—about twenty thousand people—that's less than twenty miles from

Tempe, but far enough from the Phoenix urban sprawl that when you get there, you really start feeling as though you are getting a long way from civilization. This would be a good place to spend that first night in advance of the obligatory early start. You could drive farther and roll out your sleeping bag in a state park, but it's almost worth the stop to be able to wander into a bar and get someone talking about the Superstitions, the gold, the Dutchman, and all the fools who have come and gone trying to find what has never been found. You might even ask around about treasure maps, and you might be surprised by what the answer is. Beware, however, for there are many treasure maps, and most are not for real—most, but not all.

From Apache Junction, you turn north on Arizona State Route 88—known familiarly as the "Apache Trail"—and really start to get the flavor of the Superstitions. Even the road takes you back in time—not back to the Dutchman's time, because there was no road here in the Dutchman's time—but back to 1922, when Governor George Hunt built this road as a shortcut from Phoenix to Globe. The road has been maintained but never widened since then.

As you leave Apache Junction, you can start to see the Superstitions off to the right—dry, rugged, and starting to appear dangerous. And in the afternoon, when the thunderstorms start to spike the peaks with lightning, you can smell the electricity that probably helped convince the Pima people that there was magic in these hills. The Superstitions are like a woman. They say that the lure of the Superstitions lies as much in their mystery as in their beauty.

Not far from Apache Junction, you pass the turnoff for Goldfield, the former mining town turned tourist ghost town where there were two major gold discoveries in the early 1890s that led to the development of the fruitful Black Queen and Mammoth Mines. Today Goldfield is fruitful only in its well-stocked tourist shops, and is good only as a place to buy ice cream and T-shirts. Press on; you have places to be, and if you got the early start as we admonished, you will pass Goldfield before many of the gewgaw stands are open for the day.

Continue up Route 88, and almost on cue the Apache Trail passes Arizona's tribute to Jake Walz, the 292-acre Lost Dutchman State Park with a handful of campsites, a visitors' center, and water. In this country one cannot stress the notion of water too much. From May through September, temperatures can *average* above the century mark. Pictures of this place make you think being here is like walking on the moon. Being here in July makes being here seem like walking on the sun.

Check your radiator and fill your canteen.

Beyond the Lost Dutchman State Park is the 159,700-acre Superstition Wilderness Area, which is part of the vast Tonto National Forest. The Dutchman's mine is somewhere within the Superstition Wilderness Area. Looming above his state park is the 3,000-foot Superstition Mountain itself; and visible as you wind your way north by northeast toward Government Well is the peak that has become a sort of icon for the whole ethos of mystery in the Superstition Mountains (plural). This is nowhere near the famous mine (although it is, according to most legends). There is a poster or pamphlet cover tacked to a bar we visited somewhere on a southwestern back road that pictures Superstition Mountain as a sort of Mount Rushmore of human skulls. In broad daylight it's hard to imagine, but at dusk, with the shadows creeping up the western side, there are some sights that make you wonder.

About a dozen miles from Apache Junction you will get your first glimpse of the Salt River since leaving Phoenix. The Dutchman wouldn't recognize it. Three dams—the Stewart Mountain, Mormon Flat, and Horse Mesa—that were constructed back in the 1920s have turned this part of the river into a series of lakes. As far as we are concerned, though, this is irrelevant. The Dutchman's mine is pretty far to the south—off to the left of the two-lane blacktop road on which we are now cruising.

Ten minutes or so after we catch sight of the lakes—or what is left of the Salt River—we reach the little settlement that was known as Tortilla Flat four decades before John Steinbeck coined—or borrowed—that name as a nickname for Salinas, California. In about as much time as it takes for the average pair of treasure hunters to bat around a few reminiscences of Steinbeck, the pavement of the Apache Trail turns from pavement to mere trail. It is at this point, as the rental car tires start kicking up a clatter of gravel, that you can look due south and see the most probable route to the Lost Dutchman Mine.

By now the optimistic headlong development visible back in Phoenix is a distant memory as reminders to the futility of human attempts to tame the desert begin to appear. The Reavis Ranch Trailhead that we pass about a quarter hour out of Tortilla Flat was where the trail used to take off for the resort of Pine Air, the brainchild of a gaggle of schemers from Mesa who probably made a fair piece of change selling lots here. Pine Air never existed except as a glimmer in the eye of a fast-talking salesman and as a few stakes and strings on the desert floor, but the Reavis Ranch did exist.

At the place where Tonto Creek used to flow into the Salt River there is the kind of stone structure that makes the notion of longevity come to mind quite clearly. This massive stone dam—they say it's the largest of this kind in the world—was dedicated in 1911 by Teddy Roosevelt, and it still bears his name. So, too, does the lake that crouches behind Theodore Roosevelt Dam. Maybe the only claim to fame that Theodore Roosevelt Lake can claim is that it claimed the famous *Santa Maria*. Not the most famous *Santa Maria,* obviously, but the seaplane called *Santa Maria* that Francesco de Pinedo was using in his attempt to fly around the world. He made it here from Italy in 1927, crossing the Atlantic six weeks ahead of Lindbergh, but someone was smoking around his gas tank, and the *Santa Maria* and Francesco's dream turned to ashes here in the shadow of the Superstitions. The shadows of those mountains had that effect on the dreams of the Petrasch brothers, Julia Elena Thomas, Sims Ely, and Jim Bark, and they might have that effect on yours—if you take the wrong stories too seriously.

Over your shoulder to the right as you ponder Theodore

Roosevelt Lake is Tonto National Monument, where the stock-in-trade are a cluster of pretty well preserved Salado Indian cliff dwellings that were built here at the same time Europeans were building Gothic cathedrals. These people farmed in the Salt River Valley and supplemented their diet by hunting and gathering native wildlife and plants. The Salado were fine craftsmen, producing some of the most exquisite polychrome pottery and intricately woven textiles in the Southwest—some of which have survived the centuries and are now are on display here in the visitors' center museum. Tonto National Monument was established by President Theodore Roosevelt in 1907 as one of the first national monuments to be proclaimed under the Antiquities Act of 1906.

From Tonto National Monument, Route 88 is a paved road again. The splattering of gravel under the floorboards is replaced by a quavering hum as you cruise past the cottonwoods on the twenty-nine miles of two-lane blacktop that take you southeast toward the crossroads a couple of miles from Globe, the county seat of Gila County.

Globe and Apache Junction are like the bookends of the Superstition Mountains. Apache Junction has that first breath of the country kind of flavor you get going out Phoenix, while Globe is sort of a self-contained minimetropolis in the middle of nowhere. With about seven thousand people, Globe is only a third the size of Apache Junction, but it has that self-confident, last-chance-for-gas kind of arrogance of a town that is the only game in town.

U.S. Highway 70 ends in Globe—or starts in Globe, if you prefer—dead-ending into U.S. Highway 60. Highway 70 has its other end on the Atlantic shore at Morehead City, North Carolina. It winds west through Memphis, Tennessee—the hometown of Elvis—and Roswell, New Mexico—the hometown of UFO crashes—as a sort of main street of American cult capitals, or as a conspiracy buff's Route 66. It just ends in Globe, in the shadow of the Superstitions, overwhelmed by Highway 60, which takes us back toward Phoenix under the chin of the Superstition Wilderness.

On Highway 60, you head west in the general direction of Phoenix, with the Pinal Mountains on your left and the Superstitions on your right. You will pass through the old mining town of Miami, which is not a ghost town in the strict sense of the word, although it *is* a mere ghost of its former self. When the last hint of Miami vanishes from your rearview mirror, you'll be entering the "Top of the World" country. It would greatly enhance the color of this narrative to say that at this point the terrain should make you feel as though you are "sitting on top of the world." However, the "Top of the World" to which the local lore alludes is not the top of the actual world, but a saloon that existed on a side road near the old Pinal Ranch in the early days of the twentieth century. Still, this country has, if not a top-of-the-world serenity, at least an otherworldly beauty of steep sandstone cliffs and canyons splashed with the red of a Martian landscape.

Superior, fewer than twenty miles from Miami, is another mining town with a past, and what a past. It was here in 1875—back when the Dutchman still roamed the hills to the north—that old Aaron Mason had the strike that turned into the great Silver King Mine, which is, like the Lost Dutchman Mine, a true western legend. When the armchair geologists start to claim they are sure there are no minerals of value in the Superstitions, remind them of the Silver King and of the Black Queen and Mammoth Mines over at Goldfield. Part of the purpose of this exercise of driving around the Superstitions is to illustrate that these hills truly are rich with mineral wealth. The proof is in the millions that were pulled from the mines that are well known, well documented, and still in evidence in the form of the relics that have been left behind.

When you pause awhile to listen to the wind moaning through the old wood and crumpled tin structures that are all that remain of the once-proud Silver King, it is worth pondering what would have happened if Aaron Mason had been as reclusive as Jake Walz. And vice versa. What if Mason would have kept his strike a closely held secret? What if Jake Walz had developed his claim into a sprawling operation with a crew of hundreds? Would he ever have come to know Julia Elena? Would the "Jake Walz Mine" have disgorged its phenomenal wealth, sending its proprietor to live in a vast stone mansion in Phoenix? Would it have played out, gone to seed, and been remembered as a ticky-tacky tourist trap on an Arizona state highway that would have been built but was not?

As you cross Gonzalez Pass, a few miles out of Superior, one of the most important landmarks in the Dutchman legend starts to come into view off to your right. Weaver Needle—also called Weaver's Needle—was named not for the proverbial "boy named Sue" but for a man named "Pauline." Pauline Weaver was, like Jake Walz and so many others, an eccentric character whose life and life's story are much more myth and tall tale than known fact. In the 1820s he apparently led an expedition into Arizona in search of the truth behind the same age-old tales of gold in the hills that brought the Dutchman here a generation later. Weaver's crew found that for which they searched, having stumbled on the famous placer deposits on Rich Hill near Stanton, northeast of Wickenberg.

The Rich Hill placers are the kind of place they tell about in those campfire stories of lost mines, but they were real and well documented. Like Aaron Mason's Silver King, the placers are the sort of reality that makes the lost-mine stories ring true. If Pauline Weaver found one, how many are there that are still left to find? Probably not many. It *has* been more than a century and a half. But that's no reason to stop looking, especially for mines like the Dutchman's that are buried underground in a secret place, rather than lying around on a sandbar like placer gold.

All we really need to know about Weaver is that he came through the Superstitions sometime after he struck it rich at Wickenberg, that since the 1850s a pinnacle of rock has carried his name, and that this pinnacle of rock is the keystone of most of the treasure maps to the Lost Dutchman Mine that have circulated through the years.

The clues to the Dutchman's gold are many—they say that Walz let many of them drop in his barroom chatter in the 1880s and 1890s—and many of the tales involve Weaver's Needle. The stock story is that at a certain time of day on a certain day of the year, the shadow of Weaver's Needle falls across the entrance to the Lost Dutchman Mine. This is probably true, but what time and what day? Even Jake Walz is said to have said that the rays of the setting sun fall on the mine's entrance at a certain time of day on a certain day of the year. This is probably true, but what time and what day?

The Dutchman also described a "north-tending canyon." There are plenty of those out in the Superstitions. Or was it a "west-tending canyon"? There are plenty of those out in the Superstitions, too. He also said that from his mine you could see a "military trail" but that the mine was not visible from the military trail. Or was it the other way around?

From the point where you can start to see Pauline Weaver's Needle, Highway 60 becomes a straight-shot four-lane highway that takes you back to Apache Junction, where it turns into the Phoenix-bound Superstition Freeway, and you turn off to begin the expedition that will take you into the Superstitions.

In the Footsteps of the Dutchman

In circumnavigating the Superstitions, you can get a bit of the flavor of the country, the desert, and the world in which Jake Walz lived for a third of his life, jealously guarding what may have been—and may yet prove to be—the greatest lost mine in the history of the West. Yet whatever flavor such a circumnavigation may provide, you must go into the Superstitions to taste the mystery, to smell the danger.

This country looks like a desert, but it is what the scientists call the Upper Sonoran ecosystem—which is essentially the Sonoran Desert. This, in turn, is named for the Mexican state of Sonora, which is across the border to the south. The Sonoran Desert is famous for the saguaro cactus you see everywhere and whose blossom is the Arizona state flower. You'll also be seeing the prickly pear, hedgehog, and barrel cactus, yucca, sotol, agave, and the spiky cholla—the "teddy bear" cactus.

You can look around and see the trees of the desert— the creosote bush and ocotillo, the palo verde and the mesquite—rich with the oils that make campfires burn hot and long on a cold desert night. In the early spring—February and March are the early spring here in the desert—you can see an amazing variety of colorful wildflowers. Scuttling among the hackberry bushes are squirrels, chipmunks, porcupines, jackrabbits, and rattlesnakes. If you keep your eyes peeled, you may see a whitetail or a mule deer, and if you're not careful or run out of luck, you may have to share the trail with a bobcat or a javelina—a wild pig—or even a mountain lion.

During the winter, temperatures can get down into the thirties at night, or up into the sixties during the day, but in the summer, it can stay in the seventies all night long and top 110 in the shade—if you can find the shade—by midafternoon. The sun can be intense. Take water. Wear a hat, and lather yourself with sunscreen. This is no place to work on your tan. Even if the Dutchman never had the benefit of sunscreen, don't bother to take a chance.

Wear sturdy hiking boots. The Dutchman would have done that. He had probably known—or even heard the pitiful wail of—prospectors who'd had the misfortune of having a copperhead or sidewinder sink its fangs into an unprotected ankle.

The Dutchman probably also knew the sinking, desperate feeling of being in the midafternoon heat with miles to go and not a drop left in his canteen. Today they sell bottled water virtually everywhere—from minimarts in Apache Junction to truck stops in Globe—so you have no excuse. It sounds trivial until you are out there and you really, really need a drink.

This place is a wilderness, and as the Superstition Wilderness Area, it is managed by the U.S. Forest Service,

which has built trails into and across it. But U.S. Forest
Service trails are not the neat, pretty, well-maintained trails
you find in National Park Service areas. They are steep,
rough, often hard to follow, and not for amateurs and/or
the faint of heart. Be warned and beware.

Wherever you go, don't leave without your U.S. Geological Survey topographical map and your compass. Always know your location in terms of landmarks and note
your elapsed travel time so you can plan when to turn back.

Two trails of note that are recommended locally are the
Peralta Trail, which takes off from Forest Service Road 77,
which is reached from Highway 60; and the ominous-
sounding First Water Trail, which intersects State Route 88.
Either of these trails will get you into the country around
Weaver's Needle, and wherever it is, the Lost Dutchman
Mine probably is not far away from Weaver's Needle.

To the north of the notorious Weaver's Needle you can
see Black Top Mesa, which has some Spanish-language
petroglyphs or inscriptions—seventeenth-century graffiti—
carved or scratched into some rocks on its 3,354-foot peak.
Beyond the mesa are some old mines that date back to the
nineteenth century or before. Could one of them be the Lost
Dutchman Mine, hidden in plain sight?

West of Black Top Mesa is a series of four roughly parallel north–south canyons that are visible on the U.S. Geological Survey topographical maps and that are—from
east to west—known as East Boulder Canyon, Little Boulder Canyon, West Boulder Canyon, and O'Grady Canyon.
East Boulder Canyon runs from northwest to southeast on
the downhill slope beneath the steepest cliffs of Black Top
Mesa and winds up near the base of Weaver's Needle. Little Boulder Canyon is the shortest and shallowest of the
four, and it leads essentially nowhere.

West Boulder Canyon is the longest of the four. As is
the case with both East Boulder Canyon and Little Boulder
Canyon, it starts at the plateau just northwest of Black Top
Mesa and arcs to the west like a letter "C" until it reaches
the southeast end of a broad, mile-long canyon that reaches
northwest toward the edge of the Superstition Mountains,

about a mile from Route 88. At the point where West Boulder Canyon reaches the edge of this canyon, it forks, with one fork running back into the hills toward the southwest, and with the main part tending to the southeast, toward Weaver's Needle.

O'Grady Canyon is a short spur that takes off from West Boulder Canyon near the plateau west of Black Top Mesa. There are trails through all these canyons except Little Boulder, and there are trails that crisscross the trails, so pay close attention to your topographical map.

What is important about this tangle of canyons is that Adolph Ruth came here, and Adolph Ruth had a map—maybe even *the* map.

Remember that Adolph Ruth was the son of Erwin Ruth, who had helped to smuggle a Mexican family named Peralta into the United States during the depths of the Great Depression and the scary moments of the Mexican Revolution of 1929. The Peraltas had *the* map before the Dutchman even set foot in Arizona, and Adolph Ruth brought a copy of what he believed to be *the* map with him when he went into the Superstitions in 1931. What exactly he did with the map is uncertain, but when Ruth's bullet-riddled skull was found, it was here at the fork in West Boulder Canyon.

If Adolph Ruth actually had the real map, then it doesn't take much of a stretch of the imagination to conclude that the treasure is close by West Boulder Canyon.

Another item of interest is at the opposite end of that broad mile-long canyon that extends northwest from the fork of West Boulder Canyon. Here, almost at the place where the Superstitions end, is a place known as the Massacre Grounds. This is generally believed to be the place where the Peralta pack train was ambushed by the Apaches in 1847 as they were leaving with the last load of ore from the mine. It was in this area that piles of animal bones mixed with pieces of ore were occasionally discovered during the late nineteenth century.

When he was leaving the mine on that fateful day, Don Miguel Peralta would have chosen the fastest exit from the

Superstitions and a route that was mostly downhill for the sake of his pack animals. Keep this in mind. When you are standing there on the Massacre Grounds and you factor in all the other information that is either known or generally believed, your eyes drift back toward Weaver's Needle. Once again, the trail leads back to West Boulder Canyon and the area west of Black Top Mesa.

What, then, of the story that has the shadow of the Needle falling across the entrance to the mine? If this is true, and it is also true that the mine is in the area of West Boulder Canyon and Black Top Mesa, then the shadow should be followed in the winter rather than in the summer. This is because in the summer, when the sun is in the north, the shadow would fall to the south, away from West Boulder Canyon and Black Top Mesa. This would, of course, make it easier on would-be treasure hunters, for whom 110 in the shade is a debilitating environment.

On the other hand, why would the Dutchman have spread the story about the shadow if such a story would make it easier to find the mine?

Maybe he was lying?

Maybe it wasn't the Dutchman who started the story about the shadow?

Maybe the Dutchman was just terribly enthralled by the fact that the shadow fell across the entrance to the mine?

Maybe even the Dutchman himself never went to mine in the dreadful heat of the Arizona summer?

Of course, the Peralta map that led Adolph Ruth to West Boulder Canyon and the area west of Black Top Mesa isn't the only map that purports to show the location of the Lost Dutchman Mine. Books, pamphlets, and Internet Web sites abound with stories, maps, and map fragments that have been circulating around central Arizona almost since the night Jake Walz closed his eyes for the last time.

In addition to the Weaver's Needle shadow clues, the Dutchman also described a "north-tending canyon." There are plenty of those out in the Superstitions. Or was it a "west-tending canyon"? There are plenty of those out in the Superstitions, too.

The various treasure maps that circulate from the shops in Globe and Apache Junction to the World Wide Web all include north-tending canyons, west-tending canyons, and military trails. The Superstitions, like hill country anywhere, are veritable labyrinths of canyons. These range from broad, well-defined canyons—such as the family of Boulder Canyons—to small arroyos and dry washes that are mostly too small to receive much notice from the casual hikers who trek through these hills almost every day.

One of the problems with reading treasure maps is that while they show the treasure or mine in relation to several landmarks—often including cliffs and canyons—they never tell you exactly how many of those cliffs and canyons there are between the treasure and a specific, easily definable landmark, such as exact geographic coordinates. When you get out into the field, you quickly find yourself on the horns of a dilemma. Did he mean *these* two canyons, or *those* two? Did he mean to exclude the insignificant wash between the canyons, or is *it* one of the canyons?

The Dutchman never had access to the Global Positioning System, nor did most of the people making the maps.

So what, then, do the maps show besides cliffs and canyons? They generally agree that the Lost Dutchman Mine is somewhere south of the Salt River and north of Weaver's Needle. Several indicate that the mine is on a canyon that runs north into the Salt River, but none of the Boulder Canyons do. There are various mentions of caves and springs, but the Superstitions are full of caves, and springs are dry most of the year. The maps also show many of the "old Spanish" and nineteenth-century mines that dot the area around Black Top Mesa and that are also platted on the U.S. Geological Survey topographical maps.

Jake Walz also said that from his mine you could see a "military trail" but that the mine was not visible from the military trail. Or was it the other way around? If the trail was visible from the mine and not vice versa, then that would mean that the entrance might be low to the ground, making the trail visible when the viewer was standing by the entrance but not crouching to go through it.

As with canyons, there are a lot of trails running through the Superstitions, including those built in the twentieth century by the U.S. Forest Service and those "military trails" that were used by the U.S. Army to travel between Phoenix and Globe in the years when Jake Walz was telling tales about his mine. With few exceptions the trails are all clearly indicated on the modern topographical maps, although this in itself is no clue to how long they have been here. The oldest trails are in the broadest, longest canyons, where they served the practical purpose of being a thoroughfare through the labyrinth of the Superstitions. According to the old maps, the trail that today runs parallel to the cliffs on the southwestern side of East Boulder Canyon was used as a military trail.

Also visible on the U.S. Geological Survey topographical maps are the various trails one can use to reach the interior of the Superstition Wilderness Area and the Black Top Mesa country. These include the First Water Trail, which leads into the Superstitions from a place on the Apache Trail about eight miles north of Apache Junction.

Upon reaching the Black Top Mesa country, you will have the mesa and Weaver's Needle as landmarks, and a myriad of canyons and dry washes from which to choose. Perhaps the most promising is Needle Canyon, which runs between Black Top Mesa and Bluff Springs Mountain. Sims Ely, who took his cue from Julia Elena Thomas, was one of the many who searched this area. So was John T. Clymenson, who was one of the twentieth century's most obsessive followers of the Dutchman. Before he died in 1971 at age fifty-eight, Clymenson spent years combing the sides of Black Top Mesa and Needle Canyon. Using the pen name Barry Storm, he also wrote numerous books and pamphlets on his expeditions and his theories. All of these are valuable references for understanding the Superstitions and the enormous difficulties that accompany any attempt to get into the mind of the wily Jake Walz.

However, as is the case with many lost treasure sites in the United States, *finding* the Lost Dutchman Mine is only half the battle. Actually taking out the gold would be no less a chore. Lugging a backpack full of rocks—especially when they are mostly a metal as heavy as gold—through the inhospitable desert is a substantially daunting task. Then, too, is the problem of legally taking possession of the gold. Being a national wilderness area, the Superstitions are under the jurisdiction of the U.S. Department of Agriculture, which is bound to enforce the National Wilderness Act approved by Congress in 1964. Specifically this means that you can't run a mine in a national wilderness area. Since the last day of 1983, the Department of Agriculture has specifically banned any kind of gold-digging in the Superstition Wilderness Area.

As the fiery rays of the setting sun paint the sandstone cliffs of the Superstitions, one is left to reflect on sunsets past and on the Dutchman himself, who watched them for four decades as he made his way toward Phoenix, his saddlebags bulging with enough gold to care for his immediate needs. There was no need for more. When the time came, he would disappear and reappear, traveling up one of the Boulder Canyons or up Needle Canyon, or to someplace that even Barry Storm could not have imagined.

Chapter 12

HIDDEN TREASURE AND LOST MINES IN THE MIDDLE OF NOWHERE

PLACE: *Near Jarbidge, in Elko County, Nevada*

TIME PERIOD: *1909–20*

Today there is probably no state that is more closely identified with the myth of striking it rich overnight than Nevada. People do, but many more go home having been struck down, struck dumb by loss, or having simply struck out.

Big-time gambling—or "gaming," as they like to say in Nevada—is by far the major industry there, but it is a relatively recent industry. Before the boom in big-time casinos that began in the early 1950s, Nevada had existed only as a vast, empty place that one had to cross to get to California. Before gaming transformed two tiny corners of the state, the only major boom—and it was a big one—had been the great silver rush of the 1860s, which pulled millions of pounds of silver out of the great Comstock Lode in the Reno–Virginia City area and gave the Silver State its enduring nickname.

In terms of its physical environment, Nevada is a state of stunning and often shocking contrasts. Las Vegas and the Reno–Lake Tahoe area are major concentrations of people, activity, and wealth, yet in 99 percent of the state, one can look in all directions and neither see nor hear another human being. There are counties in Nevada that are larger than Portugal but contain fewer people than a New York

City subway train. Nevada is the emptiest state in the conterminous United States, and U.S. Highway 50, which crosses Nevada at its midsection, is billed as the "Nation's (or the World's) Loneliest Highway" because one can drive for hours without seeing a place of human habitation. Much of this region is also extremely dangerous, a hot and waterless desert filled with poisonous snakes, spiders, scorpions, and gila monsters in summer, and drifting snow in winter.

U.S. Highway 50 aside, the emptiest corner of Nevada is that portion of Elko County north of Interstate 80 that is bisected only by a very lonely eighty-two-mile stretch of U.S. Highway 93 and that nestles up against the most deserted part of Idaho. Geographically, Idaho is two states. The panhandle in the north is characterized with deep canyons and heavily forested mountains, while the southern part of the state is mostly a vast, open space. This latter area is in turn characterized by an agricultural east, a virtually uninhabited west, and a huge area of lava beds in between. The lava beds constitute an almost impenetrable labyrinth with essentially no roads, even to this day. As such, the lava beds have traditionally provided an excellent hiding place for stolen loot. The steep canyons of the central panhandle also present a terrain that has proven useful for this purpose.

Between them, northern Elko County, Nevada, and Owyhee County in the southwestern corner of Idaho—the southern part of the vast Snake River Basin—have the distinction of being one of the least populated and least visited corners of the conterminous United States. Owyhee County, for example, has an area the size of Connecticut, but it has fewer than half a dozen settlements and only one paved road, Idaho Highway 51.

If the search for the treasure is as much a part of the treasure as the glittering gold in the strongbox, and the treasure within the search is the journey of self-discovery that comes from experiencing distant and remote terrain, this chapter is a tribute to that search and that treasure.

Miles from Anywhere

The most remote corner of the conterminous United States was not always that way. Today it is miles from anywhere, but for a brief moment in time, it was somewhere. There was a gold strike, then many people. That is the origin of those staples of Western lore, lost mines and ghost towns. There are several alleged locations of hidden treasure in Nevada's Elko County—and neighboring Humboldt County as well—where one would have to drive for the better part of a day on unimproved or unpaved roads just to get from a main highway to the town near which the treasure is said to be located.

Located at the dead end of a very long gravel road, the ghost town of Jarbidge can be said to be the most remote town in this entire vast empty quarter. It is not really a ghost town anymore, but it is the smallest of small towns, with a population of just fourteen. There are casino elevators in Las Vegas with larger populations.

Jarbidge has a history that dates back nearly ten thousand years, to a time when ancient hunting parties camped in nearby caves to hunt game. In about A.D. 1150, Shoshone-speaking people entered the region, camping and hunting here until the nineteenth century. In fact, the name Jarbidge—not "Jarbridge," as it is occasionally written by outsiders—comes from a Shoshone word meaning "a bad or evil spirit."

Gold was discovered here in this isolated area in 1909 by a man named Dave Bourne. Eventually, a total of $9 million—in old preinflation dollars—was produced, and in the early 1920s the Jarbidge district replaced fading Goldfield as the premier gold-producing area in Nevada. The population reached a peak of about twelve hundred in about 1920 and then declined, even though a Guggenheim holding company had industrial-scale mining operations here between 1918 and 1932. When the mine closed, the town dried up. Such is the origin of ghost towns and lost mines. Among the lost mines that dot these remote hills is that one of legendary value known simply as the Sheepherder's Lost Claim.

One of the more colorful of the lost treasures that figure in Elko County folklore is the Jarbidge Stage Treasure, which, as the name implies, is loot that was stolen in a long-ago stagecoach heist—but not just any long-ago stagecoach heist. It was on a cold, stormy December 5, 1916, that they robbed the stage from Rogerson in Jarbidge Canyon, a quarter of a mile north of the town. This larceny is said to have been the last stagecoach robbery and murder in the history of the Old West. At least part of the loot was never recovered.

In recent years, however, the area has gotten a trifle more traffic as people come in to enjoy the nearby Jarbidge Wilderness Area, with its half dozen peaks over ten thousand feet. In fact, Jarbidge is more hospitable than many of the ghost towns of the West. At the end of the road there is the Tsawhawbitts Ranch Bed and Breakfast, open seasonally. Phone ahead to (702) 488-2338 for availability. Don't plan to just drop in. There is also the Outdoor Inn, a rustic hotel with ten comfortable rooms, plus three furnished one-bedroom apartments, available by day or week and ideal for treasure hunters. The Outdoor Inn also has a full restaurant featuring home-cooked meals, and an adjacent bar for celebrating your discoveries in the old-fashioned way of buying a round for the house. Phone ahead to (702) 488-3211. Both are far from what you would find in Reno or Las Vegas, but they have what you will never find amid the bright lights of the gambling meccas—they are miles from anywhere.

Coming from a major airport, Jarbidge is a two-day drive most of the year, if you don't want to be on the gravel road at night—and we would not recommend that. Boise, Idaho, and Reno, Nevada, are the major airports that come to mind. There are smaller, closer airports in Twin Falls, Idaho, and Elko, Nevada, but the time that would be lost in changing planes makes the major-airport idea the better choice.

If you choose to fly into Reno, take Interstate 80 east

across the entire state of Nevada. It is an excellent road except in the dead of winter, but it is very long and tiring. At Wells, Nevada, turn north on U.S. Highway 93 to Jackpot. A border town catering to Idaho gamblers, Jackpot had plenty of accommodations and is a good staging point for getting an early start for the drive into Jarbidge. The next morning, get up early, avail yourself of one of those underpriced "gamblers' special" steak-and-eggs breakfasts that Nevada is famous for, fill your gas tank, and continue north on Highway 93. You'll be in Idaho before the smell of the bacon fat fades. Turn west at the town of Rogerson, eighteen miles from Jackpot.

If you are flying by way of Boise, drive east along the spectacular Snake River on Interstate 84 to exit 173. Like Interstate 80, Interstate 84 (which used to be called "Interstate 80 North") is an excellent road, except in the dead of winter, and it is not quite so long and tiring. At exit 173 turn south on U.S. Highway 93. You will cross the spectacular canyon—some call it "grand," and I won't argue—of the Snake River and immediately find yourself in Twin Falls. A medium-size town by Idaho standards, Twin Falls is a good staging point for getting an early start for the drive into Jarbidge. In the morning, fill up your gas tank and drive south twenty-one miles to Rogerson and turn west.

Driving west from Rogerson, you will be on a paved road. Note the crossings of Salmon Creek and Cedar Creek. About twenty miles from Highway 93 you will cross into Owyhee County. Ahead of you is the great emptiness. In Owyhee County there is a story of a lost placer on a stream or streambed in the vicinity of the Owyhee Mountains, but it remains so remote that it is likely to stay lost forever.

About five miles into Owyhee County you will pass through the tiny town of Three Creek—not Three *Creeks,* just singular—and you will cross the East Fork of the Bruneau River, which flows north into the Snake River. The East Fork will be your alert that the pavement will soon end.

When the paved road does end, there will be a fork. On

the right will be a dirt road that twists across the desert for seventy miles—through spectacular Bruneau Canyon—to the town of Bruneau, Idaho. To the left is a gravel road that twists and turns for twenty miles, crossing the Nevada state line to Jarbidge.

There is a dirt road alternative route to Jarbidge that is not recommended in the winter, during a heavy storm, or after a heavy storm, when a great deal of rain may have fallen. From Reno, drive east on Interstate 80, toward Wells, but take exit 301 at Elko, fifty-one miles short of Wells. Fill your gas tank in Elko and take Nevada Highway 225, a paved road, north for fifty miles to the place where it crosses the North Fork of the Humboldt River. A few miles father on Highway 225 there is an inconspicuous dirt road leading east. It will eventually take you north to a turnoff for Cole Canyon and the North Fork Campground. At this point turn east again for forty-eight miles to Jarbidge.

If you are going into Jarbidge, be prepared. As always, when you turn off a paved road, or if you are driving on an especially remote paved road, always start your drive with a full tank of gas and be prepared to turn back when your gas gauge reaches the "half full" mark. You should also carry both a properly inflated spare tire and a flashlight. Make sure you have a jack in the vehicle, and make sure everyone in the vehicle knows how to use it. In the winter, always carry chains if there is even the remotest possibility of snow or ice. Carry water and food as well as a shovel and blankets.

Once in Jarbidge, however, you are only partway there. The treasure is not in town. It is out there somewhere on those windswept hills. Even from a ghost town, one must hike for miles through the sagebrush, looking for clues that are as transitory as the desert mirages that drift through here in the summer, or the dry, crystalline snow that drifts through here in the winter.

Chapter 13

THE LOST TREASURE OF LOS PERROS DE LA NIEBLA

PLACE: *Southwestern New Mexico*

TIME PERIOD: *About 1910*

Treasure is elusive in a metaphysical as well as a physical sense because it is a search for the elusive and often impossible and because it becomes an allegory for the searcher's own voyage of self-discovery.

There is a story they used to tell in the mountains of Grant County, New Mexico, that has such a mystical element. It is the tale of ''Los Perros de la Niebla''—the Dogs of the Mist.

As the story goes, it was nearing winter in Grant County, the air was cold, the canyons were filled with mist, and you could smell the snow coming. A man and his dogs were deep in the Mogollon Mountains, hunting for a bear, when the man apparently stumbled across a streambed filled with large gold nuggets. Somehow, in his excitement, his gun is believed to have gone off accidently, mortally wounding him.

A day or so later the dogs were seen in town, and people wondered what had happened to the dogs' master. Around the neck of one dog was a torn piece of the man's shirt. On it, written in blood, were the words ''Follow Dogs. I am Dying.'' Tied up in the cloth was a huge nugget of almost pure gold.

Unlike the happy ending you'd expect if the story orig-

inated in Hollywood, searchers could not get the dogs to
lead them back to the man. They searched the misty mountains—probably until the snows finally came—but they
never found the man and they never found the gold. However, as the story goes, on misty days in those mountains
you can still hear the distant barking of Los Perros de la
Niebla.

Chasing the Dogs of the Mist

If they searched when the story was new and the trail fresh
and found nothing, then it is unlikely this treasure is going
to be found these many decades later, but people still wonder and fantasize. The tale of Los Perros de la Niebla is a
compelling story, but it has taken on the dimensions of a
myth. Should we take it more as an allegory than as a true
story? Did it really happen?

Grant County is in the southwestern corner of New Mexico, stretching from the Arizona state line to the Rio
Grande. To the south it almost touches the Mexican state
of Chihuahua. Grant County is an interesting place for treasure seekers of all kinds. In the south, around mining towns
such as Silver City, there are a lot of tales of lost mines
and stolen loot. In the north, in the rugged Gila National
Forest, which contains the Mogollon Mountains and extends deep into Catron County to the north, you can find
patches of virtually untraced back country the size of Connecticut.

There is even one canyon with tenth-century cliff dwellings that were built by the ancient pre-Anasazi Mogollon
people, and later used as one of the last outposts of the
Apache people. In fact, the earliest ruin that has been found
within the monument is a pit house of a type that was made
between the first and fourth centuries. People lived in
houses here at the time of the Roman Empire, but only their
ghosts remain. Now designated as a national monument,
this abandoned city is situated high on the southeast-facing

cliff of a side canyon overlooking the West Fork of the
Gila River. The cliff dwellers abandoned their homes by
the early fourteenth century. Why they left and where they
went are not known. Some people use the word "haunted"
up there.

The Gila Cliff Dwellings National Monument is at a
point about as deep as you can drive into the Gila National
Forest on a paved road, New Mexico Highway 15, which
extends north from Silver City, the county seat of Grant
County. The driving time is about two hours, and it is a
steep climb through the Mogollons. In turn, Silver City is
about two hours from the city of Las Cruces, New Mexico,
and either would provide a good base for an expedition into
the Mogollons. The archives at New Mexico State University in Las Cruces and the county records in Silver City
will be excellent sources of information for getting inside
the legend of Los Perros de la Niebla.

Las Cruces has an airport, but the nearest major airports
are at Albuquerque, New Mexico, and Tucson, Arizona.
Las Cruces is conveniently at the intersection of Interstate
25 from Albuquerque and Interstate 10 from Tucson 25 and
is an easy half-day drive from either Albuquerque or Tucson. To reach Silver City from Las Cruces, take Interstate
10 west sixty-two miles to Deming. At Deming, exit 82
will put you on U.S. Highway 180, and Silver City is fifty-
two miles to the northwest.

Tangible Treasure

If the treasure of Los Perros is as ethereal as the mist, then
it should be noted that there have been a great many very
tangible and very valuable treasures taken out of the southern periphery of the Mogollons.

Silver City itself was not immune to the spurts of treasure
frenzy that rippled through the West in the nineteenth century. In short, it did not get its name from flatware. Silver
City is a major mining center and has been since it was

born as boomtown in the summer of 1870 after John Bullard opened a silver mine. When the silver began to play out, copper took its place as a major area industry, specifically at the huge Santa Rita Open Pit Copper Mine, which still operates.

At an elevation of 5,920 feet, Silver City is higher than the well-known "mile-high" city up in Colorado, but on the drive north on Highway 15 you continue to climb even higher as you reach into the Mogollons. This writer has seen snow beneath the mist along Highway 15 as late as the first week of May.

The steepness is illustrated by the fact that the small, never-incorporated ghost town of Pinos Altos, about seven miles north of Silver City, has an elevation of 7,040 feet. Pinos Altos is also older than Silver City, having the distinction of being the oldest Anglo settlement in the southwestern corner of New Mexico. Dating from 1860, when the magic word "gold" was first spoken here, Pinos Altos is surrounded by a host of aging gold mines. They say that as much as $800 million in gold was extracted from the Pinos Altos mines before they closed more than half a century ago. This was back when gold was less than $40 to the ounce. Today this take would be worth more than $8 *billion*.

Among the famous gold mines in these hills that are abandoned but far from "lost" are the legendary Golden Giant, the Hardscrabble, the Hazard, and the Kept Woman. As is often the case around the gold mining districts of the West, there are also a number of "lost" mines and unclaimed claims in the hills around here. There are lost mines on Black Mountain just outside Pinos Altos and Addams's Lost Mine, which is on an unidentified red mountain north of Pinos Altos. This would place it in Gila National Forest, which contains many red sandstone mountains. This site is *probably* not to be confused with the Lost Adams Diggings in El Malpais in Cibola County. Most of the "lost" mines are literally lost and today are little more than potentially deadly holes in the pine-needle-covered ground. Walk with care in these hills.

Of course, the deeper you travel into the Mogollons, the farther you get from places where large-scale mining—even for gold—would be practical. This doesn't mean there is no gold. If $8 billion was taken from around Pinos Altos, how much is left, and where is it?

There is a story that might answer that. It takes place long, long ago, and it tells of a man and his dogs who were deep in the Mogollons hunting for a bear, when the man apparently stumbled across a streambed filled with large gold nuggets. Even today, on a quiet, misty morning, far up the West Fork of the Gila River, if you hold your breath and listen carefully, you can still hear those dogs.

Chapter 14

THE GASTON BULLOCK MEANS TREASURE

PLACE: *Concord, North Carolina*

TIME PERIOD: *1923–27*

As much as any good treasure story, the public loves a good celebrity scandal story, and the more celebrated the celebrity, the more delicious the scandal.

In the 1970s the American public was abuzz with the Watergate corruption scandal that brought down the presidency of Richard Nixon. In the 1990s the American public reveled in the tawdry series of sex scandals that dogged President Bill Clinton. By that time few Americans remembered that their country had once had a president named Warren Gamaliel Harding and that his presidency had been rocked not only by a corruption scandal, but a series of sex scandals as well. Beyond that, there were further elements that conspire to help a good scandal become a truly good story. There was a possible murder—actually, a covered-up presidential assassination—and there *was* a treasure.

On August 2, 1923, the world was informed that President Warren Gamaliel Harding had died at the Palace Hotel in San Francisco. Present at his bedside were his wife and his personal physician, General Charles Sawyer.

It was just not clear exactly how he had died. He had been ill since he left Alaska a few days earlier amid rumors of ptomaine poisoning. The official story was that he had suffered a stroke, but there was little doubt in the minds of a great many people that his death had come at the hands of his wife, the cruel and jealous Florence Kling De Wolfe Harding, a wealthy heiress whom he had married to help finance his newspaper in Marion, Ohio. If it was Warren Harding's disinterested malleability that made him the ideal presidential candidate for the boys in the smoke-filled room, it was Flossie Harding's drive and ambition that groomed Warren for the staircase that led him to that room. It was not the first time that a woman's ambition and greed for power would be the catalyst that catapulted her husband to the presidency. Nor was it to be the last.

It has been said—and it is probably true—that no U.S. president in the twentieth century *looked* more like our "central casting" idea of a president, while being more utterly incompetent. He was not the twentieth century's worst president. Certainly Harding's ineptitude prevented him from inflicting the level of damage done by Lyndon Johnson to the American economy with his tragic "Great Society" programs and to the fabric of American society with his blind obsession with the Vietnam War. Nevertheless, Harding's buffoonery was hardly comic.

Like a Turtle on a Log

Warren Gamaliel Harding was born on a farm near Blooming Grove, Ohio, during the last year of the Civil War. He aspired to little more than a comfortable living as a small-town newspaper editor in Marion, Ohio, but when he married Florence Kling De Wolfe, her lust for power became the guiding force in his life. She realized, perhaps better than he did, that the power of the media could be used as a stepping-stone to political power. She carefully crafted Warren's editorial policies to curry favor and popularity with voters, and she helped to engineer his election to the Ohio State Senate in 1898. After that, he served as lieutenant governor, and he was elected to the U.S. Senate in 1914.

In Washington Florence Harding became "the Duch-

ess,'' a name which befitted not only her powerful and regal
bearing, but her pretensions as well. She found Washington
society to her liking. It was the ultimate power center, an
environment that possessed all she craved. Only one thing
would please the Duchess more than being a senator's wife,
and that would start to come into place in a sweaty, smoke-
filled Chicago hotel room.

It was in the summer of 1920. Senator Harding was at-
tending the Republican National Convention in Chicago
when he was summoned to the suite at the Blackstone Hotel
that was registered to Harry M. Daugherty, the Ohio political boss who had gotten him elected to the Senate in
1914.

''Do you want to be president of the United States?''
asked Daugherty, his tone more declaratory than interrog-
ative.

''Um . . . sure,'' stammered the befuddled Harding. He
had no reason to believe at that moment that he would be
nominated, much less elected, nor had he any idea that
Daugherty had predicted both events several months before.

Harding did not come to Chicago for this. He came for
the poker games with his cronies, the drinks, and the jolly
stag parties that were matters of course at conventions in
those days. Harding liked parties. He was that kind of guy.
He was, as Daugherty described him after the convention,
''sunning himself like a turtle on a log, and I just pushed
him into the water.''

The night before, Daugherty had gotten together for ci-
gars with Senators Henry Cabot Lodge and James Wads-
worth, as well as kingmaker George Harvey of the J. P.
Morgan inner circle. They had decided to divert the nom-
ination away from leading candidate Leonard Wood—who
had already received more than three hundred votes on the
convention's fourth ballot—and assign the blocs of votes
they controlled to Harding, because he would be, in Wads-
worth's cynical estimation, a president who ''could be
trusted to sign the bills the Senate sent him, and not send
the Senate bills to pass.''

Once elected, Harding appointed his puppeteer, Harry

Daugherty, as attorney general, and let him serve as the power behind the throne while the president concentrated on the pleasures of life that interested him more than affairs of state. He certainly loved the ladies, and it is supposed he loved the ponies, too, for he certainly enjoyed a good card game. He wasn't always particularly lucky, however, for it is said that he lost a set of antique White House porcelain in a poker game.

As the president played, Daugherty lost no time in consolidating his own power base in the nation's capital. As the top man at the Justice Department, he was clearly safe from any prying investigation of his own activities, but just to make sure, he brought in an old friend of his, private detective William J. Burns, to head the Bureau of Investigation, the agency that would become the Federal Bureau of Investigation (FBI) in 1935. Burns ran the bureau as his own, with a mandate to lean hard and heavy on anyone who interfered with Harry M. Daugherty.

Among Burns's battalion of detectives and secret agents was Gaston Bullock Means, a shrewd and shadowy character whose résumé included having worked as an investigator for the German ambassador in 1914 on the eve of World War I. For his work in the service of a nation with whom the United States would soon be at war, Means was paid a thousand dollars a month, which is the equivalent to more than $20,000 in current dollars. Means was also a convicted con man, an investment adviser to the society set, and he had once been indicted for, though not convicted of, murder.

Born a son of landed gentry in Concord, North Carolina, Means left the University of North Carolina in 1898 a year short of graduating and went on to use his social connections to land a traveling salesman position with Cannon Mills, one of Concord's largest companies. He had gone on the road, a road that took the young southern country squire to the bright lights and big-city life of New York and Chicago.

In 1910 Means made a career change, joining Burns's detective agency to pursue a trade for which he apparently had considerable aptitude. Burns was especially fond of Means, calling him "the greatest natural detective I have ever known." Yet it was his side jobs—such as the German embassy caper—that gave Means the means to maintain a Park Avenue apartment and cruise and fleece the crème de la crème of Roaring Twenties New York society. It was in one such scam that Means was ensnared by his murder indictment. He became bodyguard and confidant to Maude King, the fun-loving twentysomething widow of the late millionaire lumber baron James C. King.

To gain the trust of the voluptuous and free-spending young Mrs. King, Means staged a phony robbery attempt, with himself cast in the role of rescuing hero. Her new Sir Galahad became her companion, party escort, and—more to his liking—investment consultant. As the story goes, Means had relieved the young widow of $150,000 by August 1917. At about this time she became suspicious, but he soothed her with kind words, sweet lies, and the suggestion that they take a little vacation.

Maude and Gaston's vacation found them in North Carolina, where a hunting trip was suggested—a cozy hunting trip with just the two of them. This is the point where, if this was a movie, the audience would start screaming "No!" to aid the poor young woman. The result of the hunting expedition was what might have been imagined by any but the poor, gullible Maude.

Conveniently, the Means murder trial was held beneath the slowly moving ceiling fans of the Concord, North Carolina, Courthouse, where a hometown jury found in favor of Gaston Bullock Means, despite expert testimony that Mrs. King's head wound could not have been self-inflicted, as Means suggested. Having put this sad affair behind him, Means was welcomed back into the fold by William J. Burns, who was headed for bigger and better things. When Burns went to Washington, Means was there.

Gaston Means earned his keep. When Burns ordered him to go behind the scenes in Congress to finesse support for the Harding administration, Means simply investigated the congressmen, documented their dirty laundry, and turned over a set of blackmail dossiers to his boss. This earned the praise of William J. Burns, and Means was promoted over the head of another young Bureau of Investigation agent—and a man with a long memory—named John Edgar Hoover. Thus began a rivalry that only the vindictive Hoover could win.

The early 1920s was a time of paradox. In his campaign slogan, Warren Gamaliel Harding had promised the American people a "return to normalcy" after the tumultuous years of World War I and the last years of Woodrow Wilson's troubled tenure in the White House. What Harding delivered was the most corrupt administration in memory. But the people seemed to love it. Harding had delivered "normalcy" and prosperity, and he enjoyed immense popularity.

Yet the corruption festered like dry rot. Two close friends whom Harding had appointed to the Veterans Bureau and the Office of the Alien Property Custodian would soon be arrested for graft, and in what would be the Harding administration's defining scandal, Secretary of the Interior Albert Fall agreed to secretly cut an illegal deal to lease government oil reserves at Teapot Dome, Wyoming, to the Sinclair Oil Company. For his trouble Fall was the recipient of $400,000—that's about $8 million in today's dollars—in gifts and "loans."

Harding himself was never implicated in the corruption. He was too busy toiling in the fields of romance.

As a Cat Loves Cream

No American president in the twentieth century until Bill Clinton was less guarded about—or less successful in guarding—his extramarital affairs than poor Warren Harding. Among the president's more notorious affairs was that with Carrie Phillips, the wife of a friend from Ohio, which dated back to 1910 and had lasted until after Harding was elected president. Both wronged spouses knew about this one and both despised poor Warren for it.

As the Harding administration gradually receded into the status of a footnote to American history, interest in his scandals would wane. However, in October 1963 a shoe box containing a hundred steamy love letters to Carrie Phillips was discovered in Marion, Ohio. They were written by Harding over a ten-year period, from 1910 to 1920, and some ran more than forty pages in length. In 1911 Harding wrote, "I love you garbed, but naked [underlined twice] more," and "Carrie, take me panting to your heaving breast" (the first line of a poem). The final missive, written during Harding's presidential campaign, promised her $5,000 a year "to avoid disgrace in the public eye, to escape ruin in the eyes of those who have trusted me in public life. . . ."

Carrie Phillips instead received a lump sum of $25,000, a monthly stipend of $2,000 after that, and a trip to the Orient, all paid for by the Republican National Committee. She stayed abroad until after Harding's death in 1923.

Those of Harding's papers that were not burned were suppressed by the Harding Memorial Association. When the association released some of these to the Ohio Historical Society in 1963, several writers went to Marion to investigate them. One of them, Frances Russell, happened to meet Phillips's legal guardian, who had her letters to and from the president. The letters were subsequently bought by Harding nephew Dr. George T. Harding III, who was pressured into giving them to the Library of Congress, but only on the condition that they stay sealed until July 29, 2014.

However, occasionally their contents have been leaked. One passage from a memo penned by Ms. Phillips and printed in the *Washington Post* in 1976, read: "There is one engulfing, enthralling rule of love, the song of your whole being which is a bit sweeter—Oh Warren! Oh Warren—when your body quivers with divine paroxysms and your soul hovers for flight with mine."

However ripe the passion in his affair with Carrie Phillips, the woman whose legacy is most fully associated with the seamy side of Warren Gamaliel Harding was a young Ohio socialite named Nan Britton, whom the president liked—in Mrs. Harding's words—as "a cat likes cream."

When Nan Britton came to the White House, the president's Secret Service detail would bring her straight to the president's office, where she and Harding would reportedly have passionate sex in a closet. With birth control being as haphazard as it was in the 1920s, something went wrong. In three decades of marriage, the Duchess had never had a child with the bumbling Warren, but now, after a few torrid months in a cloakroom, poor Nan had become pregnant.

As was often the case then—as, sadly now—men of wealth and prominence who fathered children in casual flings wrote checks but did little else to acknowledge their children. Elizabeth Ann, Warren and Nan's daughter, grew up knowing who her father was, but, because of his refusal to accept paternity, she was unable to use her father's last name.

Meanwhile, in October 1921, less than a year into her husband's first year in office, the bitter and jealous Duchess consulted a well-known Washington fortune-teller named "Madam X," and then hired none other than Gaston Bullock Means to "shadow" the president in his peccadilloes with Nan Britton.

Means went to work. He audaciously broke into Nan Britton's Chicago apartment, where he found love letters from the president, and gifts that Harding had given to Elizabeth Ann. As brazen as his burglary had been, Means returned to the apartment a second time when the Duchess demanded that he go there and steal all the baby presents the president had given his little daughter. This he did, carting off everything but the baby buggy, which was too unwieldy.

Even as the investigation of Harding's indiscretions was starting to get interesting, Means was in trouble on other fronts. He was implicated in several nefarious affairs of his own, including a will forgery and a scheme to defraud the Southeastern Express Company. News of these activities got into the papers, and undercover man Means found himself in the limelight. Harry M. Daugherty publicly dismissed him as a Justice Department investigator in February 1922 but kept him on the federal payroll.

Means watched his fortunes fade, and two years into his presidency, Harding's life was also coming apart. Nan Britton was pregnant, and all around him his political cronies were starting to tumble. Word of Albert Fall's deal in Wyoming had leaked out, and Senator Thomas J. Walsh opened the investigation that would make poor Fall take the fall that would make him the only U.S. presidential cabinet member to go to jail until Watergate.

Harding did what presidents often do when the political atmosphere in Washington becomes a bit too close for comfort—he took a trip. In July 1923 he traveled to Alaska to open the Alaska Railway, to eat some crab, and to grab some press that did not carry the phrase "Teapot Dome" in the first paragraph.

On the Alaska leg of the trip, all went well. The first American president to visit Alaska, he opened his railroad, ate his crab, and got some good—or at least nonscandalous—press. On the ship back to San Francisco, however, he fell ill. There was talk of pneumonia and of ptomaine poisoning from tainted crab. There were whispers of other things, but then there were a lot of whispers floating around at any mention of President Harding in the summer of 1923. When the ship docked in the Golden Gate City, Harding and his entourage checked into the Palace Hotel. The president went to bed, and his handlers began to issue bulletins that said his health was "improving." As for the First Lady, she was at her husband's side.

According to the *New York Times,* at 7:30 P.M. on the evening of August 2, one week after Warren Gamaliel Harding had first been reported to be sick, "utterly without warning, a slight shudder passed through his frame; he collapsed, and all recognized that the end had come. A stroke of apoplexy was the cause of his death."

Despite the official story, almost no one believed that

Harding had died of natural causes. The question on everyone's lips was the proverbial "Whodunit?"

Conspiratorial fingers pointed to the madly jealous Duchess, of course, because it was easy to see her at the end of her rope with his philandering. He was reported to have died from poisoning and, after all, poison is—the cliché says—a woman's murder weapon. Fingers also gestured in the direction of the enemies he had made and those who had something to gain by his death or something to lose by his continued existence. It was widely believed that Harry Daugherty was at the end of his political rope and that Harding was preparing to dismiss him. There was talk that Daugherty had engineered the death of his close confidant Jess Smith and that the attorney general had both the will and the means to dispose of the president as well. The means may have included Gaston Bullock Means, but there is no evidence of that. Means himself presented copious evidence that the Duchess did it.

The official cause of death was listed as natural causes, but it was Florence Kling De Wolfe Harding who denied the demands for an autopsy, and the history books still list death by natural causes—cerebral apoplexy. A year later, both she and General Sawyer—who was also present at the president's death—were also deceased.

Calvin Coolidge, Harding's vice president, was sworn in as president by his father in Plymouth, Vermont, and made his way back to the nation's capital to pick up the reins of power and the pieces of the most discredited presidential administration in history. Immediately upon their almost simultaneous return to Washington, both Coolidge and Florence Harding began cleaning house. For the First Lady suddenly turned former First Lady, this included the bittersweet pleasure of burning every love letter from Nan Britton that she could find squirreled away in the dead president's personal files. For Coolidge cleaning house would involve the disassembly of the Ohio political machine that had pulled Harding's strings. In the meantime, the Senate began its own investigations, and eventually Harry Daugherty himself was indicted.

For Gaston Bullock Means, time was running out, but his imagination was not. During Prohibition, confiscated liquor was often held in government warehouses, and this offered Means an opportunity. However, he was caught. In October 1923 he was arrested for stealing liquor from a federal warehouse, using a forgery of the secretary of the treasury's signature. Means was still free from incarceration in March 1924 when he was arrested again, this time for extorting $65,000 from some cronies by promising them he could get *their* indictments quashed. Finally, in April 1925, he was sentenced to thirty-six months in the Federal Penitentiary in Atlanta. There had reportedly been a promise that Means would get a suspended sentence in exchange for testimony at Senate hearings against Harry Daugherty and the Ohio hoodlums. If there had been a deal, it fell through. Means testified, but he still would up in Atlanta for three years.

While he was in jail, Means wrote his famous book *The Strange Death of President Harding*. In this book, published in 1930, Means told the bizarre tale of secret meetings with the Duchess, of following the president and his young mistress across several states, and of his paranoia of the sinister Harry M. Daugherty, who had beaten his rap and walked free.

When Means himself walked free in 1928, it was a changed world. As he returned to Concord, North Carolina, to ponder the rest of his life, J. Edgar Hoover was now heading the Bureau of Investigation, and he would be keeping an eye on his onetime rival.

Gaston Bullock Means's Last Scam

In the latter decades of the twentieth century it seemed like there was a "crime of the century" or a "trial of the century" nearly every five years or so, but during the first half of the century, there had been only one of each, and they both involved the kidnapping and murder of the twenty-month-old son of aviation hero Charles Augustus Lindbergh and his popular wife, Anne Morrow Lindbergh. The crime, which occurred on March 1, 1932, created a media frenzy that was unprecedented and not to be paralleled until after the television era a quarter century later. The body of the poor infant was found seventy-two days later and a suspect was arrested, tried, and promptly executed. There are many who say that Bruno Richard Hauptmann was innocent, but that, as they say, is another story.

While Gaston Bullock Means was almost certainly innocent of this "crime of the century," he saw in it an opportunity for a crime of his own. The sweet-talking detective convinced Mrs. Evalyn Walsh McLean, the estranged wife of the publisher of the *Washington Post* and owner of the Hope Diamond, that he had the connections to secure the release of the Lindbergh baby. All he needed from Mrs. McLean was absolute discretion and $104,000. Having faked two meetings with his imaginary kidnappers in South Carolina and Texas, he reported back to his benefactress that the criminals had asked for an additional $35,000. This tipped the credibility scales for Mrs. McLean. She called the police, and the police called J. Edgar Hoover's Bureau of Investigation. Hoover, whose reputation for exhaustive and vindictive investigations is unparalleled in American history, and who once described Means as "the greatest faker of all time," would personally arrest the suspect.

Convicted of grand larceny, Means was sentenced to fifteen years in the Federal Penitentiary at Fort Leavenworth, Kansas. As he went to prison, his wife went to Wynnewood Park. While her breadwinner was incarcerated, Julie Means and their children moved into the home at 9021 Fairview Road in the Maryland suburb that had been designed by Gilbert L. Rodler and that was owned by Willard D. Miller, the circulation manager of the *Washington Post*. Rumor had it that Miller had run into financial difficulties during the Depression, but there was no word on why the circulation manager of the paper was mixed up with the wife of the man who had tried to swindle the ex-wife of his boss.

In 1931 Miller had rented the Fairview Road home to J. C. Austin, who was assistant to the president of the Southern Railway, and now Miller rented it to Julie Means. How she—and her persecuted husband—could afford such a place is part of the mystery, but afford it she did. While Gaston was sleeping on a threadbare mattress and taking his meals on a tin plate, Julie whiled away the hours under the beamed ceiling of the living room, staring into the large stone fireplace with chestnut mantel flanked by bookcases and built-in pewter lamps; or looking through the French windows, across the flagstone terrace to the home's rare shrub plantings, its willows, poplars, Japanese cherries, and dogwoods and toward the Maryland hills beyond. It was a short-lived idyll, however, because in 1935 the bank foreclosed on Willard Miller. He lost the house, and Julie Means was on the move.

Gaston Bullock Means was not. He would never again smell the air of freedom. He died in December 1938 at a federal prison hospital in Springfield, Missouri.

The $104,000 was never found. If Julie Means spent it, she never said. Also lost was an estimated $500,000 that he buried on his former estate in Concord. Has it ever been found? If so, no one ever said.

Can it be found? Will you be the one? Fly to Charlotte—Mecklenburg County—North Carolina. Go in the spring, when the magnolias are in bloom. Don't go in the summer, when the humidity hanging over the lakes makes the air unbelievably sticky—and a person's perspiration stains the seersucker—and anyone in his or her right mind is inside where it's cool. Take Interstate 85 north in the direction of Greensboro, or take U.S. Highway 29 for a taste of the local flavors, and you'll be in Concord before you know it. Wheel on over to the county courthouse and ask anyone to tell you about the Gaston Bullock Means estate.

Chapter 15

JOHN DILLINGER'S LITTLE BOHEMIA CACHE

PLACE: *Northern Wisconsin*

TIME PERIOD: *1934*

During the Roaring Twenties and the early 1930s, gun-toting gangsters grabbed headlines and the attention of the public as they grabbed loot in bank heists and extortion scams throughout the nation. There have always been people who have idealized outlaws. Indeed, there has always been a undercurrent within popular culture that has placed certain outlaws—especially those who seem glamorous—on a sort of pedestal of heroism. Call it the Robin Hood syndrome. The illustrious and almost certainly fictitious Mr. Hood, with his "rob from the rich and give to the poor idealism," existed at a time when established authority was seen as being more evil and more corrupt than highwaymen and cutpurses. In the corrupt 1920s and the Depression 1930s, similar views were held with regard to established order—from banks to politicians.

Distance has always made the perpetrators of certain crimes seem glamorous. In nineteenth-century America, the dime-novel-buying public, most of whom lived east of the Mississippi, thrilled and swooned to tales of the outlaws of the West. Jesse James and Billy the Kid became romantic heroes even though they were desperate thugs who somehow were "discovered" by journalists who made their exploits—spectacular gunfights and spectacular horseback escapes—seem somehow heroic. But heroic at a distance. Had those dime-novel readers been compelled to exchange places with one of Billy the Kid's victims, the glamor would have faded in an instant. Pirates also are glamorous—at a distance. As noted elsewhere in this book, pirates were cruel men—and a few women—who were capable of torture and vicious things that are almost hard to comprehend, yet they are celebrated today on T-shirts and coffee mugs up and down the eastern seaboard. Meanwhile, today's pirates, the dreadful airliner hijackers, strike fear. They are in no way glamorous to most of the world.

Hijackers aside, it is hard to understand why popular culture embraces certain criminals and abhors others. Why are some romantic and some not? In the 1990s, people in the United States reacted with horror to the Oklahoma City Federal Building bombing and lived in mortal dread of street crime, while at the same time, teenage girls swooned to "gangsta rap," a form of popular music that glamorized a lifestyle that embraces prostitution, violence to women, and drive-by shootings. Of course, the youngsters who listened to the shouts of the "gangsta rappers" would no more want to live in an environment filled with prostitution, violence to women, and drive-by shootings than the dime-novel readers of the nineteenth century would have wished to stare into the barrel of Billy the Kid's six-shooter.

In the 1930s, during the depths of the Great Depression, another breed of gangster began to excite and thrill that corner of popular culture that loves outlaws. People such as Al Capone, Machine Gun Kelly, and Pretty Boy Floyd—not to mention the terrible Ma Barker and her boys—became cult heroes. Because of the Depression, many Americans, nearly helpless against forces they didn't understand, idealized outlaws who took what they wanted at gunpoint. Of course, while the gangsters of the 1930s committed violent murders and generally terrorized people, in many cases the crimes they committed were almost justifiable in the eyes of many people. For one thing, they robbed banks. While most people, even today, distrust banks and bankers, during the Depression a vast number of people had been seriously injured by banks. Many banks folded, sending depositors' money to oblivion while the banker walked away. In other cases banks took the homes and farms of longtime customers who fell behind on their mortgage payments.

During the 1930s a sort of Robin Hood aura was bestowed on the gangsters that made people forget how truly cruel and vicious they really were. Of all those gangsters the FBI still refers to as "lurid desperadoes," one man, John Dillinger, came to evoke this gangster era, and stirred mass emotion to a degree rarely seen in this country. Dillinger, whose name once dominated the headlines, was not Robin Hood. He was a brutal thief and a cold-blooded murderer.

From September 1933 until July 1934, he and his violent gang terrorized the Midwest, killing ten men, wounding seven others, robbing banks and police arsenals, and staging three jail breaks—killing a sheriff during one and wounding two guards in another. But from September 1933 through July 1934, John Dillinger lived on the front pages of the nation's newspapers, frightening, titillating, and selling papers.

The Making of a Mobster

John Herbert Dillinger was born on June 22, 1903, in the Oak Hill section of Indianapolis, Indiana. Oak Hill was, at that time, a middle-class residential neighborhood, and Dillinger's father was a grocer in the neighborhood. Dillinger, Sr., was a hardworking man who raised John in an atmosphere of disciplinary extremes. He was ruthless and repressive on some occasions but generous and permissive on others. John's mother died when he was three, and when his father remarried six years later, John resented his stepmother.

Meanwhile, John's erratic and violent personality began to evolve and eventually to explode. During his teens, the flaws in this perplexing personality became evident. He was frequently in trouble in school, and finally he quit school and got a job in a machine shop in Indianapolis. Although intelligent and a good worker, he soon became bored with his job. As with many problem children of any generation, Dillinger developed the habit of staying out all night. His father believed—as many parents still do—that the temptations of the big city were corrupting his teenage son. Thus it was that his father reacted—as many parents still do—by deciding to move the kid out and away from the corrupting influences of the city. Dillinger, Sr., sold his property in Indianapolis and moved the family to a farm near Mooresville, Indiana. However, as often happens in such cases, John reacted no better to rural life than he had to what he experienced in the city.

In Mooresville John Dillinger began to run wild again. He stole a car and got caught. It was a choice of jail or enlisting in the military service, and Dillinger picked the U.S. Navy. However, as often happens in such cases, he reacted no better to navy life than he had to life in Mooresville. He soon got into trouble again, and he even deserted his ship when it docked in Boston.

Discharged from the navy, Dillinger returned to Mooresville, where, in 1924, he married an old girlfriend, sixteen-year-old Beryl Hovius. The wedding—which was certainly an awkward and strained moment in the Dillinger and Hovius households—took place against the backdrop of the newlyweds' dazzling dream of bright lights and excitement of a life in Indianapolis. As "bright lights-big city" dreams often do, this one went sour. The lights were bright and the city was bigger than Mooresville, but without money a city is a difficult and unforgiving place. Dillinger had no luck finding work in the city, so he was forced to get money the way criminals usually do. He joined forces with a small-time hood and pool hustler named Ed Singleton. The dream now was for fast, easy money, the holy grail of all small-time hoods.

As the literature tells us, the chief difference between small-time hoods and successful criminals is the knowledge born of experience that fast money is almost never easy and that easy money rarely comes fast. Usually money comes neither fast nor easily. The Singleton-Dillinger gang chose, as their first "job," a grocery store holdup in Mooresville. Of course, this scheme came with the irony that Dillinger's own father was a grocer. The robbery went down with a small take and a pistol-whipped grocer who was left in a pool of blood for the trouble of trying to protect his cash drawer. However, the perps did not get far with the take from what was John Dillinger's first heist. He and Singleton were quickly apprehended.

At the arraignment, Singleton pleaded not guilty, stood trial, and was sentenced to two years. Dillinger, following his father's advice, confessed. His honesty backfired, however, and he was convicted of assault and battery with intent to rob, as well as conspiracy to commit a felony. The hapless Dillinger received joint sentences of two to fourteen years and ten to twenty years in Indiana State Prison. He was stunned by the harsh time, especially when the equally guilty Singleton got off with a mere two years.

Dillinger, who was already a sociopath with an erratic and violent personality, became a tortured, deeply bitter man in prison. He would not, however, serve a full twenty years. Had he served the full sentence, he would have emerged from jail in 1945. It would have been another time, an era that no longer belonged to the gangsters.

Today we like to think of the parole of violent felons as the misguided caprice of liberal judges, but in the early 1930s it was still an experiment based on the idealistic notion that prison actually reformed its inmates. After a mere eight and one-half years of his twenty-year sentence, John Herbert Dillinger was paroled on May 10, 1933. Many things had happened while he was in Indiana State Prison. The Roaring Twenties had ended halfway through his sentence, and the prosperity of those years has been replaced by the darkest years of the Great Depression. If John Dillinger was hard-core unemployable in 1925, he was hopeless in 1933.

Dillinger was faced with a crucial dilemma: Unemployment had reached past 25 percent, and if the average person could not find a job, there were certainly no jobs for violent ex-cons like him. Far from being rehabilitated, Dillinger was more convinced than before that crime could be made to pay. He got hold of a weapon and knocked over a bank in Bluffton, Ohio, within weeks of walking free of prison. As had happened eight and a half years earlier, Dillinger did not have long to enjoy his loot. Busted by the police in Dayton, Ohio, on September 22, he was thrown into the county jail in Lima, Ohio, to await trial.

Coincidentally, while the Lima sheriff's deputies were frisking Dillinger in advance of showing him to his accommodations, they found a document that seemed to be a plan for a prison break. Dillinger, of course, insisted that he had no knowledge of such a plan. Of course, the deputies believed him.

Four days later, using the same plans that Dillinger had in his possession, eight of Dillinger's friends escaped from Indiana State Prison, using shotguns and rifles that had been smuggled into their cells. During their escape, they shot two guards.

On October 12 three of these escaped prisoners and a parolee from the same prison showed up at the Lima jail where Dillinger was incarcerated. Pretending to be Indiana State Police officers, they told the Lima sheriff that they had come to return Dillinger to Indiana State Prison for violation of his parole. The sheriff asked to see their credentials, but of course they had none. One of the men pulled a gun, shot the sheriff, and beat him into unconsciousness. The four hoods—Harry Pierpont, Russell Clark, Charles Makley, and Harry Copeland—took the keys to the jail and freed Dillinger. They then locked the sheriff's wife and a deputy in a cell, and left the sheriff to die on the floor.

At this point neither Dillinger nor the others had violated a federal law, but local authorities asked for the assistance of the feds in identifying and locating the criminals. The U.S. Justice Department's Bureau of Investigation—the agency that would become the Federal Bureau of Investigation (FBI) in 1935—was just then beginning to earn its long-standing, albeit recently tarnished, reputation for fast and precise work. The "Bureau," as it was known, quickly identified Pierpont, Clark, Makley, and Copeland as Dillinger's accomplices. Their fingerprint cards in the Bureau of Investigation's Identification Division were flagged with red metal tags, indicating that they were wanted.

Even as the Identification Division in Washington, D.C., was doing its fast and precise work, Dillinger and his gang pulled off several bank robberies. Unlike his first two heists, both of which led to his being caught, Dillinger was suddenly successful in striking with impunity. Not only did the gang hit banks, they also plundered the police arsenals at Auburn, Indiana, and Peru, Indiana, stealing several .45-caliber Thompson submachine guns as well as a number of rifles and revolvers, a quantity of ammunition, and several bulletproof vests. Five gangsters on the run were now a small, well-equipped army. They had withering firepower, and several new gangsters had joined to become part of the action.

On December 14 John Hamilton, a Dillinger gang member, shot and killed a police detective in Chicago. A month later the Dillinger gang killed a police officer during a robbery of the First National Bank of East Chicago, Indiana. Then they expanded their reign of terror to the very corners of the United States. Dillinger and company made their way to Florida and, subsequently, to Tucson, Arizona.

It was in Tucson that the crime spree might have ended. It was here on January 23, 1934, that a fire broke out in the hotel where Clark and Makley were hiding under assumed names. Firemen recognized the men from their photographs, and local police arrested them, as well as Dillinger and Harry Pierpont. They also seized three Thompson submachine guns, two Winchester rifles mounted as machine guns, five bulletproof vests, and more than $25,000 in cash, part of it from the East Chicago robbery.

Dillinger was extradited and sequestered at the county jail in Crown Point, Indiana, to await trial for the murder of the East Chicago police officer. Authorities boasted that the jail was "escape-proof." But on March 3, 1934, Dillinger cowed the guards with what he claimed later was a wooden gun he had whittled. He forced them to open the door to his cell, then grabbed two machine guns, locked up the guards and several trustees, and fled.

It was then that Dillinger made the mistake that would cost him his life. He stole the sheriff's car and drove across the Indiana-Illinois state line, heading for Chicago. By doing that he violated the National Motor Vehicle Theft Act, which made it a federal offense to transport a stolen motor vehicle across a state line. Dillinger had, in a phrase of the vernacular that is still with us, "made it a *federal* crime." A federal complaint was sworn charging Dillinger with the theft and interstate transportation of the sheriff's car, which was recovered in Chicago. After the grand jury returned an indictment, the Bureau of Investigation became actively involved in the nationwide search for Dillinger.

Nothing would have pleased Bureau of Investigation director J. Edgar Hoover more. Since taking over from the discredited master detective William J. Burns, Hoover had cleaned house and was rapidly turning the bureau into the slick and professional crime-fighting organization it would remain for most of the rest of the century. What the egomaniacal Hoover really needed most in 1934 was a high-profile case that would give his Bureau of Investigation a high-profile public persona. In this regard John Dillinger had just become J. Edgar Hoover's new best friend.

Meanwhile, Harry Pierpont, Russell Clark, and Charles Makley were returned to Ohio and convicted of the murder of the Lima sheriff. Pierpont and Makley were sentenced to death, and Clark to life imprisonment. However, in an escape attempt, Makley was killed and Pierpont was wounded. A month later Pierpont had recovered sufficiently to be executed.

In Chicago, Dillinger joined his girlfriend, Evelyn Frechette. They then proceeded to St. Paul, Minnesota. It was here that Dillinger would team up with Homer Van Meter, Eddie Green, Tommy Carrol, and the notorious Lester

"Baby-Face Nelson" Gillis. This new version of the Dillinger gang was even more violent than the previous year's version, and their seemingly endless bank robberies were netting them trunkloads of cash.

Public Enemy Number One

By now the newspapers were following the story with rabid enthusiasm. Dillinger's crime spree was exactly the kind of thing that captivates the public, and in 1934, at the depths of the Great Depression, the public was pleased for such a diversion, however lurid and however dangerous it was for the people in the upper Midwest.

J. Edgar Hoover even joined into the media frenzy by coining the term "Public Enemy Number One" to describe John Dillinger. It sold papers, but it also put the Bureau of Investigation on the front page of those papers, which is exactly what Hoover wanted. Of course, what the Bureau of Investigation now had to do was to actually *catch* the Dillinger gang.

On March 30, 1934, a Bureau of Investigation agent talked to the manager of the Lincoln Court Apartments in St. Paul, who reported two suspicious tenants, "Mr. and Mrs. Hellman," who acted nervous and refused to admit the apartment caretaker. The Bureau of Investigation began a surveillance of the "Hellmans'" apartment immediately. The next day an agent and a police officer knocked on the door of the apartment. Evelyn "Mrs. Hellman" Frechette opened the door but quickly slammed it shut. The agent called for reinforcements to surround the building.

While they were waiting for backup, the agents and police officers saw a man enter a hall near the Hellmans' apartment. The man was Homer Van Meter. When questioned, he drew a gun, and shots were exchanged. During the gunfight Van Meter fled the building and then forced a truck driver at gunpoint to drive him to Eddie Green's apartment. Suddenly the door of the "Hellmans'" apartment opened and the muzzle of a Thompson submachine gun began spraying the hallway with .45-caliber lead. Under cover of the machine-gun fire, Dillinger and Evelyn Frechette fled through a back door. They, too, drove to Green's apartment, where Dillinger was treated for a bullet wound that he had received in their escape from the "Hellmans'" hideout.

At the Lincoln Court Apartments, the Bureau of Investigation found a tommy gun with the stock removed, two automatic rifles, one .33-caliber Colt automatic with twenty-shot magazine clips, and two bulletproof vests. Meanwhile, across town, other agents located one of Eddie Green's hideouts where he and Bessie Skinner had been living as "Mr. and Mrs. Stephens." On April 3, when Green was located, he attempted to draw his gun, but was shot by the agents. He died in a hospital eight days later.

Dillinger and Evelyn Frechette managed to get away. They fled to Mooresville, Indiana, where they stayed with Dillinger's father and half brother until his wound healed. At this point Evelyn made the mistake that may have saved her life. She went to Chicago to visit a friend—and was arrested by the Bureau of Investigation. She was taken to St. Paul for trial on a charge of conspiracy to harbor a fugitive. She was convicted, fined $1,000, and sentenced to two years in prison. Eddie Green's girlfriend Bessie Skinner got fifteen months on the same charge. The gallant authorities apparently decided not to charge the ladies with armed robbery.

Meanwhile, Dillinger and Van Meter had robbed a police station at Warsaw, Indiana, of guns and bulletproof vests. They split up, and Dillinger hid out for a time on the Upper Peninsula of Michigan. The Bureau of Investigation managed to locate him, but he slipped away just ahead of a posse of bureau agents dispatched there by airplane.

Little Bohemia

In April 1934, soon after John Dillinger had outwitted the Bureau of Investigation on the Upper Peninsula, the bureau received a tip. It seemed there had been a sudden influx of rather suspicious guests at the Little Bohemia Lodge, a rural getaway overlooking Little Star Lake in the summer resort town of Manitowish Waters, about fifty miles north of Rhinelander, Wisconsin. One of them sounded like John Dillinger and another like "Baby-Face Nelson." Dillinger, Nelson, and their pals had secretly checked into the rustic lodge for a "vacation."

Late on the cold afternoon of April 22, 1934, a Bureau of Investigation task force set out from Rhinelander in rented cars, headed for Little Bohemia. Two of these cars broke down en route, and, in the uncommonly cold April weather, some of the agents had to make the trip standing on the running boards of the other cars. Two miles from the resort, the car lights were turned off and the posse proceeded through the darkness.

When the cars reached the resort, dogs began barking. The agents spread out to surround the lodge, and as they approached, machine-gun fire rattled down on them from the roof. Swiftly, the agents took cover. One of them hurried to a telephone booth to give directions to additional agents who had arrived in Rhinelander to back up the operation.

While the agent was on the telephone, the operator broke in to tell him there was trouble at another cottage, about two miles away. Special Agent W. Carter Baum, another Bureau of Investigation man, and a local constable went there and found a parked car that the constable recognized as belonging to a local resident. They pulled up and identified themselves. Inside the car, "Baby-Face Nelson" was holding three local residents at gunpoint.

He turned, leveled a revolver at the lawmen's car, and ordered them to step out, but without waiting for them to comply, Nelson opened fire. Baum was killed, and the constable and the other agent were severely wounded. Nelson jumped into the Ford they had been using and fled.

Meanwhile, when the gun battle had subsided at the Little Bohemia Lodge, three bystanders were wounded and one had been killed. Dillinger was gone. When the agents entered the lodge the next morning, they found only three frightened women. Dillinger and five others had fled through a back window before the agents surrounded the house.

Before he left the area, however, Dillinger reportedly buried $200,000 in several suitcases in the thick woods behind the Little Bohemia.

The Lady in Red

In Washington, Bureau of Investigation director J. Edgar Hoover assigned Special Agent Samuel A. Cowley to head the bureau's investigative efforts against Dillinger. Cowley set up headquarters in Chicago, where he and Melvin Purvis, special agent in charge of the Chicago office, planned their strategy. A squad of agents under Cowley worked with East Chicago, Indiana, policemen in tracking down all tips and rumors.

Late in the afternoon of Saturday, July 21, 1934, the proprietress of a house of ill repute in Gary, Indiana, contacted one of the East Chicago police officers with information. This woman called herself Anna Sage; however, her real name was Ana Cumpanas, and she had entered the United States from her native Romania in 1914. Because of the nature of her profession, she was considered an undesirable alien by the Immigration and Naturalization Service, and deportation proceedings had been started, so she was interested in the notion of trading the Bureau of Investigation some information about Dillinger for their help in preventing her deportation—plus the cash reward being offered in the Dillinger case.

At a meeting with Anna Sage, Agents Cowley and Purvis were cautious. They promised her the reward if her information led to Dillinger's capture, but said all they could do was call her cooperation to the attention of the Department of Labor, which at that time handled deportation matters. Satisfied, Anna told the agents that a girlfriend of hers, Polly Hamilton, had visited her establishment with Dillinger. Anna was sure it was him and claimed she had recognized him from a newspaper photograph.

Anna Sage then told the agents that she, Polly Hamilton, and Dillinger would probably be going to the movies the following evening at either the Biograph or the Marbro Theater. She said that she would notify them when the theater was chosen. She also said that she would wear a red dress so they could identify her.

On Sunday, July 22, Cowley ordered all the agents of the Chicago office to stand by for "urgent duty." They waited. Finally, Anna Sage called to confirm the plans. They *were* going to the movies, but she still did not know which theater. With this in mind, Cowley decided to send agents and policemen to both theaters. At 8:30 P.M. Anna Sage, John Dillinger, and Polly Hamilton strolled into the Biograph Theater, where Clark Gable was starring in *Manhattan Melodrama*. Purvis phoned Cowley, who shifted the other men from the Marbro to the Biograph.

Cowley then phoned his boss for final instructions. They had "Public Enemy Number One" cornered at last. J. Edgar Hoover was desperate for the collar, but equally anxious for no civilians to get hurt, as they had been at the Little Bohemia debacle. He cautioned Cowley to wait outside rather than risk a shooting match inside the crowded theater, and each man was instructed not to unnecessarily endanger himself. Cowley then added that if Dillinger offered any resistance, it would be each man for himself.

At 10:30 P.M. Dillinger, with his two female companions on either side, walked out of the theater and turned to his left. As they walked past the doorway in which Purvis was standing, Purvis lit a cigar as a signal for the other men to close in. Dillinger quickly realized what was happening and acted by instinct. He grabbed a pistol from his right trouser pocket and ran toward an alley.

Five shots were fired from the guns of three Bureau of Investigation agents—Charles B. Winstead, Clarence O. Hurt, and Herman E. Hollis. Three of the shots hit Dillinger, and he fell facedown on the pavement. At 10:50 P.M. on July 22, 1934, John Dillinger was pronounced dead in a little room in the Alexian Brothers Hospital. Agents Winstead, Hurt, and Hollis were each commended by J. Edgar Hoover for "fearlessness and courageous action." None of them ever said who actually killed Dillinger.

Eventually twenty-seven persons were convicted in federal courts on charges of harboring, and aiding and abetting John Dillinger and his cronies during their reign of terror. "Baby-Face Nelson" was fatally wounded on November 27, 1934, in a gun battle with Bureau of Investigation agents in which Special Agents Cowley and Hollis also were killed.

Gangsters of a different sort would return in the 1980s to control large sections of America's cities with impunity, but for the time being the events of that sultry July night in Chicago marked the beginning of the end of the first gangster era.

What Happened to Dillinger's Last Cache?

John Herbert Dillinger died in a hail of bullets and was buried in Crown Point Cemetery in Indianapolis, Indiana. He never had a chance to spend most of the money he had stolen. Most of the gangsters—with Al Capone a notable exception—did not. On the other hand, much of the loot stolen by the gangsters was never recovered.

The most notorious of the caches is the $200,000 in currency that Dillinger buried in the woods behind the Little Bohemia Lodge. Because he had so little time to carry out this task, it is thought that the hiding place is quite close to the lodge, but many attempts to find it—including one filmed for television—have failed to locate it.

The Little Bohemia is still there on Little Star Lake in

Manitowish Waters, Wisconsin, but it is a restaurant now and no longer a lodge. All but eleven of the original twenty-five acres have been sold. Manitowish Waters is a very small town in a very remote corner of Wisconsin that is really a long way from the beaten track. People come in the summer to fish, relax, eat sausages, and drink beer. During the rest of the year it's the kind of small town that most people just dream about.

Getting to Manitowish Waters from the outside world is not easy. I suppose that if it were, Manitowish Waters wouldn't be the kind of place where the "summer people" love to go. It's a long day's drive from either Minneapolis or Milwaukee—which are the sites of the nearest major airports—and a good half day from Eau Claire or Green Bay, Wisconsin.

From Minneapolis, take Interstate 94 east to Wisconsin exit 52. Follow Highway 29 east—bypassing Eau Claire—to Wausau. From Eau Claire simply take Highway 29. From Milwaukee take Interstate 94 west to Madison and continue to exit 108 on the Wisconsin River near Portage. Exit 108 will put you on Wisconsin Route 78, which is another freeway, headed due north. Stay on this freeway, which will become U.S. Highway 51 within a few miles. Stay in the direction of Stevens Point and Wausau. You'll reach Stevens Point in about an hour from Portage. It's the better part of a second hour to Wausau, but Highway 51 is a freeway the whole distance.

From Wausau it is still nearly a hundred miles to Manitowish Waters, and the Highway 51 freeway ends just fifteen miles north of Wausau, at the town of Merrill. From here Highway 51 simplifies into the same two-lane road that John Dillinger took when he headed toward Minneapolis on the morning of April 23, 1934.

The adrenaline was pumping from the shoot-out the night before. What thoughts went through his mind as he raced south through the Wisconsin pines on this exact same road with the sound of tommy guns still ringing in his ears? Was he thinking of Chicago and the lady in red? Did he still have thoughts of Evelyn Frechette, doing time for "harboring'' him? Was the gangster thinking of the $200,000? When was he thinking of going back?

And now we *are* going back to Manitowish Waters, back to the woods. A half hour out of Merrill you pass Muskellunge Lake and the U.S. Highway 2 turnoff to Rhinelander. It was from here that the Bureau of Investigation agents headed north in the fading light of that fateful April evening so long ago. Coming out of Rhinelander, they probably took Wisconsin Highway 47, which parallels U.S. Highway 51. At Woodruff, thirty miles north of the Highway 2 junction, Highways 47 and 51 come together. Highway 51 continues due north, and Highway 47 angles to the northwest. This was the route the Bureau of Investigation agents took, and it was almost certainly John Dillinger's escape route as he headed toward Minneapolis in a stolen car.

At Woodruff, turn left. Take Highway 47 out through the lake country, across Lac du Flambeau Indian Reservation. It is only twenty-two miles from Woodruff to Manitowish Waters. What must have been on Dillinger's mind? Could he have been thinking that the loot probably would be discovered at first light? Could he have imagined that the $200,000 would have remained undiscovered for so long?

As we drive through these woods with their beautiful lakes and tall trees casting long shadows, we wonder ''where.'' Could it have been somewhere out here, and *not* behind the Little Bohemia? There is a story that a man showed up in Manitowish Waters a few years ago claiming to be Homer Van Meter's cousin. He said that the loot had been stashed somewhere down around the town of Tomahawk, about sixty miles south on U.S. Highway 51. Does he know where?

At last the sign reads ''Entering Manitowish Waters.''

They say that the true treasure in a treasure hunt is more in the hunt than in the treasure. The treasure is elusive, but the joy of the hunt is with us always. The currency that Dillinger buried in 1934 may now be a damp, shapeless pulp, but the Little Bohemia is still here and if you ask, they will show you that the bullet holes from the fateful shoot-out are also still here. There are still sausages, still beer, and there will always be the beautiful lakes and tall trees casting long shadows.

Chapter 16

THE PADRE LARUE/DOC NOSS/VICTORIO PEAK TROVE

PLACE: *Victorio Peak, New Mexico*

TIME PERIOD: *1937–97*

The stories of mystery, suspicion, and superstition associated with lost treasure are often intertwined with stories of crimes and conspiracies. Few crimes in modern times sparked more suspicion and more conspiracy theories than the Watergate scandal of the 1970s. In 1972 a team of burglars with murky dossiers and Central Intelligence Agency connections were arrested as they tried to break into the Democratic National Committee offices at the Watergate building in Washington, D.C. It turned out that they were part of a covert effort on behalf of the reelection efforts of then president Richard Milhous Nixon. Nixon was in fact reelected, but in the meantime he became involved in efforts to cover up the sinister implications of the Watergate burglary. Historic, high-profile congressional hearings were held, and by 1974 he was compelled to resign to avoid impeachment.

Though the fact was overshadowed at the time, the hearings also brought to light another curious cover-up, that of a treasure trove on federal land in New Mexico. The story of this trove would have all the elements of "thriller" fiction: Spanish gold, a fake doctor, Nazi secret weapons, mysterious deaths, connections to secret military test sites, the Watergate affair, and even a member of the O. J. Simpson Dream Team. It was too complex and convoluted to make for believable fiction—it was *fact*.

In 1973, during the congressional Watergate hearings, conspirator and former White House counsel John Dean casually mentioned to the Senate committee that gadfly attorney—and later O. J. Simpson Dream Team member— F. Lee Bailey represented a mysterious cadre of treasure hunters who had enlisted the aid of the Nixon White House in the search for "a hundred tons of gold bullion" that were buried in a cave in New Mexico.

The thread of the story went back to 1937, when a group of people was deer hunting near Victorio Peak in the Hembrillo Basin, not far from the Trinity site, where the U.S. Army would detonate the first nuclear weapon only eight years later. One of the men was a mercurial con man named Milton "Doc" Noss, who had done time in Texas for passing himself off as a podiatrist. As the legend goes—and the legend is supported by papers he filed with the New Mexico State Land Office—Noss discovered the opening of a cave, lowered a rope, and climbed down sixty feet with a flashlight.

In the cave Noss first found the skeletons of twenty-seven people who'd been tied up and left to die in the cave. Upon a further search of the cave he found Spanish armor, guns, jewelry, saddles, swords, other equipment, and a box of letters dated prior to 1880. In one of the smaller subterranean chambers Noss found an old Wells Fargo chest, guns, swords, saddles, jewels, and a stack of leather pouches containing gold.

Noss also found 292 ingots of gold bullion. Assuming that each weighs 40 pounds, which is probable, and based on the typical size of a gold ingot from the Spanish period, this would be a total gross weight of 11,680 pounds. Assuming that the ingots would have a gold content of at least 60 percent, which is again typical, there would be 7,008 pounds of gold. At a price of $350 per ounce, the 292 ingots would have a value of $39.24 million, sufficient to get the attention of most treasure hunters. One variation on the story tells that he found 16,000 bars of gold "stacked like cordwood'' in the cavern. These would have a value of $2.15 billion, *more* than sufficient to get the attention of most treasure hunters.

While the national media were preoccupied with the Watergate affair and gave the gold bullion affair little mention, the ears of treasure hunters perked up. The stumbling block was that the cache was on military land and hence not accessible to the general public in those dark days at the depths of the cold war.

How Did It Get There?

While there is some disagreement over the details concerning the original source of the treasure, it is generally believed to be the early nineteenth-century Padre Felipe LaRue treasure, which was discovered and rehidden by Colonel A. J. Fountain in about 1880 and discussed in Henry I. James's 1953 book *The Curse of the San Andres.*

Felipe LaRue—also referred to as Philippe LaRue or Felipe LaRuz—was a French-born Franciscan missionary priest working in Mexico, who operated a mine known to legend throughout the Southwest as the Padre LaRue Mine. It is alleged to be south of Victorio Peak in the Organ Mountain country of New Mexico's Hembrillo Basin.

LaRue was the son of a wealthy French nobleman who joined the Franciscan order in a fit of rebellion against his family. The idealistic lad was forcibly sent to—or volunteered for—duty with the missions in Mexico. He apparently arrived in Chihuahua in about 1798, and there are various stories about him being a discipline problem and/or being particularly sympathetic to the plight of poor Indians. Either or both may be true and would fit the further details of the tale. Eventually he decided to leave Chihuahua and head north. There are several alternate explanations for why he undertook the trip. In the version that paints him as rebellious and idealistic, he stole some mules from either the archdiocese or the Spanish governor and headed north to found a mission, where he was free to do as he pleased without the administrative control of the church hierarchy.

In another version, which paints him as merely idealistic, he was running a small mission in Chihuahua when he met a cared for an old Spanish soldier with a deathbed yarn about a fabulous vein of gold just two days north of what is now El Paso, Texas. The good padre decided that his poor mission could use the gold to finance its good works, so he decided to go to find it. In any case, Padre LaRue made his way north into the Hembrillo Basin.

Located in what is now Dona Ana County, New Mexico, the basin is west of the rugged San Andres Mountains at the mouth of a vast, waterless plain that the explorer Francisco Vásquez de Coronado dubbed Jornada del Muerto— meaning the "Journey of Death"—when he traveled through here in 1540. Although they established outposts farther west in the Rio Grande Valley, few Spaniards had ever ventured back between 1540 and the time that LaRue arrived here. He brought with him several other monks and possibly two dozen Indians, although the Indians spoken of in the stories may have been living in the area when the monks arrived. They set up what amounted to a semipermanent settlement near a springs, built some buildings, and began irrigating for fields. If they had not known about the gold ahead of time, they soon discovered a vein of ore and started a mining and smelting operation, with the Indians as laborers.

A couple of years later, church authorities got wind of the mine and decided that the gold—or at least a share of it—belonged not to LaRue's little colony but to the church hierarchy. In another variation of this part of the story, it was the Spanish authorities who got wind of the mine and decided the gold belonged not to LaRue's little colony but to the Spanish colonial government of Mexico. Technically—if it was a Spanish soldier who revealed the location of the mine to LaRue—this may have been true.

When the priest heard that they were coming, he and his team hid the many gold ingots that had accumulated from the smelting activity—possibly in the Victorio Peak cave. To make a long story short, the Spanish arrived and found the hiding place but not the mine. They tortured Padre LaRue, the monks, and the Indians to death without finding out where the mine was and left empty-handed, probably planning to return for the stashed treasure. This may have never happened, because in 1810 the Mexicans revolted and threw the Spanish and their brutal army out of the land they'd ruled for three hundred years.

Jornada del Muerto remained relatively untouched through most of the nineteenth century, although Apache raiding parties tended to favor this area where they could be relatively secure from being hassled by U.S. Cavalry troops. The Mescalero Apache chief Victorio used the Hembrillo Basin as a base for raids on settlements in the Rio Grande Valley and elsewhere. Victorio Peak was named for the chief after a battle near the mountain on April 7, 1880, in which he routed a U.S. Army force. There is also a story that Victorio had found Padre LaRue's cache and was fighting to protect it. In addition, there is a story that Colonel Fountain found the Padre's treasure in 1880. This would explain the letters dated before 1880 and the Wells Fargo artifacts that Doc Noss reported. In any case, after 1880 the secret would be safe for another fifty-seven years.

A Doctor in the House

In November 1937 the secret known to Padre LaRue, and possibly to Victorio and/or Colonel Fountain, was stumbled upon by a deer-hunting Milton "Doc" Noss. As the story goes, Noss had climbed Victorio Peak to survey the terrain, but it started to rain, so he took shelter in a natural opening on top. In a small subterranean chamber there he moved a large boulder and found a shaft leading down into the mountain.

An alternative version of the story tells that a man named

Matt Gilmore, whose family grazed goats near Victorio Peak, had first shown the cave to Doc Noss in 1936. It was also mentioned in a White Sands Missile Range public affairs release that the U.S. Secret Service—the branch of the U.S. Treasury Department that investigates counterfeiting—had reported the possibility of gold or faked gold having been stashed in a cave by Doc Noss as part of a bunco scam. If the Secret Service did release such a story, it would certainly be the sort of tale that would be seized upon by conspiracy theorists as a smoke screen to denigrate a "legitimate" lost-treasure story. If they wanted to do such a thing, this is, of course, the kind of story they would tell. On the other hand, Doc Noss *was* a swindler and a con man, and there are rumors that he used to buy copper ingots and have them electroplated with gold to use in scams.

According to the variation of the legend that believes the treasure was really there, Doc Noss later returned to this place with his wife, Ova—also known as "Babe." While she stayed on the surface, the doctor climbed down several hundred feet into a large subterranean chamber with a stream running through it that he described to Ova as being "large enough to drive a train into."

Between 1937 and 1939 Doc and Ova Noss worked to remove the treasure, although Babe herself never actually went into the cave. Nor did Doc show her exactly where he rehid the treasure. He told her it was for her own good. He was afraid she might get hurt down there in the hole, and he was afraid she might be kidnapped and forced to tell the location. As Ova waited patiently, the doctor undertook the difficult task of lifting eighty-eight ingots from the cave. Because it was then illegal for Americans to possess gold bullion, Noss stashed the bars elsewhere. Only two other people, a pair of Mexican-American boys who briefly helped Noss, are known to have seen the cave, and no one knows where he cached the eighty-eight ingots. As to what happened to the two boys, again the stories vary. In one version, one of the boys died and the other disappeared. In another, one of them, named Benny Samaniego, was interviewed in 1963 and told of "stacks of gold bars, skeletons, armor, old guns, and statues.'' Another, Benny Sedillo, described the gold ingots as being extremely heavy and recalled being threatened by Noss should he reveal the location of the cavern.

In 1939 the removal of the loot ended when the doctor became a bit too greedy. In the children's folk tale about the golden goose, the boy became so impatient waiting for the golden eggs that he cut open the goose, killing it and stopping forever the flow of golden eggs. In 1939 Doc Noss was impatient with a narrow space in the entrance to the treasure chamber that was hard to squeeze through. In an effort to widen it using dynamite, he blew it shut and was never able to open it again.

With the shaft blown shut, Doc Noss apparently sought help in financing an effort to reopen it. It has never been satisfactorily explained why he tried to raise money for this effort when he had already taken so much gold out of the trove. Perhaps he planned to borrow it and never repay it. The doctor's trail becomes hard to follow in subsequent years, but it seems that he involved a large number of people in a major effort in 1941. During World War II he divorced Ova, moved to Arkansas, and remarried, although not necessarily in that order.

After the war the doctor took a job working in Alice, Texas for a man named Charley Ryan. During 1948 Noss apparently talked him into traveling with him to New Mexico "to check on the mine." Noss also talked Ryan into financing—of all things—a lead-mining operation on Victorio Peak.

Noss and Ryan arrived in New Mexico and rented a house in the town of Hatch, about forty-five miles north of Las Cruces in the Rio Grande Valley. However, they soon discovered that Doc's plucky ex-wife, Ova, was controlling the Victorio Peak site, and claiming to have a state permit that allowed her to prospect there. Noss allegedly told Ryan not to worry, and they filed claims on sites north of Victorio Peak that contained some lead-bearing ore. It wasn't too long before Ryan figured that he had been conned by the wiley Noss, and Ryan stopped the lead-mining operations in March 1949. He told Noss that he was leaving New Mexico and that he'd called the Dona Ana County sheriff to arrest Noss for fraud. Noss threatened to kill Ryan and pulled his gun, but Ryan was quicker.

In a shoot-out worthy of an Old West that was a half century gone, Ryan's second bullet brought Milton Noss's colorful life to an abrupt end. On May 26, after a two-day trial in Las Cruces, Charley Ryan was found not guilty based on grounds of self-defense.

Ova Noss would always claim that the doctor's death was murder. He had, she said, failed to produce gold bars he'd promised to Ryan. This was all dutifully reported in the media at the time. Everybody loves a murder where treasure is involved.

In Search of a Treasure Lost

The existence of—and the memories of—Samaniego and Sedillo notwithstanding, it is generally believed that with Doc Noss dead, there was no living person who knew the exact location of the shaft that led to the Victorio Peak treasure trove. Certainly Ova Noss did not know, for she would spend the rest of her life trying to rediscover a place to which she had been so near, yet so far. Indeed, the treasure discovered by Doc Noss would become the obsession of many over the latter half of the twentieth century.

Ova Noss had come back into the search in 1952. Since it was still illegal for U.S. citizens to possess gold bullion, any such gold was legally required to be redeemed for currency. Records show that in 1952, three years after the shooting, Ova Noss showed up at the Denver Mint inquiring whether "Milton Noss had made any deposits of gold at the mint from November 1937 to March 1949." The Denver Mint said "no," but mint officials added that Ova should report any gold that did turn up. Coincidentally, Denver Mint records *did* show that in 1939 a man named Charles Usher of Santa Monica, California, had brought in a gold bar that he had obtained secondhand from a man described as "Doc Noss from New Mexico."

By 1952, however, it had become very much harder to wander around Victorio Peak than it had been in 1937. The place in the middle of nowhere that nobody had wanted was now very popular. Before World War II, the Hembrillo Basin and the Jornada del Muerto to the north were about as far off the beaten track as one could get, but after the war the area took on an importance that few could have imagined in 1937. The U.S. Army owned most of these desolate badlands, and had used the Trinity Site at the head of Jornada del Muerto to test the first nuclear weapon, in July 1945.

After the war the army established the White Sands Missile Range to test a new generation of rockets that would be climbing from the New Mexico desert to the edge of outer space by 1950. Indeed, it was to White Sands in 1945 that the U.S. Army had brought Wernher von Braun and German scientists who had developed the V-2 rockets that were formerly Adolf Hitler's secret weapon but that would now form the foundation of the evolution of the Saturn rocket that would take Americans to the moon in 1969.

By 1950 the U.S. Army needed more space to test-fire their arsenal of captured Nazi V-2s and other weapons, and they began leasing or commandeering additional land. On July 13 the army entered into a lease agreement with a rancher named Roy Henderson for the land where Victorio Peak is located. It was here that the Gilmore family had grazed sheep, and it had, of course, been Matt Gilmore who said he had taken Doc Noss to Hembrillo Basin in 1936 to show him a cave.

On November 14, 1951, the U.S. government officially took the step that would legally preclude any further efforts to find Doc Noss's treasure trove. Public Land Order 703 was issued, withdrawing all White Sands Missile Range lands—now including Victorio Peak—from "prospecting, entry, location, and purchase under mining laws," thus reserving their use for military purposes.

While there is some doubt whether Ova Noss ever had

a state or federal prospecting permit for the area, Public
Land Order 703 apparently didn't stop her from continuing
to claim that she had such rights, nor from selling gold
mining stock. According to a White Sands Missile Range
public affairs release nearly forty years later, on January 5,
1953, "Ova Noss assigned 4 percent of her Victorio Peak
interests to J. L. Fowler of Enid, Oklahoma, who, in turn,
sold parts to at least ten persons in Oklahoma and Kansas.
In February 1955, a Mrs. Miller of Caldwell, Texas, wrote
to the Denver Mint concerning the purchase of gold mining
stock from Ova Noss."

As time went on, only the military had access to the area,
but stories about the gold still circulated around New Mexico, and the doctor's cache did not go undisturbed. In 1958
U.S. Air Force captain Leonard Fiege, based at Holloman
Air Force Base, adjacent to White Sands Missile Range,
was hunting in the Hembrillo Basin when he and three
companions stumbled across the entrance to a cave on Victorio Peak. He and a man named Berclett entered the cave
and found the subterranean chamber filled with gold bars
that Doc Noss had described. They explored it and then
caved in the entrance to prevent anyone from disturbing
their discovery.

For an inexplicable period of three years, apparently
nothing happened, but in 1961 Fiege went to his base commander in an effort to gain official access to his 1958 discovery. In May 1961 Major General John G. Shinkle, the
White Sands Missile Range base commander, received a
letter from the Holloman Air Force Base commander requesting that Captain Fiege be allowed to enter Victorio
Peak to "get evidence," which they would then provide to
the U.S. Treasury Department.

On May 29 Fiege met with General Shinkle to tell him
about the cave and to say that it would be "a simple
matter" to recover a few bars of gold. Shinkle said that the
request couldn't be granted without higher authority, so
Captain Fiege began a circuitous crawl through the chain
of command. He went to the Denver Mint, which contacted
the secretary of the army, who, on July 30, gave Shinkle

permission to allow the investigation of Victorio Peak. Because it was still illegal for U.S. citizens to own gold, the Secret Service, the enforcement branch of the Treasury Department, also was notified.

On August 5 a group including Fiege and Berclett, as well as General Shinkle, a number of White Sands Missile Range military police, and Special Agent L. E. Boggs of the Treasury Department went to Victorio Peak. They tried to reopen the caved-in entrance, but after five days of digging they were unable to. Shinkle ordered a halt, but on September 20 he told the Secret Service that he was going to give Fiege one more chance.

White Sands Missile Range records indicate that in late October two men named Bradley and Gray entered Hembrillo Basin and approached the workers. They demanded a piece of the action or, they said, they would tell Ova Noss. The White Sands Missile Range military police escorting Fiege ordered them to leave the missile range, since they were trespassing, but on November 1 the New Mexico State land commissioner notified the U.S. Army that Ova Noss was accusing them of mining her treasure. General Shinkle ordered all work to stop on November 3, and informed the secretary of the army and local officials that this had been done and that no gold had been found.

Attorneys for Ova Noss demanded that she have access to the cave, but were informed by White Sands Missile Range that the area was closed to personnel not associated with missile tests. Because there were numerous rumors that the U.S. Army itself was digging for the treasure, the army added that it officially regarded Fiege as a claimant to the treasure and that the service itself did not conduct any official or unofficial search at the peak for its own benefit.

About a year later the Gaddis Mining Company of Denver Colorado, under a $100,000 contract to the Denver Mint, and the Museum of New Mexico approached the U.S. Army at White Sands Missile Range seeking permission to enter and dig at Victorio Peak. Though it would not be revealed until the late 1970s, Ova Noss was working in cooperation with Gaddis but had wished that their association not be disclosed.

Because the state of New Mexico had sponsored the request, the army recognized the state's interest in a possible archaeological find. On June 20, 1963, a license was granted by the U.S. Army for a thirty-day exploration, although the period would later be extended through to September 17. This activity began with simultaneous archaeological, seismic, and gravity surveys. According to Chester Johnson, a museum representative on the project, a 4.5-inch rock bit was used to test the places indicated by survey that might be caverns. Drill holes varied from 18 to 175 feet in depth, depending on location, and about 80 holes were drilled. Gaddis also drove their own tunnel 218 feet into the side of Victorio Peak in an attempt to gain access to the lower regions, but this failed. The project is reported to have cost $250,000 and to have found nothing. White Sands Missile Range records show that the army filed a claim of $7,640.54 in October 1963 with the state for reimbursement for logistical support.

Despite $250,000 down the hole for no return, the Museum of New Mexico and Gaddis Mining continued to make inquiries about the site through the 1960s, and the publicity that surrounded the 1962 dig brought a number of other parties out of the woodwork. A mysterious pair who called themselves D. Richardson and R. Tyler showed up at White Sands Missile Range asking for permission to locate "lost treasure," and in 1969 the army was contacted by a Fort Worth law firm representing Violet Yancy, Doc Noss's second wife. She had paperwork claiming that the doctor had bequeathed her 76 percent of the stash. She said he left the remainder to Ova.

Ova Noss, meanwhile, appeared to be one of the few interested parties *not* to visit White Sands Missile Range in the 1960s, although she and her son, Harold Beckwith, were secretly involved with the Gaddis firm. Although this fact would not be officially revealed for many years, rumors to that effect were in circulation during the 1960s.

On June 2, 1973, during the Watergate hearings columnist Jack Anderson reported that F. Lee Bailey was involved in a consortium of never-named individuals who were trying to gain access to the treasure at White Sands Missile Range. According to Anderson's column, Bailey had a sample gold ingot assayed. This bar—whose provenance was not revealed—turned out to be 60 percent gold and 40 percent copper, which was consistent with the composition of ingots that dated from the Spanish period through the beginning of the nineteenth century. But this "recipe" also was consistent with the composition of jewelers' gold, which suggested to some that it was a hoax involving an ingot created recently from melted jewelry.

The Watergate connection came when Bailey discussed the gold with Attorney General John Mitchell, asking for his support in getting permission to gain access to White Sands Missile Range. Bailey reportedly said that if he could have a helicopter and permission to get into White Sands Missile Range, he'd have the gold in half an hour. Mitchell, in turn, shared the treasure tale with White House staffers H. R. Haldeman and John Dean. All three were intrigued, but all were otherwise occupied. Each was involved in the Watergate conspiracy—and all three eventually did jail time for their part in the scandal.

It was never demonstrated that there was a clear connection between the Victorio Peak affair and the Watergate conspirators, but because Dean mentioned the gold during his Senate Watergate investigation testimony, the gold became linked to Watergate.

Meanwhile, conspiracy theorists, who seemed to be everywhere during the Watergate years, were whispering that the U.S. Army had already retrieved much of the gold hidden in the cave. They pointed to the considerable road-building and heavy equipment work done during 1963 as evidence that the army was up to something at the site. The army continued to deny that it had any interest in digging for treasure.

As the names of the Watergate conspirators filled the papers daily, Bailey's mysterious consortium remained mysterious, although one of its members is believed to have been a man named Fred Drolte, who was wanted by federal authorities on an arms smuggling charge. Bailey succeeded in getting the state of New Mexico to approve a search by promising the state a 25 percent cut, but the U.S. Army had jurisdiction, and that left Bailey and the unnamed consortium at an impasse.

Meanwhile, equally unknown persons penetrated the perimeter of White Sands Missile Range and dynamited a side canyon east of Victorio Peak, destroying some Indian pictographs that were believed to identify the location of the treasure. After this the army set up a security post, staffed by military police, west of Victorio Peak.

The publicity that came of the Watergate connection and the army's reaction to the dynamite attack brought the Doc Noss gold into the headlines as never before, and White Sands Missile Range was deluged with inquiries and proposals from psychics, would-be treasure seekers, and "friends" of Doc Noss, each of whom claimed to be *the* executor of the doctor's final wishes.

By 1975 the possession of gold by U.S. citizens had been legalized for the first time since 1934, and on March 5, 1975, a federal judge in Albuquerque ruled that the army had the right to restrict access to Victorio Peak *but* that eventually it would have to make arrangements for a search. The U.S. Army took the official position that it wanted the affair put to bed once and for all, and the only way to do that was to search for the gold. The dilemma the army was in was fairly straightforward. It did not want to go into the gold-mining business itself, but neither could it pick or choose among the claimants. To let them all in simultaneously would have resulted in a shoot-out and/or a disaster of unimaginable proportions.

Finally, White Sands Missile Range accepted a proposal from F. Lee Bailey, who had arranged with Norman Scott, a Florida-based, internationally known treasure hunter, to lead an expedition under the banner of a consortium of six interested parties dubbed "Expeditions Unlimited." On March 19, 1977, the search was on for the first time since the Gaddis Mining Company and the Museum of New

Mexico pulled out in 1963. The Expeditions Unlimited people were there in force for what was called Operation Goldfinder, but they were considerably outnumbered by the worldwide print media and television vans. Even Dan Rather was on hand to tape a segment for *60 Minutes*.

As in 1963, the only gold that was found was discovered by those renting equipment, selling refreshments, or providing motel rooms for interested parties. Stanford Research Institute brought sophisticated ground radar in from California, and this confirmed the existence of vast subterranean chambers, but still, no gold or artifacts were retrieved. There were a number of suggested reasons for this. While ground radar readings showed the underground caverns, it also showed several hundred feet of debris filling the entrance. With this in mind, it was easy to argue that the two weeks allowed for Operation Goldfinder were too short.

It has also been said that Expeditions International failed because of its lack of knowledge of Victorio Peak, although Gaddis Mining Company also had failed, and it had the benefit of its association with Ova Noss, who allegedly had the best information about the site.

However, Ova Noss was not included in the Expeditions Unlimited consortium, and she died in 1979 with Doc's gold still in its hiding place—or still believing the doctor's greatest scam. Eight years after her death, Ova's grandson, Terry Delonas, announced the beginning of another search effort, which would be called the Victorio Peak Project. It would be undertaken by another consortium—this time including Noss relatives—and would be called the Ova Noss Family Partnership.

Norman Scott came back into the picture to join forces with Terry Delonas as Ova Noss Family Partnership project manager, and in 1989 they went to the Department of the Army for permission to get onto White Sands Missile Range. The base commander, Major General Thomas Jones, said that the Ova Noss Family Partnership would be given access to Victorio Peak on the condition that the treasure hunters would stay out of the way of missile firings and U.S. Air Force gunnery range activities and that they would have to reimburse the army for any support activities they would provide. The Defense Authorization Act of 1990 allowed direct reimbursement to the army and White Sands Missile Range, and an escrow account, was set up. The Ova Noss Family Partnership would pay into this account, and expenses would then be deducted and paid to White Sands Missile Range.

On January 8, 1990, so they could begin an environmental and engineering survey of Victorio Peak, the Ova Noss Family Partnership paid White Sands Missile Range $54,000 for such services as security at the peak by the military police and road grading. Lambert Dolphin, the geophysicist who had been involved with Operation Goldfinder, returned to do ground radar work, and Les Smith, who had worked with Gaddis Mining Company in 1963, also was on hand.

On June 14 the Ova Noss Family Partnership handed White Sands Missile Range an environmental assessment for the search prepared by EcoPlan Incorporated of Albuquerque that included an archaeological overview by Human Systems Research of Mesilla, New Mexico. In short, the Ova Noss Family Partnership proposed to "improve the roads so drilling equipment can be put on the peak, locate and define the treasure cavern by drilling bore holes and using ground sensing radar, get to the cavern by tunneling or boring, explore the cavern for treasure and cultural antiquities, document and remove anything found, close all entrances to the peak, and restore the landscape by approved reclamation methods."

When the cavern was located, the Ova Noss Family Partnership hoped to use one of seven existing holes to reach the cavern with a Roadheader tunneling machine, which grinds itself into the rock using circulating rotary heads, or through the classic "drill and blast" method of hard-rock tunneling. If this was not possible, they planned to bore a hole straight through the limestone by erecting a 140-foot rig and drilling a 42-inch hole. The boring operation would run 24 hours a day with an estimated progress of eight to

16 feet per day. The Ova Noss Family Partnership estimated that it would take 20 to 50 days to penetrate 400 feet into Victorio Peak. When the cavern would be reached, a 36-inch steel sleeve would be inserted into the hole to allow access to the subterranean chamber. On completion of the operation, the sleeve would be welded shut and covered or filled with dirt.

In May 1990, Dolphin used a new ground-penetrating radar, described as being 20 times more powerful than the one used in 1977, to image the peak's interior. He identified a subterranean chamber 200 feet below the old 218-foot Gaddis tunnel that was completed in 1963, which was consistent with recollections of Doc Noss having said that he went 300 to 400 feet into the peak. As Dolphin described it technically, this area was below the limestone reef material in the peak in a region of soft shale that probably eroded out, leaving a chamber with crumbling walls and a very hard ceiling. He believed that Noss may have entered the peak on top and worked his way down to the subterranean chamber where the gold was located.

On April 4, 1991, a licensing agreement was signed by Terry Delonas for the Ova Noss Family Partnership, and by Brigadier General Ronald Hite (as commanding general of White Sands Missile Range) for the Department of the Army. The agreement gave the Ova Noss Family Partnership one year to conduct their exploration within a one-mile radius of Victorio Peak. The Ova Noss Family Partnership would be allowed to keep the ''treasure,'' while ''all archaeological resources, antiquities, or items of historical or cultural interest . . . whenever located on White Sands Missile Range shall remain the property of the government'' because artifacts must be dealt with by White Sands Missile Range according to federal law. It was noted that ''archaeological resources, antiquities, or items of historical or cultural interest'' included baskets, pottery, rock carvings, arrowheads, and jewelry, while ''treasure'' included ''coins, gold or silver bullion, precious metals (not including metals with radioactive value), precious cut and uncut gems (not including jewelry or gems set in valuable ornaments), unset and loose jewels, and related valuables.''

To control the site and prevent any possible fraud, the Ova Noss Family Partnership people had to consent ''to a thorough search of their persons, vehicles, equipment, and any other personal property by government security personnel.''

By the spring of 1996 a tunnel had been drilled at the base of the reef that extended more than 1,000 horizontal feet. In the course of excavation, there has been very significant correlation between fissures and void pockets encountered and the location of seismic anomalies. In other words, the ground radar studies had painted an accurate picture of where the subterranean chambers were.

However, on March 15, 1996, the U.S. Army evicted the Ova Noss Family Partnership from White Sands Missile Range. The reason, as stated by the U.S. Army, was that the Ova Noss Family Partnership had stopped paying into the escrow account. For its part, the Ova Noss Family Partnership maintained that it had already paid more than $800,000 over four years, while White Sands Missile Range had never satisfactorily itemized its expenses. Army deputy assistant secretary Paul Johnson replied that the billing had been ''fair and reasonable.''

The Ova Noss Family Partnership filed suit on April 4, 1997, against the army and White Sands Missile Range in the Court of Federal Claims, seeking damages in excess of $600,000 and hiring as its attorney William Casselman II, who had served as deputy special assistant to President Nixon from 1969 to 1971 and as counsel to President Ford from 1974 to 1975.

Meanwhile, the Ova Noss Family Partnership also claimed that it had been forced to abandon $100,000 worth of supplies and equipment at the Victorio Peak site, and on June 25, 1997, the Department of Justice informed the Ova Noss Family Partnership counsel that White Sands Missile Range intended to sell or destroy supplies and equipment, and add to the amounts White Sands Missile Range claimed it was owed. The Ova Noss Family Partnership then offered to remove the supplies and equipment, including explosives, at a cost of only $2,000. When this offer was refused and further negotiations broke down, the Ova Noss Family Partnership countersued the army on July 8. A compromise was reached in which the Ova Noss Family Partnership's property at Victorio Peak would not be sold or destroyed, but they would pay the army $2,603 to remove explosives and a leaking oil drum from the peak.

And so it goes. As the Ova Noss Family Partnership and White Sands Missile Range ran up legal bills that dwarfed any sum that Doc Noss ever put in his pocket during his lifetime, Victorio Peak stood as silent witness to events that spanned two centuries—the violent deaths of Padre Felipe LaRue and Doc Noss, and the greed of many who had followed their trail into the Jornada del Muerto.

Making a House Call

Following the trail of Padre LaRue and Doc Noss to Victorio Peak is a relatively easy chore. It still is in the middle of the nowhere, but the roads are good. Fly to El Paso, Texas, and take Interstate 10 west—actually it runs north from El Paso, but the signs call it "west"—along the Rio Grande to Las Cruces, New Mexico. Or fly directly to Las Cruces. Here you can visit the courtroom where Charley Ryan was acquitted of murdering Doc Noss.

From Las Cruces, U.S. Highway 70 east is a four-lane that will take you across the Organ Mountains, which rise steeply from the Rio Grande Valley. From 5,719-foot San Augustin Pass you can look down into the Hembrillo Basin. Off to your left, and stretching for as far as the eye can see, is the Jornada del Muerto, and if the name confused you on first reading, one look at the place will shed all doubts about why old Francisco Vásquez de Coronado named it thus. Across the Hembrillo Basin are the San Andres Mountains, and beyond them is White Sands National Monument.

Just about everything you see looking east from San Augustin Pass—except White Sands National Monument—is of White Sand Missile Range or part of the Holloman Air Force Base gunnery range. Victorio Peak sits there in White Sands Missile Range, immediately adjacent to the "Yonder Area," a sort of Area 51 of the Holloman Air Force Base range, subject to bombing attacks or missile firings. On the eastern side of the peak, in a rock outcropping, is a cross that is about four feet high and three feet wide. There are many legends dealing with this cross. Some folks will tell you that it is the "X" that marks the spot, but geologists that the horizontal bar is formed by the action of acidic water, much like water dissolves limestone to form cave decorations, while the vertical stroke is caused by water running down the rock in the same path for centuries. Nearby is a black crevice that some people say is soot from Padre LaRue's smelter.

If you could get close enough—and you probably can't—you would see the bulldozer trails and the equipment left from the Gaddis operation in 1963, Operation Goldfinder in 1977, and the Ova Noss Family Partnership activities of the 1990s. Somewhere up on Victorio Peak there may be a hundred tons of gold—or even 320 tons, if the 16,000-gold-ingot story is true. But you'll never know. The U.S. Army will never let you get close enough.

The gold may be there, and it may not be. Maybe it never was. It may remain hidden, as much in a cloak of mystery as in rock and gravel. What can be said for certain is that the death of Doc Noss opened the door to speculation, just as it closed off any knowledge of the true location of the treasure. Indeed, there may be no treasure, or there may be several, if one counts the original site, plus the place or places where Doc Noss hid his eighty-eight ingots.

The speculation has spawned a myriad of tales, and many of those were ultimately documented in press releases issued between 1990 and 1992 by Jim Eckles of the U.S. Army's White Sands Missile Range Public Affairs Office.

There are the numerous stories about the doctor's various scams. There are even rumors that the treasure has already been secretly extracted by the U.S. Army. As Ova Noss

Family Partnership attorney William Casselman said: "I believe that the Noss treasure exists or existed. I can't speculate as to whether it's still in the peak or not."

Maybe Doc Noss is laughing in his grave at having duped three generations of treasure hunters with a fantastically convincing hoax, or maybe the fabled billions are still there.

There are so many stories being told in the barrooms and back rooms—from Las Cruces to Tularosa, and on up to Carrizozo and San Antonio on the Rio Grande (where there is a business card with a bat on it pinned to a barroom ceiling)—that it is impossible to tell fact from fancy.

But this is the way it is with tales of lost, buried, or stolen treasure. Any and all of the stories *could* be true.

Postscript

TAKING IT TO THE FIELD

.

As we said in the Introduction, this book is about the search as much as it is about the treasure. There are stories of treasure and of the searchers who have looked for it and who have almost found it. There also have been actual directions to the vicinity of the place where it is hidden. This postscript is for those readers who have decided to follow that mysterious lure of the shiny metal and go into the field to stand in the same arroyo as the Dutchman, or to smell the same cold, salty air as Captain Kidd.

This is where you cross the line from imagining the sting of the Atlantic gale or desert scorpion and actually feeling them. Herein lie the dangers of embracing reality and chasing the ''dogs of the mist'' through real mist. As you begin this adventure, you should know that there are no guarantees of ultimate success, only guarantees of failure without proper planning. You should begin with the expectation that your search will be as much a search for adventure as for treasure.

As you have seen in reading the tales we have chosen to present, legends of lost, hidden, or buried treasure are typically unclear or ambiguous about specific locations. It is understandable that the more specific the directions to the site, the more likely the treasure has already been found.

In some cases, legends are based on place names that may have been used in the eighteenth or nineteenth century but that are no longer current.

You should start by narrowing things down as much as possible, and to do so, we suggest that you get your hands on a gas station or auto club road map or highway atlas of the state where the site is located. Nearly every town, road, mountain range and river mentioned as a landmark in this book will be on such a map or atlas. By following the directions in this book and your road map, you should be able to mark the general location of the site within a specific county. When you have done this, narrow your geographic scope with an even more detailed map.

The U.S. Geological Survey (USGS) publishes highly detailed 1:24,000-scale topographic maps and more general 1:100,000-scale maps of the entire United States. U.S. Geological Survey topographic, or "topo" maps, are incredibly detailed and among the best maps published anywhere in the world. Your road map may show towns with populations of fewer than fifty, but a topographical map will show individual buildings within the town, windmills on the edge of town, and the contours of small hills and gullies, as well as dry streambeds and ponds the size of a large living room and dirt roads you might miss driving past.

To give you an idea of how detailed these maps are, the state of Arizona takes up a page and a half in a typical highway atlas. This map shows all paved and many unpaved roads in perfect clarity, and it shows towns from Phoenix down to those with populations of fewer than fifty. In this map the state is about fourteen inches wide. If one used a set of U.S. Geological Survey 1:24,000 maps to form a map of Arizona, the state would be more than eighty *feet* wide!

It is really counterproductive to attempt any actual fieldwork without a topographical map, and you should keep your topographical map with you at all times while you are in the field. They are inexpensive, yet they are the single most important tool you can have. Spend the extra money and buy maps of adjacent areas if there is *any* chance you will be working in that area, or that you will have to drive or hike through an adjacent area to get from a main road to your goal.

You should begin by requesting the *Index to Topographic and Other Map Coverage* for the specific state or states, and such indices are available, free, from the US Geological Survey. They are a guide to all the topographical maps available for the state, and they will help you pinpoint the specific map or maps you need. These, in turn, may be purchased for a nominal fee from the regional U.S. Geological Survey center in your area (consult your white pages under the U.S. Government section), or by contacting the U.S. Geological Survey's Map Distribution/Map Sales office at Building 810 in Denver, Colorado. You may phone (800) 872-6277 for more information.

While the topographical map is essential, there is other research work to be done that is extremely useful. In this book, we have given many of the particulars about the legend or legends surrounding each treasure. This may have been enough to get you interested and to get you started, but many of these stories have been the subjects of entire books, or even entire shelves of books. You should, at the very least, go to your library and/or bookstore and thumb through a few of these. In short, you should know as much as possible about the circumstances behind the treasures you're seeking. When you are in the field, standing in the same arroyo as the Dutchman, or smelling the same cold, salty air as Captain Kidd, you will want to know as much as there is to know.

It is also useful to know as much as you can about the history and geography of the region into which you will be traveling. Your library and/or bookstore will have guidebooks, and all the states have tourist bureaus that will be happy to supply you with maps and many lovely brochures. Another useful library pursuit is to immerse yourself in the historic period when the treasure was hidden or when the mines were in operation. All historic events occur in the context of time as well as place. If you are going to be looking for pirate treasure, read a good book about the pirates and their times. If your quarry was hidden during the

Civil War, read about Civil War battles and campaigns that took place in the area.

If the treasure was hidden by a specific person such as Captain Kidd or Jesse James, reading a biography of that person will help give you some background information that may be vital later in your search. Gold-mining activity in a specific area typically was confined to a short time span, and histories of many of these "booms" have been written and are available in bookstores or libraries. Back issues of regional newspapers are also valuable and can be used to clarify specific minutia. In some cases entire books have been written about specific treasures.

Just as your road map was useful in orienting you to a general area or section of a specific state, it will also show you how to drive there. If you are planning to fly, the nearest airport also will be shown, and "nearest airports" are mentioned in this book as well. Once you arrive, continue your research work by going to a local library and/or bookstore. As noted above, you should know as much as possible about the circumstances behind the treasures you're seeking, and no matter how good your library was at home, local libraries are always the best place to flesh out your basic knowledge of an area and its history. Most libraries have a local history section, and many libraries and county historical museums are staffed by knowledgeable people who love to answer questions about local history and local lore. They may know—or may be able to refer you to people who know—more about a specific event or treasure than has ever been written in a book.

Going to museums and/or archives near the site is also useful, whether it be the state or local museum and/or archive. It would not be unusual to find a person or persons at such an institution who would have a great deal of unpublished information about the treasure you seek. As with maps, the closer you focus, the better the information and the greater the detail. Often the most comprehensive information will be in the county seat, or in the largest town in the area, which may be across the county, or even across the state, line. Another useful stop in the county seat will be at the county land office or the county recorder's office. This will be helpful if a treasure is associated with land that was once owned by a specific individual, or if there is anything about a mining claim in the area.

Because historical events happen in the context of time as well as place, it is often useful to look in back issues of the local or county newspaper. This will reveal helpful details and information to narrow down or pinpoint the date of an event you may have read about, or that exist in the hazy memory of an old-timer with whom you may have spoken. It is also always amazing to see how much information that was known—and printed in the papers—is utterly forgotten in all subsequent published accounts!

Finding the treasure once you've reached what you think is the site takes a little intuition and a lot of patience and luck. Here you're on your own. You have to put yourself in the place of the person who buried it, and ask "Where would *I* have put it?"

In the Rockies or the Sierra Nevada, placer gold can be found the old-fashioned way—with a gold pan. You take a pan of gravel from a shallow place in the stream and swirl the water in it, allowing the gravel to gradually wash out. The heavier gold will work its way to the bottom and will be clearly visible when most of the gravel is gone.

When you have fine-tuned your search from state to county to locality, and have pinpointed it to a specific section of the most detailed U.S. Geological Survey topographical map, the treasure still may not be obvious. Many treasure hunters now use metal detectors. These tools have revolutionized the search for lost and buried treasure. They originated a half century ago as a military tool to find buried land mines, and were eventually adapted for civilian use in searching for buried metallic objects such as coins and artifacts.

Modern metal detectors are quite rugged and sophisticated instruments. They weigh between two and five pounds and can be operated easily with one hand. Some can be adapted for mounting to your belt. Depending on type, metal detectors can be used to find metallic objects buried as deep as twelve inches or more. They also can be adjusted to discriminate among objects. For example, many modern detectors can be programmed to reject aluminum can pull tabs and bottle caps while reporting coins. Many metal detectors are waterproof, and some are designed for use underwater.

Metal detectors are widely available, with the average price for a good metal detector being between $400 and $600. Of course, there are both cheaper and more advanced models. As with purchasing any other tool or piece of equipment, you should investigate the detectors with the features you need that are available in your price range, and do some comparison shopping. After you have compared and selected a metal detector—and before going into the field—practice with it in a controlled situation. Start with something as simple as having a friend bury some pocket change in your backyard. The next step would be to bury a variety of objects so you could get the feel for how your detector reacts to bottle caps, nails, and larger metal objects.

A good publication to read before selecting a metal detector is *Metal Detector Information,* which is published by Tesoro Electronics, a leading maker of metal detectors. It contains information about Tesoro metal detectors, of course, but also a good deal of useful information about the selection and use of metal detectors in general, and a list of dealers throughout the United States who sell metal detectors and related equipment. For more information contact Tesoro Electronics, Inc., at 715 White Spar Road in Prescott, Arizona 86301. Their telephone number is (520) 771-2646.

The actual process of digging will be determined by the lay of the land and many other factors that will be obvious when you get to the site. Not all "buried treasures" are actually buried. Some may be hidden elsewhere, such as in a building; and others may be in the open and easy to see if you know where to look, or in a place that is so remote that no one has been there in a hundred years. It may be disguised as something else.

In the case of those that *are* buried, many will have been

buried for more than a century. Clues have probably shifted or are gone. In the case of pirate treasure on shorelines, winds, tides, and hurricanes will have changed major features—perhaps several times over. In the three hundred years since Captain Kidd's time, an island may have been eroded and washed away, while another may have formed nearby. If the cache was on the former island, it will now be at the bottom of the sea under tons of sand and gravel, and searching the "new" island will be as pointless as digging in your neighbor's yard. Floods and landslides may have buried the treasure deeper or even pushed it to a different place. As indicated above, it is always good to consult local sources, whether they be historic records, coastal charts, or old-timers with long memories.

Dangers in the Field

When you have passed the last gas station at the edge of the nearest town and have pointed your rented car in the direction of the treasure, you have entered the real world of that site. It has passed from being an idea described on paper in this book or another, beyond the descriptions of an old-timer in a tavern or library. The real world is dangerous. The real world is not safe. Remember that there are people who have died for many of these treasures, either looking for them or trying to keep them from being taken or found. At this point you should have done everything you can to protect yourself from danger. Many of the sites listed in this book are in wilderness areas where there are serious hazards. Fieldwork can be dangerous. If you are used to the dangers of an urban environment, you must accustom yourself to an environment with none of those dangers, but with a vast palette of perils that must be recognized and prepared for.

If the field into which you are going is in the wilderness, use utmost caution when traveling there. When out of the sight of paved roads and familiar landmarks (on foot or in a vehicle), always carry your detailed topographic map and compass. Also carry adequate food and water. In areas where specifically required, stay on marked trails and/or roads.

When hiking in the wilderness, or when driving on unpaved roads or off-road areas, always carry a watch and allow plenty of time for your trip. Consider distance, elevation, weight being carried, physical condition (of yourself, your traveling companions, and your vehicle), weather, and hours of daylight. Check the latest weather forecast, and be prepared for sudden changes in weather. Even in summer, cool, wet conditions, if accompanied by winds, can cause hypothermia. On warm, sunny days, even if it is not particularly "hot," people can be subject to heat exhaustion.

If you are going into the wilderness in search of a treasure site, whether it is in this book, or something you identified from another source, consider the time of year when you are making the trip. It can make a big difference. Climate conditions that are uncomfortable in a populated area may turn deadly in the wilderness. Simply put, there are certain times of year when expeditions into wilderness areas should not be attempted. Hiking in snow-covered mountains, especially the Cascades, Rockies, and Sierra Nevada, should not be attempted in winter. Extensive desert excursions in the summer, such as into California's Death Valley and the deserts of Arizona or New Mexico, where temperatures can stay well above a hundred degrees from dawn to dusk, should never be attempted.

When you turn off a paved road, or if you are driving on an especially remote paved road, always start your drive with a *full tank of gas* and turn back when your gas gauge has reached the "half full" mark. Also, carry both a properly inflated spare tire and a flashlight. Make sure you have a jack in the vehicle, and make sure everyone in the vehicle knows how to use it. In the winter, always carry chains if there is even the remotest possibility of snow or ice.

When exploring coastal areas always be aware of waves, undertows, and tides. Each year dozens of people are stranded by incoming tides when taking dangerous chances or not paying attention. Whether you are on the rocky coast of Maine, or the dunes of offshore islands of New Jersey or North Carolina, be vigilant, especially in stormy weather.

Also take care when digging or working with loose rock, or in caves and crevices. A small push on a seemingly solid rock could create a landslide that could kill you or trap you. If you are traveling alone it could be days before you are found. Even if you are traveling in a group, it could take a dangerous length of time before your companions can summon help.

In the hills and mountains of the West one is likely to come across an abandoned mine shaft, and it is certainly tempting to go in and explore it. We strenuously advise you to resist such a temptation. Just don't do it. Many years of inattention, water seepage, the effects of freezing and thawing, and possible seismic activity have rendered virtually every abandoned mine in the country prone to imminent collapse, cave-in, or flooding.

It is best to observe mine shafts from the entrance and speculate about caches left outside. In fact, there probably was none. The mine was abandoned for a reason. Whoever sank that shaft in the first place, walked away because it played out. There is almost certainly nothing of value inside. There is certainly nothing inside that is worth your life.

If you come across a naturally occurring cave or cavern, use extreme caution if you think about entering it. Naturally occurring caves may be less fragile than mine shafts, but they, too, can experience water seepage, the effects of freezing and thawing, and can be susceptible to seismic activity. They, too, can come crashing in on top of you. Beware of loose, fallen, or falling rock, and do not enter a cave if there is potential danger from such rock.

It is also strongly suggested that you stay away from caves if you have claustrophobia or difficulty with directions and navigation. In caves and caverns *always* carry an *extra* flashlight and *two* sets of extra sets of batteries. Also beware of predators, which range from poisonous insects and reptiles to bears. Bat caves, which are common in Texas and the Southwest, are a hazard not for the bats themselves, which are almost certainly harmless, but for deadly disease germs often present in bat guano, which litters the floor of bat caves. If there is any possibility of danger, just say no. Stay out of the cave. Do you really want to be walking through bat guano, with more of it raining on your head from above?

The little creatures of field and forest can be more dangerous than they appear, and should be regarded with an appreciation for the hazards they present. Even insects, especially ticks carrying Lyme disease or Rocky Mountain spotted fever, can be dangerous. Always carry insect repellent.

Especially in the desert and the bayous of the Gulf Coast, be wary of poisonous snakes, gila monsters, scorpions, and tarantulas. In the case of scorpions, it has been said that the smaller they are, the more deadly they are.

Larger animals, such as mountain lions and wild pigs, are particularly dangerous and can strike without warning. In Minnesota, Montana, and the Upper Peninsula of Michigan, wolves have been making a comeback to areas from which they were once eradicated, and they are particularly vicious if you tangle with them.

In the northern Rockies of Idaho, Montana, and Wyoming you may encounter grizzly bears, which are especially aggressive and dangerous. Respecting bears and learning proper behavior in their territory will help, so that if you encounter a bear, neither of you will suffer needlessly from the experience. Most bears tend to avoid people. Even in the national parks of the Rockies and the West, and in Alaska, surprisingly few people even see bears, though they are plentiful. If you are in grizzly country, make your presence known, especially where the terrain or vegetation makes it hard to see. Bears will avoid you if they can, and they can if they know you're coming. Always let bears know you are there. Make noise, sing, talk loudly, or tie a bell to your pack. If possible, travel with a group. Groups are noisier and easier for bears to detect. Avoid thick brush.

If you can't, try to walk with the wind at your back so your scent will warn bears of your presence. Contrary to popular belief, bears can see almost as well as people, but they trust their noses much more than their eyes or ears.

Attacks are rare, and chances are, you are not in danger. A standing bear is usually curious, not threatening. Most bears are interested only in protecting food, cubs, or their territory. If they see you as not being a threat, they will move on. Remember to let the bear know you are human. Talk to the bear in a normal voice and help the bear recognize you. If a bear cannot tell what you are, it may come closer or stand on its hind legs to get a better look or smell. You may try to back away slowly and diagonally, but if the bear follows, don't run, because you can't outrun a bear. They have been clocked at speeds of up to thirty-five miles per hour, and like dogs, they will chase fleeing animals. Bears often make bluff charges, sometimes to within ten feet of their adversary, without making contact. Continue waving your arms and talking to the bear. If the bear gets too close, raise your voice, bang pots and pans, or use noisemakers. However, never imitate bear sounds or make a high-pitched squeal.

If a grizzly bear actually touches you, fall to the ground and play dead. Lie flat on your stomach, or curl up in a ball with your hands behind your neck. Typically a brown bear will break off its attack once it feels the threat has been eliminated. Remain motionless for as long as possible. If you move, a brown bear may return and renew its attack, and you must again play dead. However, if you are attacked by a black bear, fight back vigorously.

If you are inexperienced with firearms in emergency situations, you are more likely to be injured by a gun than by a large mammal such as a mountain lion or a bear, and it is illegal to carry firearms in most national and state parks. Even heavy handguns, such as a .44 Magnum, may be inadequate in emergency situations, especially in untrained hands. A .300 Magnum rifle or a twelve-gauge shotgun with rifled slugs are appropriate weapons if you have to shoot a bear, but killing bears, except with a proper hunting license—and none is available for grizzlies—or in cases of provable self-defense, is illegal and vigorously prosecuted. Defensive aerosol sprays that contain capsicum (red pepper extract) have become popular since the 1980s, and indeed have been used with some success for protection against large mammals such as bears. These sprays may be effective at a range of six to eight yards. However, they are not foolproof and shouldn't be used as a substitute for common sense. If they are discharged upwind or in a vehicle, they can disable the user.

Leave nothing to chance. Always inquire locally about specific predators, hazards, and road conditions. Always pay attention to changes in tides and weather. Take full responsibility for your own physical safety and that of your traveling companions.

Do nothing reckless or dangerous, or infringe on the property rights of others. Carry water, wear adequate footwear, and do not deliberately put yourself in danger. The odds of incurring physical injury in potentially dangerous situations are always much greater than the odds of finding buried treasure anywhere.

Recovering Buried Treasure

Everyone knows how to dig. Most of us have gone into our backyard with a shovel to turn a bit of soil. We know how it feels to push the shovel in and lift a shovelful of dirt. However, when it is in your neighbor's backyard that you lift that shovelful of dirt, you are trespassing. An innocent act becomes a crime. So it is with digging for buried treasure.

When Captain Kidd made landfall on a deserted Block Island beach or a godforsaken strip of Jersey shore three hundred years ago, it is likely that this ground was owned by no one, save for a deed on file in London granting it to the duke of York or someone like him who would never actually see or set foot on the ground. When the Dutchman filed his claims, the land on which the claim was filed did not belong legally to anyone. Of course, to the Pima or Apache who were there earlier, the concept of property rights was that land was just there, as it had been and always would be, and therefore could belong to nobody. However, today, all the land in the United States belongs to *somebody*. Even the vast, empty spaces in the West belong to the Department of the Interior's Bureau of Land Management. Technically it belongs to all of us, but the Bureau of Land Management writes the rules on who can dig, and for what.

With this caveat, a search for treasure is merely a stroll or a hike until you turn the first shovelful of topsoil. In most open areas, especially in the West, your ability to come and go is fairly unrestricted, but your ability to dig and remove property is restricted. On private land, whether it is a million-acre ranch in Montana or in your neighbor's yard, you can't dig or take things without permission. Thus, before you dig, you should have done everything you can to protect yourself from danger and to keep from infringing on the safety or property rights of others. You are responsible for determining the ownership of the land onto which you will be traveling—and into which you'll be digging—in search of the treasure.

The full responsibility for determining the ownership of the land is on your shoulders. So is the responsibility for understanding whatever restrictions there may be on various activities undertaken on that land, and for making necessary arrangements with the owner for access to nonpublic land. There is no such thing as starting to dig and waiting to see whether anyone comes out to stop you. If you let it go that far, you could find yourself explaining your treasure hunt to an unsympathetic judge, or to an angry cowboy with a rifle trained at your head.

Always make necessary arrangements with the owner for access to nonpublic land. Do not cross fences without permission. Trespassing is a crime not taken lightly in most rural areas.

In the West, where there may not be a neat fence on the

property line, it may be hard to determine where public land ends and private land begins. A site that you suppose to be on public land—to which access is not restricted—may actually be on private or Native American land that may not be posted. Some sites are on military bombing ranges where access is strictly forbidden and extremely dangerous.

Beyond the notion of trespassing is the notion of taking property away with you. One of the most important questions to consider in the search for buried or hidden treasure is your legal right to take possession of it and keep it as your own property. Military reservations and ranges excepted, you may travel freely in most federal and state public lands. You may follow maps and look for and at anything you wish. However, in most cases you may not dig for or remove natural features or artifacts without permission in the form of a permit. While laws concerning the recovery of sunken treasure found beneath international waters in the world's oceans are quite liberal, laws governing treasure troves on land or in coastal waterways can be quite restrictive.

Generally there are three types of land ownership in the United States: government-owned, privately owned, and foreign-government-owned. The latter includes embassies and consulates of foreign countries, which are legally considered to be the "soil" of the country in question. These are mostly very small. They include single buildings or small compounds, such as the embassies in Washington D.C., or office buildings or even office suites, such as consulates in cities such as New York and San Francisco, or the U.N. missions in New York City. Because of their small size, the unlikeliness of treasure on their premises, and the fact that they are not generally open to the public, we have chosen not to cover them.

If you are planning to dig—or even walk—on private land, you need to have the permission of the private-land owner. Just as you would not dig in your neighbor's yard—nor want him digging in yours—you should not be caught wandering or digging in a stranger's yard, ranch, or grazing range. You should obey "No Trespassing" signs and not cross fences without permission. Unfortunately, in open, unfenced country, people may not realize when they cross property boundaries, but it is still your responsibility to know where you are.

While property owners are generally lenient with people who wander across unfenced property lines accidentally, they are not legally obligated to condone anything that appears to be trespassing. They certainly will take a dim view of people digging on their land and removing items of value. While the courts have generally ruled that it is illegal or improper to shoot and/or kill trespassers, you should not attempt to sacrifice your life to test case law.

The origins of abandoned, lost, and mislaid property, all of which have very specific legal definitions, are rooted in English common law. Over the years, legal title to these various categories of property have been decided by the courts. In some cases, in the "absence of statute," the finder has been found to be entitled to items that "all the world save the true owner" didn't know about. When in doubt, check with local authorities and/or consult an attorney who understands the applicable local laws.

The category of private land includes property owned by individuals (such as houses and condominiums), owned by families (such as farms or vacation homes), owned by companies (such as factories or farms), or owned by organizations (such as Scout camps, churches, or private schools). Also included are Indian reservations, which are tribally owned, although they contain houses and other property that may belong to individuals, who may or may not be members of the tribe.

People entering private land become subject to laws governing private property rights, whether or not the boundaries are fenced or marked. To avoid misunderstandings we recommend contact with the local land office having jurisdiction in the area prior to any searching or collecting.

Government land includes property owned by city, county, or state government, although most government-owned land is federal property. Some of this government-owned land is used for government offices, museums, or maintenance facilities. In terms of overall acreage, however, most government land is set aside as parks, which are theoretically for the recreational use of everyone. Some government areas, such as in the National Forest System or in the case of Bureau of Land Management grazing lands, are leased for commercial use.

Most government land is theoretically "public," and as such has generally open access (sometimes through a nominal fee), although, as noted above some government land, such as military bases, is restricted and no public access is permitted. In the case of Indian reservations, the tribes may function as a government entity in controlling the land, or it may be administered by the Bureau of Indian Affairs, which is part of the U.S. Department of the Interior. Indian land, however it is managed, generally has very restricted access. It is best to assume that all parts of reservations—except for public highways, commercial buildings, and specifically marked areas—is private and that no access is allowed. Again, when in doubt, determine ownership before going onto any land.

When you are entering public land you are subject to state or federal law, whether or not the boundaries are fenced or marked. To avoid misunderstandings, we recommend contact with the local office having jurisdiction over the public lands prior to any searching or collecting. It is important to note that entering on or disturbing any publicly owned land will almost certainly be subject to rules and regulations of the agency controlling that property. Then seeking permission from an agency to enter a specific area, consent given to enter will almost certainly contain limitations with respect to any property found on the land.

Just as taking property from your neighbor's yard without permission is illegal, so, too, is taking property from public land without permission. We have all heard stories about people pocketing Indian arrowheads found on public land. Even this is technically forbidden. Since the passage of the Antiquities Act of 1906, it has been illegal to excavate or appropriate artifacts—including arrowheads—on public land without permission. This would include hunting for treasure, artifacts, and gold in any form other than as found in its natural mineral condition. The reason is to preserve, enable study of, and understand our nation's heritage. Collecting artifacts from the surface or unsupervised digging is not constructive.

Unauthorized activities are seen as being destructive of potentially important archaeological information about the context in which artifacts are found. Federal agencies are charged with managing historic and archaeological resources for the benefit of the American public. The theory is that if these disappear, artifact by artifact, soon so many chapters to the story are missing and that the story cannot be told.

Another issue that may arise regarding treasure troves, especially on public land in remote areas, is the discovery of human remains. In the chapter in this book concerning the treasure discovered on Victorio Peak in New Mexico by Doc Noss, he reported finding the skeletons of persons who were evidently murdered—having first been tortured. In other cases, a treasure discovery might be near or associated with a tomb or graveyard. (Egypt isn't the only place where treasure is found in tombs.) It may be a pre-Columbian Indian burial site or a cemetery that was still in use in 1960. In either case, the discovery of human remains of any kind is a serious matter, and it should be reported immediately to the local police or sheriff's office.

The Specific Legal Requirements

While we have discussed the issues in general terms, it is important that you know and understand the specific laws and statutes that govern the search for treasure on public land. Parenthetically, this understanding will help understand the history of searches for various buried treasure discussed in the main body of this text.

To begin with, it depends on what part of the country

you are in when you begin the search. Anyone who has spent time in various parts of the United States knows there are vast regional differences, especially between the East and the West. Nowhere are these differences more pronounced than with land ownership. Whereas in the eastern part of the United States most land is in private hands, in the West, specifically the Rocky Mountain states, most of the land is owned by the federal government. In the East, most federal departments and agencies occupy and administer only the land occupied by and surrounding their own offices, buildings, and facilities. In the West there are numerous blocks of federal land that are larger than entire eastern states.

The two largest federal landowners are the Department of the Interior and the Department of Agriculture, but the Department of Defense and the Department of Energy also are major landowners. The federal government's three largest land managers are the Bureau of Land Management (BLM) within the Department of the Interior, which oversees 270 million acres; the U.S. Forest Service (USFS) within the Department of Agriculture, which oversees 191 million acres; and the National Park Service (NPS) within the Department of the Interior, which administers 80 million acres of national parks, national monuments, national recreation areas, and other sites.

As mentioned above, also within the Department of the Interior is the Bureau of Indian Affairs (BIA), which exists to assist Native Americans to manage their own affairs under a trust relationship with the federal government. Under various treaties, property rights on Indian reservations generally lie with individuals or with a specific tribe or tribal entity. Thus any inquiry regarding the search for property on Native American land should be directed to the tribal council or similar body that is associated with the specific tribe in question.

The primary legal statutes that control the federal governments authority to deal with requests to search for treasure troves on public lands are the Archaeological Resources Protection Act (ARPA) of 1979 (Public Law 96–

95; 93 Stat. 721; 16 USC 470a et seq.) and Section 4 of
the Federal Property Services Administrative Act (40 USC
310). Since most material remains that treasure trove salvagers seek to recover from the public lands are archaeological resources, ARPA is the dominant statutory authority
governing their excavation and disposition. Uniform regulations found at 43 CFR Part 7 implement ARPA and define
the classes of material remains subject to its provisions.
Under 43 CFR Part 7.3, archaeological resources are defined as "any material remains of human life or activities
which are at least 100 years of age, and which are of archaeological interest." This clearly includes remains that
would, by definition, be considered treasure troves. (*Black's
Law Dictionary* defines treasure troves as "money or coin,
gold, silver, plate, or bullion found hidden in the earth or
other private place, the owner thereof being unknown.")

With few exceptions, access to Department of Agriculture and Department of the Interior land is generally open
with minimal restriction, although treasure hunting and/or
removal of artifacts is restricted. Check with proper authorities to determine whether the area is closed to entry
for mineral exploration. Excavation of archaeological resources on Bureau of Land Management land without a
Bureau of Land Management–issued cultural resource use
permit is prohibited if these resources are on public lands.
Archaeological resources on public lands recovered in the
course of an authorized excavation remain the property of
the United States in perpetuity.

The excavation and recovery of material remains that are
fewer than a hundred years old are protected by the Antiquities Act of 1906 (16 USC 432) and the Bureau of Land
Management's "Organic Act," the Federal Land Policy
and Management Act (FLPMA; 43 USC 1701). A fifty-year
threshold is a consideration that comes into play for the
Bureau of Land Management only when determining the
eligibility of a cultural property for the National Register
of Historic Places (Section 101 of National Historic Preservation Act [NHPA] and 36 CFR Part 60) and deciding
whether such a property is subject to the provisions of Sec-

tion 106 of the National Historic Preservation Act of 1966 (NHPA; 16 USC 470), and its implementing regulations, 36 CFR Part 800.

Section 106 requires federal agencies to consider the effects of their actions on historic properties, and is intended to avoid unnecessary harm to historic properties from federal or federally approved actions. Ordinarily, cultural properties that are fewer than fifty years of age are not eligible for the National Register, nor are they subject to the provisions of NHPA.

As we have noted above, the recovery of human remains is a serious matter. If you stumble across a human skeleton, it must be reported. In most cases, tell the local sheriff. If it is in a national park, tell a park ranger; if it is in a national forest, tell a forest ranger, and so on. In any case, they will know what to do, and you will have done your duty and fulfilled your legal obligation.

Discovery of Native American graves is a particularly important issue. Once they were treated as an archaeological find, but in recent years, as the tribes have begun to take control of their own heritage, such graves are treated with a great deal more respect. As the sheriff or ranger may tell you, if archaeological resources, including treasure troves, are associated with Native American human remains or burials, the provisions of the Native American Graves Protection and Repatriation Act (NAGPRA; Public Law 101–601; 104 Statute 3048; 25 USC 3001) come into play. Since passage of NAGPRA in November 1990, the Bureau of Land Management must comply with Section 3 of the act, which places ownership or control of Native American human remains and "associated funerary objects" with Native Americans. Associated funerary objects are defined in section 2(3)(A) as "objects that, as a part of the death rite or ceremony of a culture, are reasonably believed to have been placed with the individual human remains either at the time of death or later." Any treasure troves found in association with Native American burials would be subject to repatriation or disposition to a culturally affiliated Indian tribe or Native Hawaiian organization.

The federal government is also authorized to confiscate archaeological remains, whether they are found on a national park in the West or a Civil War battlefield in the South. Under the law, the artifacts can include arrowheads and Indian pottery as well as wagon wheels and Colonial-era muskets. "Artifacts" may also mean jewelry, gold coins, and gold bullion. The specific statute that controls the federal government's authority to deal with a potential treasure hunter's offer to recover treasure troves from the public lands is Section 4 of the Federal Property Services Administrative Act, 40 USC 310; 40 USC 310 authorizes the administrator of the General Services Administration (GSA) to "make such contracts and provisions as he may deem for the interest of the government, for the preservation, sale, or collection of any property, or the proceeds thereof, which may have been wrecked, abandoned, or become derelict, being within the jurisdiction of the United States, and which ought to come to the United States, and in such contract to allow compensation to any person giving information thereof, or who shall actually preserve, collect, surrender, or pay over the same, as the administrator of General Services may deem just and reasonable. No costs or claim shall, however, become chargeable to the United States in so obtaining, preserving, collecting, receiving, or making available property, debts, dues, or interests, which shall not be paid from such moneys as shall be realized and received from the property so collected, under each separate agreement."

While the General Services Administration has never issued regulations implementing 40 USC 310, it is responsible for issuing contracts to search for treasure troves on federal lands. Of course, such contracts are subject to the land managing agency's approval and incorporation of any provisions or restrictions. The gross value of any treasure troves recovered, exclusive of items that are determined to be archaeological resources, is normally shared on a 50–50 percent basis with the offerer.

It is stated in 40 USC 310 that contracts for the search and recovery of treasure troves are entered into with the stipulation that no cost and expense be incurred by the government. Potential treasure hunters, on the other hand, may be liable for considerable expense in meeting all the legal and agency requirements. The General Services Administration requires payment of a nonrefundable service charge of $500 to cover administrative costs of processing treasure trove requests. Potential treasure hunters may also be required to post an appropriate bond to cover an agency's costs associated with an approved search. Also, a treasure hunter is required to comply with Section 106 of the NHPA, which requires a treasure hunter to obtain the services of appropriately qualified specialists to complete an archaeological inventory and evaluation of any search area to be disturbed.

Before deciding whether to permit a search, the General Services Administration and the land managing agency require submission of a current U.S. Geological Survey or similarly scaled map showing the exact location of a search area and documentation and/or evidence that provides sufficient information to allow the land managing agency to determine the validity of the proposal. Such documentation might include maps, historical accounts, photographs, and/or any other records that would help validate a treasure hunter's claim.

A treasure hunter must also be prepared to describe the treasure trove that he or she expects to find, estimate the value of such troves, and delineate the search methods to be employed in the recovery. Upon receipt of the above information, the General Services Administration sends it to the jurisdictional agency for a decision on whether to allow a search. If the Bureau of Land Management is the jurisdictional agency, it will deny or approve the search based on the assessment of the supportive documentation a treasure hunter provides to the General Services Administration. Particularly important is the submission of corroborative data that make it possible for the Bureau of Land Management to verify with reasonable certainty that treasure troves, strictly speaking, might be found in a search area. If there is any indication that archaeological resources are the target of the treasure hunter's search, the search will generally be denied.

The Archaeological Resources Protection Act of 1979 and the Federal Property Services Administrative Act apply regardless of the time the archaeological resource and/or the treasure trove was abandoned or deposited on public lands.

However, not all federal agencies follow identical procedures with respect to processing requests by treasure hunters to search for treasure troves. The Fish and Wildlife Service (FWS), for example, has developed regulations at 50 CFR Part 27 prohibiting certain acts on national wildlife refuges; among the prohibited acts is the search for buried treasure, treasure troves, and valuable semiprecious rocks, stones, or mineral specimens (see 50 CFR Part 27.63) unless specifically permitted under the Fish and Wildlife Service's regulations found at 50 CFR Part 26, subpart D— Permits. Thus the Fish and Wildlife Service is set up to prohibit the search for treasure troves under their own internal regulations unless this use is specifically authorized. Because the Bureau of Land Management does not have its own regulations setting out prohibited acts on public lands, we work through the General Services Administration's regulations and appeal procedures for processing treasure trove applications.

While Bureau of Land Management areas are usually readily accessible, National Park Service areas are more tightly controlled and usually require an entrance fee. National parks are areas set aside by Congress to "conserve the scenery and the natural and historic objects and the wildlife therein and to provide for the enjoyment of the same in such manner and by such means as will leave them unimpaired for the enjoyment of future generations." Therefore, any object or item found in a National Park Service area is considered to belong to all the people of the United States, not just the individual who found it. Consequently, hunting for or taking any objects in National Park Service areas is generally prohibited.

Ironically, burying treasure also would be prohibited in National Park Service areas under 36 CFR 2.1, which deals with preservation of natural, cultural, and archaeological resources. Regulations also prohibit possession, removal, or disturbance of any mineral resource in all parks unless specifically permitted for a particular park area. A recreational activity along these lines is gold panning. This is currently permitted by regulation only at the Whiskeytown unit of Whiskeytown-Shasta-Trinity National Recreation Area in northern California and also in a few park areas in Alaska.

The National Forest System (NFS) lands managed by the United States Forest Service, which include national wilderness areas as well as national forests, are generally less restrictive than national parks. Some people have expressed concern with apparent discrepancies between the Archaeological Resource Protection Act (ARPA) and U.S. Forest Service regulations found at 36 CFR 261.2. The ARPA as amended refers to items a hundred years or older. A person cannot be prosecuted under this statute if the items in question are fewer than a hundred years old. But the Archaeological Resources Protection Act of 1979 is not the only statute protecting historic resources.

Title 16 of the U.S. Code, Section 551, grants the secretary of agriculture the authority to make provisions for the protection of NFS lands. Title 36 Part 60 of the CFR describes agencies' responsibilities to evaluate historic resources for the National Register of Historic Places, for which a property must be fifty years old or older. Based on this, 36 CFR 261.2 defines "archaeological resource" as "any material remains of prehistoric or historic human life or activities that are of archaeological interest and are at least fifty years of age, and the physical site, location, or context in which they are found." This is seen as not being in conflict with the Archaeological Resources Protection Act of 1979, but rather in addition to it.

Persons can be prosecuted under 36 CFR 261.9, which prohibits damage to or theft of property, including items of historical significance that are fifty years old or older. The fifty-year time period exists only for sites (the archaeological context), not general forest areas, where no artifact would be expected to be found. However, people do not normally want to search in areas where there is no chance of locating anything. Therefore, the very fact of looking for artifacts is in conflict with the regulation because any item located could be within an identifiable site.

These days, searching for buried treasure often includes use of a metal detector. The use of metal detectors on NFS lands, outside of developed recreation sites, requires specific authorization. Use of metal detectors within developed recreation sites is generally allowed without authorization unless a special closure for the area is in effect. A person interested in using a metal detector, or collecting on NFS lands, should contact the office having jurisdiction on the lands they plan to visit to determine the specific regulations that may apply. In National Park Service areas the use of metal detectors is specifically prohibited by a regulation in 36 CFR 2.1(a)(7).

Department of Defense land consists primarily of military bases. Access to such bases for any purpose is usually restricted severely, and indeed at some military areas (most of them well posted) the "use of deadly force is authorized" to deal with trespassers. Access for the purpose of digging for treasure would be virtually impossible, but a written inquiry addressed to the base commander would be a first step in determining whether an exception could be made. The name, rank, and address of the base commander (or an alternate channel) could probably be obtained by phoning the base or by inquiring at the main gate of the base. The Victorio Peak treasure we have discussed at length in this book is a good example of a treasure on military land, and the various efforts that have been made to recover it.

Open land administered by the Department of Energy typically includes nuclear weapons facilities and is as restricted as much as, if not more than, military bases. Again, a phone call or a main gate inquiry would be a good place to start, but the odds for access are effectively nonexistent.

In the case of state government-owned land, laws similar to the federal statutes are on the books to severely restrict or ban the excavation or taking of artifacts on public lands without permission. Activities involving tampering with graves, cemeteries, or human remains are illegal in all states. In some cases permits may be obtained for paleontological researchers to excavate prehistoric remains, but these are severely restricted. In general one may assume that the governments of each state consider, as the Texas Historical Commission states, that "unregulated treasure hunting is inimical to the best interest and stated policy of the state, because of its potential for adversely affecting significant cultural resource sites."

As one might imagine, the laws governing treasure hunting, while generally similar, vary greatly from state to state in their specifics. For example, the use of metal detectors is restricted or banned in some states but is widely acceptable in others.

With this in mind, and to learn as much as possible about the specific laws of the states for this book, we contacted the office of the attorney general in all fifty states. Since this is the department charged with enforcing the laws of the state, one would naturally assume that they could tell you what the state laws state.

For the most part, however, these offices responded that they were not authorized to provide legal advice to private individuals or businesses (which was not our request). Apparently their lack of authorization includes telling you what the law says. Six states were very helpful and supplied detailed information in reply to our request. These were Louisiana, Maryland, Montana, North Dakota, Texas, and Virginia. Five states—Mississippi, Nebraska, North Carolina, Oregon, and South Dakota—provided limited information.

In most cases the states relied simply by suggesting that would-be treasure hunters seek the services of an attorney practicing law in the state, and to rely on his or her advice. This is expensive, but it could save a great deal of aggravation later. Another suggestion we would offer would be to contact the sheriff's office in the county where the treasure is thought to be located. They would be able to refer you to the agency in control of the area or to tell you specifically what you can and cannot do in a specific place where you might hope to dig for treasure. They will do it for a lot less cost than a lawyer, and since they are the agency that will arrest you if you break the law, what they tell you is—in most cases—exactly what you need to know.

What Do You Do with It When You Find It?

Finding lost or buried treasure is like winning the lottery. The odds are stacked so deep against it that when it happens, there is a moment of disbelief. Your head spins, and you stand speechless. Many people before you have tried and have failed, but you have done it. There may be a dull clank as your shovel strikes the strongbox or sea chest that has lain buried for more than a hundred years on a deserted beach or in a windswept coulee by a desperate, frightened thief who intended to come back for it but who died from lead poisoning after saying too much to preserve his life but too little to allow his assassins to accomplish what you have now achieved.

People react to finding treasure in different ways, almost always in some form of disbelief. Some gasp. Some scream. Many will begin to dig with bare hands to free the strongbox or sea chest from the ground. If the box is wooden, it will crumble. If it is metal, it probably will be intact. Hopefully it will not be empty. Many are, and some contain currency that was once valuable but now has deteriorated into a pulpy mush. Most metals will deteriorate. Iron will rust, copper will corrode, and silver will tarnish. Gold, on the other hand, being largely chemically nonreactive, will probably be dirty, but will have otherwise survived. One can imagine the dazzling brilliance of the sun reflected from the golden surface for the first time since one's grandfather's father was a young man.

Assuming you have filed all the necessary paperwork and have obtained all the necessary permissions, the treasure is yours. This is less, of course, the portion you have promised to the owner of the land and all applicable taxes and fees.

The question now at hand is what to do with the treasure and how to turn it into spendable money. Long gone are the days when you could walk into a saloon and buy a round of drinks with a bag of gold dust, and the $20 gold pieces that are likely to be found—which were once common—are now unacceptable as legal tender in most retail transactions. Most bank tellers will not know what they are. Most bank tellers are too young to have ever seen a silver dollar, much less an American-minted gold coin.

There are various ways to authenticate old coins and to establish the value of gold bullion and other valuables. Gold and silver coins are commonly and freely traded in the United States, and many have collectible value in addition to the value of the metal in them. Coins with certain dates are highly sought by collectors and will occasionally be worth much more than a coin of equivalent weight having a more common date.

Gold dealers advise us that the first thing that you should *not* do when you have discovered gold coins is to wash or clean them. This may actually decrease their value. They should be cleaned professionally by a reputable coin dealer.

How much is the treasure worth? The spot price for gold, silver, and other precious metals changes daily and is published each day in major newspapers. This price is the "melt" value of "raw" gold. On top of this, dealers will pay a "premium" depending on the collectible value of the piece. This premium is usually governed by the condition of the piece, or the date, although an "old" piece is not necessarily more valuable than a newer one. There are certain twentieth-century coins that are more valuable than many nineteenth- and some eighteenth-century coins.

The once-common $20 gold pieces weigh 96 percent of an ounce because at the time they were minted, .96 ounce was worth exactly $20. The United States was on the gold standard then, and gold had an exact and finite value in dollars. In the 1970s the value exceeded $800 per ounce, and in the 1990s the "melt" value of $20 gold pieces was $300 to $500. However, depending on condition and date, they could be worth $2,000 to $5,000 apiece. There was one case in 1995 when several were found in freshly minted condition with a rare date. They were encrusted in dirt but were professionally cleaned, and they sold for $20,000 apiece.

Such premiums—or value above and beyond "melt" value—are paid not only on coins, but also on bullion and bars, and even on nuggets. Many dealers and collectors will pay a premium on nuggets if they are particularly attractive.

Because modern U.S. banks are not typically equipped to deal with anything other than paper transactions and currently issued currency and American coins, it is virtually impossible to redeem gold at an ordinary bank. If a bank *did* give you cash for gold, it would not be for more than "melt" value, and it is easy to imagine that most bankers would not be willing to part with more than face value. Thus, to redeem the gold for real money at a reasonable rate, look at listings under "Coin Dealers" or "Gold Dealers" in the yellow pages of your phone book, or that of a major city near your home. The larger the city, the more choices you are likely to have.

Such dealers also often purchase bars or bullion, or can refer you to someone who does. You should call several to get a feel for someone with whom you'd be comfortable doing business. In addition to buying coins and precious metals, such dealers will offer an appraisal service and cleaning service for a fee. Coin dealers will also be able to advise you on the value of U.S. currency. Antique U.S. currency typically has collectible value above face value, but Confederate and most foreign currency usually does not.

Some coin dealers may also deal in antiques and collectibles, including gold jewelry and precious stones. They will often be able to appraise these objects, or refer you to a reputable antiques dealer who can.

Not wishing to spill cold water on anyone's dreams, it must be pointed out that there will be tax implications regarding the discovery of treasure. If it is determined that you do in fact have ownership rights to the treasure you have discovered, you should ask your tax adviser or tax preparer how to list the find on your state and federal tax return.

Appendix A

CHECKLIST OF THINGS TO TAKE ON A TREASURE HUNT

When you embark on a treasure hunt, it is essential to be fully prepared. Do not proceed unless you are sure you are acting legally and are not endangering your health or safety. Having done this, be sure you have the necessary provisions and the necessary tools.

You may be able to drive to the site in an ordinary car, or you may need an off-road vehicle. You may have to hike for an hour or several days. In each case you should be absolutely sure you are capable of making the trip and have all the food, water, and gas you need for a *round trip* and for the length of time you plan to spend at the site. Before you leave, create a realistic checklist of things you will need.

The following are essentials for any search, even if most of the trip to the site is in a vehicle:

1. Your topographical map.
2. Water bottle or canteen.
3. A reliable compass.
4. A reliable watch.
5. A flashlight (never a priority at 10:00 A.M., but often a vital necessity eight hours later).
6. First aid kit.

7. Proper footwear.
8. Proper hat and coat, considering temperature and possibility of rain or snow.
9. Sunscreen or sun block.
10. Day pack or larger pack to carry the other items, unless you'll be within five to ten minutes of your vehicle. You'll want your hands free.
11. A properly inflated spare tire and a jack.

The following are important, though not necessarily essential for a search:

1. An extra flashlight and *two* sets of extra sets of batteries (if you will be entering a cave).
2. Matches or lighter.
3. Gloves.
4. Shovel, pick, gold pan, and/or metal detector.
5. Rope (usually not necessary, but often useful).
6. Hacksaw blade (for removing the padlock from the strongbox).

The following are important if you are going to be spending the night outdoors. You should also be prepared by knowing how to camp. Often some advice from people at a camping supply store and one or two nights at a drive-in campground are all it takes, but information and experience are essential. In addition to the items listed above, you should take:

1. A sleeping bag and (if desired) a pillow.
2. A lightweight tent you can carry easily.
3. Insect repellent (even if invisible in the daytime, insects come out of nowhere at sundown).
4. Food that can be prepared at the campsite.
5. A camp stove and food serving utensils.
6. Extra plastic bags.
7. Water purification tablets.
8. Toiletries (including soap and toothpaste) and toilet paper.

Appendix B

FINDING A DEALER TO REDEEM YOUR TREASURE

In choosing a gold dealer or a coin dealer, look for one who is a member of a national professional trade organization that screens the dealers and helps to maintain a high level of honesty, integrity, and fairness. The following organizations can provide a list of members in your area, or can tell you whether a specific dealer is a member:

American Numismatic Association (ANA)
818 North Cascade Avenue
Colorado Springs, CO 80903-3279
(719) 632-2646

Numismatic Guaranty Corporation of America (NGC)
P.O. Box 1776
Parsippany, NJ 07054
(201) 984-6222

Professional Coin Grading Service (PCGS)
P.O. Box 9458
Newport Beach, CA 92658
(714) 833-0600

Professional Numismatic Guild (PNG)
3950 Concordia Lane
Fallbrook, CA 92028
(619) 728-1300